More praise for **Iwo Jima**

"The tales of valor and humanity, as told by veterans of the battle, reveal the magnitude of their remarkable accomplishment during this pivotal campaign of the Pacific war."
   —Walter Anderson, former Marine and magazine publisher

"A superb collection of 22 oral histories from Iwo Jima veterans . . . [who] make for a good mix of officers and enlisted men. . . . A unique and compelling book; strongly recommended for all collections."   —*Library Journal*

"Smith has cast his net widely and generated interviews with a wide range of veterans, so his book affords a broader-than-usual view of the battle. . . . Eminently readable and historiographically useful."   —Roland Green, *Booklist*

"Vivid . . . Smith's succeeds in conveying this then-and-now dimension of the island and its bitter place in history."
   —Thomas Mullen, *America in WWII*

"Writers and historians will continue to study and document the iconic battle which killed 6,821 Americans, wounded nearly 20,000 more and killed more than 20,000 Japanese and capture the details for posterity. But Smith's work will rank with some of the best, primarily because he has followed the lead of the great oral historian Studs Terkel and let a wide range of regular Marines, sailors and airmen who did the fighting tell their stories in their own words. These men give a clear historical perspective of what the campaign was like for those who fought and died there and why it was necessary to sustain such monumental losses of young Americans to invade and secure the island."

—Ray Elliot, *Spearhead*

"A long overdue work. . . . The real value of Smith's book lies in the fact that the stories we read are told in the voices of those who experienced the fight. While the memories might be dimmed or distorted by the expanding years between the event and now, most of the survivors tell their tales as if the events had occurred yesterday, instead of nearly 60 years ago."

—GySgt John Boring (USMC), *Leatherneck*

Iwo Jima

ALSO BY
LARRY SMITH

BEYOND GLORY:
*Medal of Honor Heroes
in Their Own Words*

THE FEW AND THE PROUD:
*Marine Corps Drill Instructors
in Their Own Words*

THE ORIGINAL:
A Novel

A U. S. Liberator bomber takes part in an air attack on Iwo Jima in September 1944, five months before the invasion. Mount Suribachi, lower right, and the two airstrips, Motomoya Nos. 1 and 2, are visible.

U.S. Air Force photo

Iwo Jima

World War II Veterans Remember the Greatest Battle of the Pacific

LARRY SMITH

W. W. NORTON & COMPANY

New York · London

The poem on page 295 by Hitomaro, translated by Kenneth Roxroth, from *One Hundred Poems from the Japanese*, copyright © 1955 by New Directions Publishing Corp. Reprinted by permission of New Directions Publishing Corp.

The extracts on pages 298–299 from *So Sad to Fall in Battle* by Kumiko Kakehashi, translation copyright © 2007 by Shinchosha Co., Ltd. Copyright © 2005 by Kumiko Kakehashi. Used by permission of Presidio Press, an imprint of The Ballantine Publishing Group, a division of Random House, Inc.

For information about permission
to reproduce selections from this book,
write to Permissions, W. W. Norton & Company, Inc.,
500 Fifth Avenue, New York, NY 10110

For information about special discounts for bulk purchases, please contact
W. W. Norton Special Sales at specialsales@wwnorton.com or 800-233-4830

Manufacturing by Courier Westford
Book design by Charlotte Staub
Production manager: Julia Druskin

Library of Congress Cataloging-in-Publication Data

Iwo Jima : World War II veterans remember the greatest battle
of the Pacific / [edited by] Larry Smith. — 1st ed.
p. cm.
ISBN 978-0-393-06234-2 (hbk.)
1. Iwo Jima, Battle of, Japan, 1945—Personal narratives,
American. I. Smith, Larry (Larry Earl)
D767.99.I9I95 2008
940.54'2528—dc22
2008001301

ISBN 978-0-393-33491-3 pbk.

W. W. Norton & Company, Inc.
500 Fifth Avenue, New York, N.Y. 10110
www.wwnorton.com

W. W. Norton & Company Ltd.
Castle House, 75/76 Wells Street, London W1T 3QT

1 2 3 4 5 6 7 8 9 0

TO
Barney Barnum, John Ripley,
Iron Mike Mervosh, and the veterans of Iwo Jima
and to all marines,
everywhere

CONTENTS

OLD MEN FORGET, yet all shall be forgot but he'll remember, with advantages, what feats he did that day.

—WILLIAM SHAKESPEARE, *Henry V*

CARLISLE: My Lord, wise men ne'er sit and wail their woes, but presently prevent the ways to wail. To fear the foe, since fear oppresseth strength, gives in your weakness strength unto your foe, and so your follies fight against yourself. Fear, and be slain. No worse can come to fight. And fight and die is death destroying death, where fearing dying pays death servile breath.

—WILLIAM SHAKESPEARE, *Richard II*

KANGOKU ROCK

N

KITANO POINT

KITA

362-B

NISHI

AIRFIELD NO. 3
(UNDER CONSTRUCTION)

ORANGE 1   O-2

ORANGE 2

362-A

MOTOYAMA

362-C

KAMA ROCK

WHITE 1

WHITE 2   O-1

AIRFIELD NO. 2

382

TACHIWA POINT   O-2

MINAMI

BROWN 1

5 ✕
✕ 4

BROWN 2

QUARRY   O-1

PURPLE

EAST BOAT BASIN

23 ⚌ 25

BLUE 2

BLUE 1 (1/25 and 3/25 landed abreast)

YELLOW 2

YELLOW 1

28 ⚌ 27

RED 2
FUTATSU ROCK
RED 1

MOUNT SURIBACHI

GREEN

TOBIISHI POINT

LANDING PLAN
IWO JIMA

1000   500   0   1000
YARDS

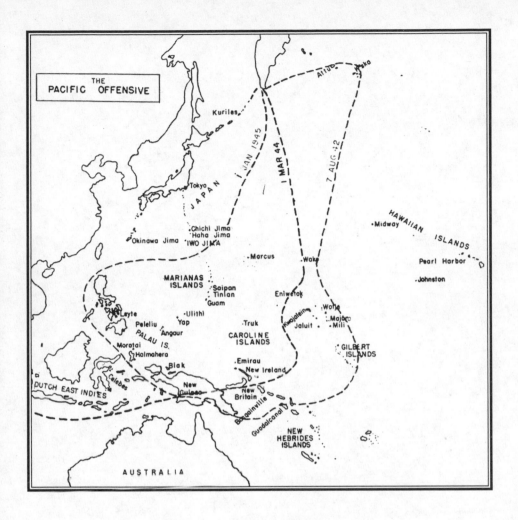

THE
PACIFIC OFFENSIVE

INTRODUCTION

They are all in their eighties now. They have had occupations, sweethearts, wives, children, even great-grandchildren. But once they stood trembling, hearts pounding, laden with weapons, ammunition, and assault packs as the amtracs and Higgins boats careened over sickening waves toward the black sands of Iwo Jima. They are survivors of one of the great battles of history, the campaign to conquer a small island in the far Pacific. Most were eighteen or nineteen years old when the boats dropped them off at the surf's edge. They were teenagers charging up those horrible ashy, slippery beaches into a torrent of artillery, mortar, and machine-gun fire, with death and destruction all around them. Hundreds surrendered their lives on the spot while those who were to survive struggled frantically to get off the beach. They were kids. They are old now. They are dying by the hundreds, age taking them instead of bullets or shrapnel. Yet thousands hold Purple Hearts, the decoration of the wounded. Twenty-two of them tell their stories in this book.

February 19, 1945, dawned bleak but manageable. That morning nearly eight hundred vessels, ranging from battleships, cruisers, and destroyers to transports and LSTs (landing ship, tanks), lay offshore. Aboard the transports were seventy thousand marines from three divisions charged with conquering eight square miles defended by twenty-two thousand Japanese soldiers fighting out of caves, bunkers, and tunnels. The Japanese knew the Americans were coming and the emperor personally had sent the brilliant general Tadamichi Kuribayashi to defend Iwo Jima. Implicit in the order was a fight to the death. The general arrived in June 1944, eight months prior to the invasion. *Iwo Jima* means "Sulfur Island," and the Japanese had carved an extensive network of mining tunnels that ran in all directions. Kuribayashi had his own soldiers work alongside Korean laborers to widen, deepen, and extend the sandstone tunnels so that there were more than sixteen miles of passageways. Some of the tunnels ran three stories underground. The island is volcanic, and the heat must have been dreadful.

Early that morning the amphibious craft, amtracs and Higgins boats, embarked from a fleet of forty-three transport ships. The fleet was a floating city, serving fifty thousand meals of steak and eggs to marines about to go ashore. The Fifth Marine Division had trained more than a year for this battle alone. Fleet Admiral Chester Nimitz was in overall charge in the Pacific. Admiral Ray Spruance was in command of the Fifth Fleet. Under him was Admiral Kelly Turner, the commander of the Fifth Amphibious Corps. General Harry Schmidt was in command of the landing force. Superfluous in the command structure but superior to Schmidt was General Holland "Howling Mad" Smith. Planning for the battle had been under way for more than a year. The Marines were *on* the ground; the Japanese were *in* the ground, and they were ready for the siege. Each man was told to fight to the death, but not before taking at least ten marines with him. They survived on half a cup of water daily and a handful of rice, yet they held out for thirty-six days. The last five days they had neither food nor water.

On the first day alone the Marines suffered 2,420 casualties, including more than 500 killed. Before the campaign was over, 13 of 24 battalion commanders fell, while 15 doctors were killed, along with 195 Navy corpsmen, who were medics on the battlefields. In those thirty-six days, 28,000 marines and soldiers—American and Japanese—were killed, and 16,000 were wounded. In the first ten days the Fourth Division lost 4,000 marines getting from the landing beaches to an assembly point you could walk to in twenty minutes—if you were not under fire. There have been few more disastrous military encounters in American history. Iwo Jima remains the Marine Corps's deadliest campaign. Some have compared Iwo Jima with the battle of Gettysburg, where 40,000 died, and with Belleau Wood in World War I, where the casualties, killed and wounded, reached 9,770. At the end of the fighting, the American dead totaled 6,821. It was the only campaign the Marines ever fought in which they took more casualties than the enemy. Every foot of the island was contested, and the fighting was so intense that several battle sites became legendary: Nishi Ridge; the Quarry; Cushman's Pocket; Hills 362 Able, Baker, and Charlie; the Meatgrinder, consisting of the Amphitheater, Hill 382, and Turkey Knob. Then there were Bloody Gorge and Kitano Point.

Most famous of all but no more difficult than these places was Mount Suribachi, where on the fourth day a team of six men went up in the morning and raised the American flag. Then, a few hours later, a second team of six raised a second flag because the first was not large enough. Joe Rosenthal, an Associated Press photographer, captured an indelible image of this moment. Indeed, Rosenthal's shot became one of the most famous images of all of World War II, if not the entire twentieth century. The photo shows six men straining to raise a heavy pole on a bleak hilltop against a gray sky. None of their faces can be seen, but you can see the flag flapping over them.

The photo also generated considerable controversy. The story has been told more than once, notably by James Bradley in *Flags of Our Fathers* and by Hal Buell in *Uncommon Valor, Common Virtue: Iwo Jima and the Photograph that Captured America*. More recently of course, *Flags of Our Fathers* has been filmed by Clint Eastwood. While the old-timers were glad to see a movie about

Iwo finally come to the screen more than sixty years after, they were dismayed by its lack of focus on the battle itself and in its portrayal of A. A. Vandegrift, the commandant, who in obscene terms sends the alcoholic Ira Hayes, the Pima Indian who was one of the flag raisers, back to his unit. They were also disappointed by other liberties taken with the facts. Chuck Lindberg, the last living flag raiser, tells the story from his perspective in Chapter 14. Just before, Norman Hatch, a combat cameraman, explains in Chapter 13 how he clarified for the commandant of the Marine Corps how the flag raisings took place.

Better received was a companion film, *Letters from Iwo Jima*, based on letters written by Kuribayashi and others, depicting the battle from the Japanese point of view. It was shot almost exclusively inside caves and tunnels like those occupied by the Japanese soldiery. Another film foray that received mixed reviews from veterans was *Windtalkers*, about the Navajo Indians who served the Marines in radio communication, using their indecipherable tongue in a code the Japanese could not break. One code talker, Samuel Tso, recounts his story in this book. Rather than tell the dramatic story of this elite group, the movie focused on a character who was instructed to shoot the code talker in the event of capture.

Such unwelcome publicity, or perhaps the unwelcome memories, inspired by the film may have encouraged the Japanese in June 2007 to restore to the island its old name of Iwo To, which has the same written characters and meaning. The Associated Press reported that it was known as Iwo To to the thousand or more civilians who lived there prior to the outbreak of the war and that it mistakenly came to be called Iwo Jima by Japanese Navy officers who moved in to fortify it after the civilians were evacuated in 1944.

There were three thousand yards of beach, designated green, red, yellow, and blue, and essentially three axes of attack, right, center, and left, each with its own division, numbering twenty thousand men. Elements of the Fifth Division were to cross the skinny south end of the island, just eight hundred yards. Their mission was to turn left, isolate, capture, and cut off Mount Suribachi, then do an about-face and move up the left, or west, side. The Third Division was assigned to the center of the island, and the Fourth was to seize Motoyama No. 1, the airfield, then pivot and go all the way to the north. One regiment of the Third Division, roughly thirty-three hundred men, was held in reserve and never released for the battle. That remains a sore point to this day because their presence and firepower were so badly needed. Units in combat could not be given any rest, and so many were being killed and wounded that raw replacements were funneled directly into the battle. These green soldiers were slaughtered because there was no time to assimilate them into experienced units.

Colonel John Ripley, USMC (Ret.) (Chapter 24), a former director of the History and Museums Division of the Marine Corps and a leading authority on the campaign to conquer Iwo Jima, is careful to avoid saying that one division or another bore the brunt of the action "because it's simply not true." He adds, "All three divisions shared equally in the struggle, along each axis of attack." The Fifth Division captured Suribachi and raised the flags, he notes, but "nobody talks about the hell it went through after Suribachi. It lost six flag raisers, including Mike Strank, Harold Hansen, and Harlon Block (three from each event), plus the battalion commander, Colonel Chandler Johnson, the commander of 2-28, in the seizure of Hill 362 Able, one of the toughest nuts of all, right off Nishi Ridge."

Ripley adds, "From this point on these guys are nose down, fighting like hell to get up here to Bloody Gorge at the northern tip of the island and the last pocket of resistance. Then it takes nine full days for an entire division, the Fifth Marine Division, to seize a piece of ground so narrow you could throw a baseball across it. I have been down in there. There are reinforced bunkers opposing each other; the ground is just unbelievable. So the Fifth Division was bled white up here. They never get any credit for that.

"We used damn near four tons of TNT and also plastic and ten thousand gallons of thickened fuel for flamethrowing, predominantly Zippo tanks, every day for nine straight days. Day after bloody day, a whole division. The Fifth Division had four thousand seventy-two casualties trying to take this position. And it's never talked about. It's one of the toughest battles ever, for any service, anywhere: the seizure of Bloody Gorge.

"Seldom in Marine Corps history has there been a comparable battle for such a tiny piece of ground, requiring so much effort, so much in the way of casualties, and yet the history books don't identify it as such. It's just part of the battle of Iwo Jima, and perhaps that's as it should be.

"Bloody Gorge alone would convince you of Kuribayashi's genius. By this time no Japanese had eaten or had any water for five straight days. They never had any sort of sustenance compared to what our marines had, but at the same time they fought and fought and fought, and what a hell of a job they did."

On March 14, after more than three weeks of horrific fighting, the island was declared secure. The invasion of Okinawa had been planned for April 1, and it was important to get the amphibious shipping back to prepare. So Iwo was declared secure on Day twenty-four. "That's when they had the ceremonial flag raising down there at Fifth Division cemetery," Ripley says, "yet we would fight like banshees for another two weeks, including Bloody Gorge."

Finally, on D plus thirty-four, or thirty-five days after the invasion began on February 19, the island was declared secure for a second time, and various units were directed to turn in their weapons and ordnance, link and ball ammunition, ranging from belted machine-gun rounds to eight-shot rifle clips, all live rounds that could not be taken aboard ship, plus exploding ordnance such as grenades, mortars, rockets, TNT, and plastic explosives. Just when everyone thought the battle was finally over, a force of three hundred enemy made its way down near Motoyama or Airfield No. 1 and slaughtered forty-four pilots sleeping in tents before they themselves were annihilated. Lieutenant Robert

Merklein, a P-51 pilot, narrowly escaped death that night. In Chapter 19, he describes what happened.

After the Marines departed, according to Patrick Mooney, another authority on the campaign, Army garrison forces of the 147th Infantry took over. They continued the work of hunting stragglers, recovering weapons and equipment, and disposing of Japanese bodies. More than 1,600 additional Japanese surrendered while at least 800 more were killed. The Marines captured only 216 of the enemy during the entire battle. Perhaps not widely known is the fact that, after March 26, 1945, Army occupation troops captured 867 and killed 1,602 over the next few years. The Japanese would come out at night to steal food, clothing, and water. Many of the later casualties were Korean laborers who had been impressed by the Japanese to carve out the tunnels. On January 8, 1949, the last known enemy walked out and surrendered to a Navy lieutenant. This Japanese soldier had apparently found a copy of the military newspaper *Stars and Stripes* that showed on its front page Douglas MacArthur and Emperor Hirohito standing together in Tokyo. He figured that if Hirohito was standing, and MacArthur wasn't bowing, the Japanese had lost the war.

I visited Iwo Jima with Colonel Warren Wiedhahn USMC (Ret.) and his Military Historical Tours on March 8, 2006. We met in Los Angeles before flying on to Hawaii and Guam as a unit. "You will never be the same once you set foot on the black sands of Iwo Jima," Colonel Wiedhahn said. Many Iwo veterans were on the trip, and he had them stand and tell a little about themselves. After several had spoken, he noted how among the veterans there almost invariably recurred the phrase "And then I was wounded." As I grew more familiar with what had taken place, my old newspaperman's curiosity got the best of me. A number of questions began to emerge, and I have sought to answer them through the stories of the men in this book. When talking to each of them, I sought to focus on personal experience as well as what I saw as the four major elements to the story: the landing; the raising of the flags on Suribachi; the at times seemingly hopeless attempt to conquer the rest of the island; and the arrival of the B-29s, which had been one of two major objectives of the invasion.

First, how did the invading American force keep from being annihilated and driven off the beaches? General Kuribayashi placed his artillery, machine guns, and riflemen from Mount Suribachi on the south end all the way to the Quarry on the north, so that the entire four thousand yards of shoreline were utterly bracketed, enfiladed by guns and artillery from every direction except the east, where the American ships lay offshore. Even after the assault was under way, he waited an hour or more, until several waves of marines had landed, before unleashing his artillery. The carnage was appalling. Joe Rosenthal said later the bullets and artillery were so thick it was like trying to run through rain without getting wet.

Second, what really happened with the flag raisings, and how did it get sorted out? There's the lingering false assertion that the Rosenthal photograph, the model for the Marine Corps Memorial in Washington, D.C., was faked. And who actually raised the flags? At last count, the number of men claiming to have helped raise them numbered 1,632. The last living flag raiser, Chuck Lindberg (no relation to the pilot), died in Edina, Minnesota, on June 24, 2007, only a few weeks after recounting his story for this book (Chapter 14).

Third, what happened to the twenty-one thousand defenders? And what became of Lieutenant General Tadamichi Kuribayashi, the Japanese commander? He had accepted the assignment of defending Iwo Jima, which was considered part of the Japanese homeland, to the death. He knew he could not win; he could only delay the American advance. During his nine months there he inspired his troops, devised a brilliant strategy of defense, and found time to write forty-one selfless and tender letters to his wife and children in Tokyo. No one has solved the mystery of his death. Recent accounts that have him commanding that last attack on Motoyama No. 1 conflict with prevailing knowledge over the previous fifty years. You'll read about the discovery of Kuribayashi's chief of staff's remains in Chapter 22; the general's remains have never been found.

Fourth, was it worth it? At the time the Allied commanders offered two reasons for the invasion. The Army Air Corps was sending B-29 Superfortresses by the hundreds to bomb Tokyo and other targets in Japan. These planes flew out of Saipan and Tinian, more than a thousand miles one way to Japan, and then back. Iwo, a territory under Japanese mandate, was at the halfway point, 750 miles from Tokyo. Forces there could alert the mainland that the B-29s were coming. That had to be stopped. The Air Corps strategists also knew that Iwo had two fully equipped airfields. These essential strips would provide a place where B-29s damaged or with engine trouble could stop on the way back.

Finally, what has happened to the place since? More than twenty years after the end of hostilities the Johnson administration returned ownership of Iwo Jima to Japan. The American flag was lowered there at 12:15 p.m. on June 26, 1968, and was replaced minutes later by the Rising Sun. Thousands of old marines, including many of those in this book, are still angry about it. Though the Japanese were reluctant to allow it, the terms of what was called the Status of Forces Agreement stipulated that the Marine Corps would have access to the island in perpetuity. I wanted to see how many men had gone back and how they felt about that tiny island they had nearly given their lives for.

The poet William Butler Yeats wrote, "An aged man is but a paltry thing, a tattered coat upon a stick," and so it is with many of these old vets, some widowed, some getting about with walkers, toting hearing aids, memories uncertain, while many others remain vigorous and feisty, full of energy, their recollections sharp. Many, like Domenick Tutalo and Norman Hatch and Cyril O'Brien, are still working. Mike Mervosh, eighty-two, can still do nine one-handed push-ups. More than sixty years have passed since they labored onto the beaches of Iwo Jima. It is poignant to see pictures of them as dashing, uniformed, handsome young men and to encounter them now. The war that shaped their lives is far in the past, yet still vivid in their memories. Where relevant, I have supplied specific dates, times, and facts without intruding otherwise. This book does not presume to offer a definitive account of what has been called the thirty-six days in hell of Iwo Jima, although it does strive for accuracy. Rather, it is a series of snapshots offering a glimpse into the lives of twenty-two men who took part in various aspects of the conflict and how they have fared since. Their stories speak for themselves.

ACKNOWLEDGMENTS

This book could not have been written without the splendid help and advice of the Medal of Honor recipient Colonel Harvey H. "Barney" Barnum, USMC (Ret.); the kindness and courtesy of Colonel Warren Wiedhahn, USMC (Ret.), of Military Historical Tours; and Colonel John W. Ripley, USMC (Ret.). I was led to its subject by Sergeant Major Mike Mervosh, USMC (Ret.), and some of his Iwo Jima comrades, all of whom were gracious, accommodating, and helpful. In addition to donating their time and their invaluable memories to this book, many of the men gave me permission to reproduce pictures from their personal collections and allowed me to photograph them. I am grateful for their generosity. I also wish to thank Gerry Byrne of *Parade*, John Butler, Keiko Hirano, Masahide Mizoguchi, Rosa Ogawa, Lee Kravitz, and Lou Leventhal, for helping me with facts, and Jonathan Au, for rescuing vital copy that seemed irretrievably lost in the computer.

Iwo Jima

The battle begins. The first wave of marines in amtracs approaches the beach on D-day, February 19, at 9:00 A.M. with Mount Suribachi in the background. The island smokes from the Navy shelling and aircraft bombing.

AP Wide World Photo, from the U.S. Navy

PART ONE

The Invasion

There were four assault regiments, representing the Fourth and Fifth Divisions. The run from ship to shore took about half an hour. The first landing came at 9:02 a.m., and in a short while there were six thousand marines on the beach. The first waves came in on LVTs or tracked amphibious vehicles called amtracs. Subsequent units came in on Higgins boats, known as LCVPs (landing craft, vehicle, personnel). The beach segments were designated green, red, yellow, and blue.

The Japanese commander Kuribayashi had spurned conventional wisdom of protecting the shoreline from invaders and instead held his fire till the three thousand yards of beach were crammed with marines, and then shortly after 10:00 a.m., he opened up from caves, tunnel mouths, and fifteen hundred pillboxes with heavy artillery, giant mortars, rockets, and antitank weapons. All the weapons had been preregistered for accuracy.

American intelligence had reported the sand would cause no

problems, but this was dead wrong. The steeply terraced soft black volcanic sand immobilized every type of vehicle, and soon there was a terrible jam-up along the beach and the marines themselves had trouble moving in it. The effect of the barrage was devastating, but still the Marines managed to land 30,000 men the first day. Casualties on the first day totaled 2,420, including 501 killed.

The weather turned bad, the beaches were closed, and there was chaos everywhere, but the marines kept coming. Colonel Joseph Alexander, in his definitive account of the campaign, quotes one observer: "The wreckage was indescribable. For two miles the debris was so thick that there were only a few places where landing craft could still get in. The wrecked hulls of scores of landing boats testified to one price we had to pay to put our troops ashore. Tanks and half-tracks lay crippled where they had bogged down in the coarse sand. Amphibian tractors, victims of mines and well-aimed shells, lay flopped on their backs. Cranes, brought ashore to unload cargo, tilted at insane angles, and bulldozers were smashed in their own roadways."

On the third night, fifty kamikaze planes from Katari Air Base near Yokosuka attacked offshore, crashing into and sinking the escort carrier USS *Bismarck Sea*, damaging several others, and putting the USS *Saratoga* out of the war. All the kamikazes were lost. The number of casualties from these attacks and shore fire during the battle totaled 2,798, including 1,917 wounded.

In the first five chapters, an infantryman, a sailor, an amtrac driver, an operations officer, and a flamethrower talk about the opening days of the fight.

1

CORPORAL RICHARD NUMMER

**Weapons Company, Twenty-eighth Marines,
Fifth Marine Division**

*For forty years I never even talked about it or
nothing, but soon as I seen that flag I knew I
was the one put the hole in it. Not too many
people know there's a hole in the flag.*

Standing in the backyard of his home
north of Detroit in the summer of 2006,
eighty-year-old Richard Nummer holds
the bayonet he took from the body of
Siguo Kubo, a Japanese soldier he shot
dead during the campaign for Iwo Jima
in February–March 1945.

Corporal Richard Nummer,
right, and his foxhole buddy Al
Esposito, from New York, have
their picture taken atop Mount
Suribachi on February 24, 1945,
with a camera recovered from
the body of a slain marine.

I met with Richard Nummer at his modest home in East Detroit in the summer of 2006 before the Marine Corps opened its new museum in Quantico, Virginia. He was eighty years old, lively and talkative. We hit it off immediately. It turned out he had quit school to join the Corps in 1942. He added that sixty-three years later, in 2005, he received an honorary diploma from his alma mater, East Detroit High School. "They finally got the government to give you a thing saying they appreciate what you did. So I got my honorary diploma. All those years later I finally became a high school graduate." Richard laughed when he said this. "I still got the cap and gown they gave me."

"I went in with the fifth wave. When we got off the ship, we went around and around in circles, rendezvoused, so they could start letting different waves go in, you know, one right after another. So when we went in with the other waves, it seemed like there was no action at all. But just about the time I got there, around ten o'clock or ten-thirty, we start running in, that's when they really opened up.

"I was in a Higgins boat. The ramp went down in front. Our gun, a thirty-seven millimeter on wheels you pulled with a truck, was on the other boat, an LST [landing ship, tank], I think. At that time I was with Headquarters Company of the Twenty-eighth Marines.

"When I hit the shore, like I say, we ran up. There were not too many bodies when we first landed. I saw about ten. The first wounded guy I seen his jaw was gone. He was running back, and a couple corpsmen were trying to tackle him so they could get morphine into him. I don't know if he made it or not.

"But as you ran up, you'd tap a guy on the shoulder, and he'd run up a little farther and you'd get in his hole. He was supposed to get up and go to next hole when you tapped him, like leapfrogging. So I get in this hole and tap the guy on the shoulder and, nothing. He was gone. There was shell holes all over from the aircraft. I jumped in this one hole. It was pretty good, but right above me I could see all this sand getting hit with bullets from up above, coming right down. Anyhow, I laid there. You couldn't move. Every time you'd just move an arm or something you'd draw fire.

"I was pinned down there for maybe five minutes. I had a New Testament with some of the Psalms included, here in my pocket, so I opened that up, and I read the Twenty-third Psalm. And I just finished that, put it back in my pocket, when a shell hit, and I don't know nothing till the next day. [Richard had been knocked out cold.] I guess it was the concussion from that shell hitting close by. There were bodies all around there. I lay there twenty-four hours. Anyway, next morning I woke up, and when I got up to where my group was, the rest of the company, the sergeant just shook his head. He said, 'We had you down KIA.' Killed in action. 'Cause I was laying there with the dead.

"Our gun maybe didn't get hit, but it could have got stuck in sand. You couldn't use them until they got some bigger vehicles to pull them out of the sand and up onto the beach. Each ground section of artillery was supposed to be with one of these companies.

"Anyways, Combat Team Twenty-eight crossed the neck at the base of the island and turned toward Suribachi. They got the Thirty-sevens up, and they were firing at anything they could see on Suribachi. They kept putting the shells in so fast and shooting them that the lines and grooves were just round after a while, and the barrels were no good at all [heat melted the rifled grooves inside the barrels, so the shells could not rotate. The grooves give them accuracy and velocity]. They were almost disabled. So we got stuck with infantry in the attack on Suribachi, and then, four days later, on February 23, the first flag went up. Louis Lowery got that first photograph. I knew him real well. He was on the ship with me. He slept almost right next to me. So, oh boy, that didn't mean the war was over for us, but at least we got something going. The whole thing was supposed to take three days. I was there thirty-seven days, the whole time, and one day more.

"I didn't go up with Lowery on the first flag raising. Some of us decided we was going to climb up Suribachi for a closer look, so we started going to the top. It probably took us forty-five minutes. Suribachi was pretty much taken out when we went up. We got there about the same time as this group arrived for the second flag raising. And they was just putting the flag up. We saw it go up, and we were just walking around up on top, looking down. A lot of pictures were being taken, but nobody knew this was going to be anything famous. We went up there because that's where our group was. We were up there maybe an hour or so, and they decided our outfit, the Twenty-eighth, had got hit so bad we had to wait for replacements. And they said, 'You're going to stay right here.'

"So we were the first marines to sleep on top of Suribachi, six feet from the flag. I have a picture of my buddy and me sitting there. My buddy Al Esposito from New Jersey found a camera in the pack of a dead marine, and we had our picture taken with that. I was six feet tall and weighed a hundred sixty. We were taking turns on guard duty. Every hour we'd wake the other one up, kept changing like that. We was the closest foxhole to the flag, which was like right here, off my right shoulder. So he just got to sleep, and I kinda dozed off. At that time this was probably the safest place on the island because the rest of it was all downhill. There were about forty of us up there. Anyway, I heard this noise and I turned around and I thought it was a Jap, so I shot. But it wasn't a Jap; it was the flag, snapping in the wind. I told Esposito next morning, I said, 'Jeez, look what I did.' He said, 'What the heck did you do that for?' I says, 'Well, I thought it was a Jap.'*

"If you ever go to Washington, D.C., that flag is in the Navy

---

*The use of the word *Jap* to describe the enemy was commonplace during the war, and it is repeated throughout this text by the marines who fought at Iwo Jima. The correct word, of course, is *Japanese*.

Yard. Both flags are there [they have since been moved to the new Marine Corps Museum in Quantico, Virginia]. The first time I went for an Iwo reunion was twenty years ago. Reagan was president then, and we went to White House, met him and his wife and the first George Bush, and then we went over to Arlington Cemetery, where they got the flag raising statue, and soon as I went in that museum and seen the flag, I knew.

"For forty years I never even talked about it or nothing, but soon as I seen that flag I knew I was the one put the hole in it. Not too many people know there's a hole in the flag. It's right there in the second stripe. Here it's probably the most famous picture ever taken, and I stuck my little hole in it. I should have been court-martialed. At that time, of course, nobody knew it was going to be famous, not until we got back to Hawaii a month later and seen the pictures and all.

"I knew right away, but all those years I never told anybody. In fact, the Marine Corps don't even know about it. This guy was here last December [2005] it was the first time I ever told anybody about it. He come here and like interviewed me. They're coming out with a picture, and this is the guy that does Clint Eastwood's sound and all that. He was here, and he came here to try get this worked into the picture. But after he left, I got a phone call from him saying the picture was too far in the making, so it probably wouldn't be mentioned.

"We were up on Suribachi five days while we waited for reinforcements. We lost five hundred ten men in four days of fighting. The reinforcements came on February 27, which was my birthday. I turned nineteen on Iwo Jima. We'd go down every day to work on the graves detail. They'd give you big black gloves that reached up to your elbow, for picking up the dead. That was our job. We'd pick up these bodies and put them on the truck, and off they'd go. They'd bury them in trenches. They were all brought back to the States later on.

"You saw some real bad sights there. No masks, and the smell and the flies were terrible. This one guy we picked up, somebody said,

'There's John Basilone' [Basilone was a notable marine who'd received the Medal of Honor for action on Guadalcanal]. He wasn't in the Twenty-eighth. I think he was in the Twenty-sixth or Twenty-seventh. He got it the first day I guess, but he laid there for all that time. A lot of the bodies were there for five days already. We didn't fool with dog tags at all. You got your name stenciled across your back. For every dead Jap, I seen twenty-five dead marines easy. The Japanese would pick up their dead at night and drag them inside the caves, and we never knew exactly how many we got.

"A lot of times we'd lose two or three marines and cover them up with a blanket or a poncho. During the night the Japs would come and crawl in there, and some would take their uniforms off so you didn't always know if it was a marine or not. Then the burial detail would come around. When we was on burial detail, we always had to watch out there wasn't a Jap among 'em waiting for us, with a rifle or a grenade, whatever they could find. They'd try to get as many of us as they could.

"We just piled the bodies on the truck, and then they took them to where the cemetery was going to be. We did that for five days. We were walking around almost like zombies, you know? We had all this death on our mind, and we knew it was going to go on farther, and is this the end of us or what? We did this, and went back and forth to the beach to get supplies and stuff.

"We finally got into combat when we got down to the other end. We were on the front lines there. I had an M1 all the time. At night we'd put our thirty-seven millimeters in a row and put canister in, so if the enemy came, you could wipe out a whole bunch of them. But they never made a banzai attack except on that last day. Some days you stayed right where you was. All day long you didn't move.

"We were down to the other end about a week, and one night off in the distance I could see somebody running around. We had different password codes. You'd yell 'tree,' and the person was supposed to answer with the name of a tree. And then you'd yell, 'president,' and the answer would come back: 'Roosevelt!' So quite a ways off here this guy come running. It was just getting dark. Two buddies in the hole with me, and I had the first watch that night. It was going to be an hour off, an hour on.

"This figure kept coming closer and it was getting darker, and I said to the guys, 'There's somebody out there, but I think it's a marine.' And they said you don't want to shoot another marine, but he shouldn't be out there. So he come closer. A hundred yards away was a lot of rocks and stuff, and he kept coming, coming; he had a rifle, got closer and closer, so pretty soon he got close enough to where he could hear me, and I yelled out, 'Tree!' And he's supposed to yell back, 'Oak,' or whatever. 'President!' Nothing. 'Car!' He's supposed to yell back, 'Ford,' or whatever. So then I started over. About twice I went through the thing. Nothing. So then I said, 'Bukyosterol.' That means 'Drop your weapon.' But he kept coming, and he's almost right here. And the guys got up and said, 'Shoot!' My finger just froze on the trigger, and down he went. So that was the first one I got.

"Now he laid in the rocks, and I must have got him in the belly somewhere. I thought I killed him, and now I'm really shaken up because I thought it was a marine. So he started talking in Japanese. We didn't know what he was saying, but farther on you could hear the other ones answering him. So he was trying to give away our position. We started throwing flares out there to see where he was. Meantime the whole group was all lined up with our guys. We knew they were coming. One of them hit the trip flare, and that lit up the field right in front, so quite a few Japs got killed. Next morning my lieutenant came up, his name was Manning, Robert Manning. He come up, and he said, 'Who had the machine gun last night that started all this?'

"They said, 'That was no machine gun. That was Nummer over there, with his M1.' So he come over to me and shook my hand and said, 'Good going, kid.' He was from Bougainville and different campaigns before that. He says, 'Go on out there now, and any souvenirs on him, they're yours.' So I went out there. 'Wait a minute!' he says. One of the guys brought a rope, put the rope around his leg and pulled it, and sure enough, he had two or three grenades underneath. If he hadn't told me that, I would have gotten blowed up. That was one of the tricks they had. He probably shoved them under himself as he was dying. Those grenades were little black things as big as your fist that just had a piece of rope, and you pulled that out and put it underneath you and it wouldn't blow. Sometimes they'd hit them on their helmet to get them started.

"The grenades blew him up. I got his wallet and his bayonet. I still got the bayonet in the other room there. Then the lieutenant says, 'Well, you probably saved some of these guys' lives. I'll talk to you about it later on.' I didn't know if I was going to get some kind of medal or what.

"He left, and this was a terrible thing: He left, and he wasn't gone long. He said, 'You try to get some sleep now.' So I got in the hole and I just about went to sleep and they woke me up. They said the lieutenant just got killed. And he wasn't that far away from us. The reason he got killed he was crawling out to another guy laying there wounded and he was pulling him back. A sniper got him. It took us another two, maybe three days just to get to his body.

"One of our sergeants was named Duffy, from New York. There was this other kid named Hood. He drove the lieutenant's jeep. Here the war's going on, and the two of them get into a fistfight. They couldn't get the lieutenant's ring off because his hands were all swelled up, so the sergeant said, 'We're going to cut his finger off to send his wife back his ring.' And the other guy, Hood, said, 'No, just cut the ring off.' So they got in a big fistfight over this. We were aboard ship when we heard his wife just had a baby. He never seen the baby.

"Before we landed on Iwo, I had boils all over, so they put me in sick bay aboard ship, and the doctor come in and said, 'We got a new drug we're going to try on you; it's called penicillin.' So I was one of the first to get penicillin. They shot you in the rear end; I think I got three of them, and all the infection concentrated in one big boil on my knee. Even when I was on Iwo, I had boils pretty bad. A corpsman said, 'You're in more pain than some of these guys that got hit,' and he told me, 'We can get you off the island.' I said, 'No, you're not getting me off the island, not for boils.' So I stayed right there. Why leave if I was still in good enough shape to fight? Just because you had boils? Did I think I was going to make it or not? Every night you'd say, 'Well, I wonder if this is going to be it.' You never knew.

"I got a little story about Ira Hayes [Hayes was the Pima Indian who helped raise the second flag and whose life was romanticized after he died drunk in an irrigation ditch on the reservation in New Mexico in the 1950s. A movie about his life was made starring Tony Curtis, and Johnny Cash had a hit song called the "Ballad of Ira Hayes"].There were six guys in that flag-raising picture, and three of them got killed before we left the island. Bradley was left, Ira Hayes and Rene Gagnon. Bradley, his son came to one of the reunions. He's the one that wrote the story about *Flags of Our Fathers*. But Ira Hayes was the only one I knew real well. After we got back to Hawaii, they went on the seventh war loan drive in the States, and he got drinking quite a bit, had his problems with drinking. They were making a big hero out of these three guys, and Ira Hayes just couldn't see it. He said, 'Anybody could do the same thing we did. It's the dead guys that should be . . . ,' so anyway, they sent him back to us.

"He was probably in the States three, four months, and he come back to our outfit. In our tent we had one of the code talkers, his name was Thompson. And Ira come into the tent, and everybody shook his hand, one thing and another. He started drinking right away, beer, you know, we had it in the tent. And he wouldn't leave until all the beer was gone. If there was any left, he'd shove it in all around his belt. He'd be gone for days, nobody knew where he was at. It's a shame."

[Richard shows me a Japanese flag inscribed with various cities and explains.]

"After the war ended, I had occupation duty in Japan, nine months in Sasebo. Iwo Jima was the only battle I was in, but right after that we was getting ready to hit Japan and the bomb went off, which saved a lot of our lives. From Sasebo, not long after the war was over, we went to Nagasaki, where the second atom bomb was dropped. We were drinking their water and everything else. I was home about five years when I woke up with a gray streak. What the heck? The doctor said, 'I think you had a slight stroke.' My one eyebrow on the side was gray. They didn't know about this radiation stuff at that time. I got out a corporal in July of '46. When I got back, I couldn't even get a beer: I wasn't old enough."

[When the book *The Spearhead*, relating the history of the Fifth Marine Division, came out, Richard's name was not in it. He wrote to Washington and received a letter from Lieutenant Colonel H. W. Edwards at the Historical Branch, written on March 15, 1954. The key paragraph reads: "As a member of Weapons Company, 28th Marines, Fifth Marine Division, you sailed on board the USS *Talledega* for Iwo Jima, at sea 1–4 February 1945, at Enwietok (*sic*) in the Marshall Islands 5–6 February, at sea 7–10 February, at Saipan 11–16 February, at sea 17–18, arrived and disembarked for action against the enemy at Iwo Jima 18 February. You were engaged in action on Iwo Jima from 18 February (*sic*) until 26 March on which date you embarked on the USS *Winged Arrow* to return to base. You sailed from Iwo Jima on 27 March."]

[Richard has one last story.]

"I had this wallet from this guy that I shot that night when the lieutenant was also killed, different things, so forty years later I saw all this stuff that I had. It was no good to me, so I thought I'll send it back. I was all over different places, Japanese restaurants, and I was trying to get this stuff sent back. I was in Denver at a car show, and there were these three Japanese. I didn't know if they were Japanese, Koreans, or Chinese so I asked, 'Any of you guys Japanese?' One says, 'Yeah, we're Japanese.' So I says I got some stuff I'd like to send back to Japan. One guy says, 'I'm going back in a month, back to Japan,' and he says, 'I'll take the stuff with me.' So I packed it all up and sent it to him in Denver, where he was at, and he left for Japan. About a year later I still hadn't heard anything, so I was really disgusted. I had his address and everything, so I wrote him.

"And lo and behold, the same day I wrote him I got the first letter, from the daughter of this guy that I'd shot. She was forty years old, born after he left. Never knew her father at all. I got the letter here from her. She was so happy that she knew finally what happened to her dad.

"Besides the wallet, I sent diaries and different stuff, flags that had names on them."

[Here is the handwritten letter from the daughter.]

Dear Mr. Nummer:

Allow me to write to you. My name is Mrs. Kimie Sato, a daughter of Siguo Kubo, who was a soldier died on Iwo Jima. I received my father's notebook and three articles from you via Mr. Yamamoto six years ago [sic]. I heard you will go to Iwo Jima on March 14. How I wish I could go there and see you and say my thanks to you. However I cannot go there because of many restrictions. I was very excited and my heart was choked with the memories of my grandparents and my mother who died in 1981 when I handed the articles left by my father six [sic] years ago. They are my treasures for me now.

As you know I was born ten days after my father had departed for the front.

Thank you very much for your kindness and also I want to express my heartfelt thanks for Mr. Yamamoto and the Welfare Ministry. I received many congratulations from my friends and my relatives after the newspaper reported the ceremony of the return. I hear you are ill in bed. How do you feel these days?

Although I guess you had a pain of both physical and mental injuries I am sure that your warm and heartfelt kindness will impress the deceased and their families. I am praying for you that you may get better quickly for your friends and your family and you will have good days. If you go to Iwo Jima on March 14, please contact Mr. Takada if possible who will join the ceremony there.

Thank you again and I hope you will feel better soon.

Sincerely,
Kimie Sato

"That was the year I went to Iwo Jima—1995, the fiftieth anniversary. When I got there, the plane landed, and we was the last ones to get to where they had the ceremony. They announced my name on the loudspeaker to come to the podium. So I went to the podium, and there was a package for me. Now here I get a package and I don't know—a hand grenade?—what's in there. My son and I got on the side and we opened it up and she had a nice tie for me, coasters, a tablecloth, different stuff she was so proud for me to have. Some thought I was wrong by sending the stuff back, but I don't think so. It was no good to me, that stuff, but to her it meant the whole world."

Did she know Richard Nummer had shot her father?

"No, I never did tell her that. Couldn't do that."

Following publication of Richard Nummer's story, members of the Fifth Marine Division challenged his account of shooting a hole in the flag, which he stoutly maintained was true. Pointing out that he had kept quiet about it for forty years, he asked, "Why would I make that up?" It was noted that the hole in the flag is square in shape, inconsistent with a bullet hole, but the flag flew many days and was thoroughly frayed when it did come down. Richard later spoke with Ray Elliott, author and editor of the Fifth Marine Division newsletter *Spearhead*, and offered to take a lie detector test. Elliott was inclined to believe him.

2

SEAMAN JAMES BUSH
Water Tender Third Class
USS *Terror*, Cruiser Mine Layer

We had the flag over the body in the canvas, and we'd go through the whole service, and they'd say, "Now we commend this body to the deep," and we'd pick up the board, and the bag would slide straight out and down into the water. It would disappear in a hurry.

Civilian James Bush, eighty-one, at home in Ajo, Arizona, in October 2006.

Water Tender Third Class, James Bush, in a photo taken in San Diego in 1944.

Jim Bush and I were roommates on Guam in March 2006 on his first return to Iwo Jima since 1945. He was affable, talkative, and friendly, and we got along just fine. I interviewed him in our hotel room on Tuesday before we made the day trip to Iwo. I asked what had brought him back to the site of the battle. "I saw something about it on the History Channel one time," he said, "and I wondered how you got there. I couldn't afford it then anyway. Then a few months back I saw a little mention in the paper about this Military Historical Tour, and I called, and they sent me this literature, and I'm out here— sixty-one years later."

"I'll be eighty May 16, 2006. I was born in New Mexico, and we moved to Arizona when I was nine. I joined the Navy in May of 1943, stayed in a little over two years. I joined at seventeen so I would not have to sign up for the draft.

"We brought all our wounded from Iwo Jima to Saipan at the end of February in 1945, resupplied, and went and anchored in a big lagoon at Ulithi, where we went ashore to swim and dive and eat and drink beer. There was nothing there but beach. The beer was Iron City.

"The story of how we got the beer started in Pearl Harbor in January, when we were all fueled up and loading the last of our supplies. Some new young officer pulled up alongside the ship in a weapons carrier and parked it near the end of our gangplank. We told him, 'Don't park there,' because we were unloading trucks and putting supplies on the ship. He said he would park where he wanted to. He was a real starchy-looking guy with a uniform that was too large for him. He didn't look any older than me, and I was going on nineteen.

"We'd already put all the supplies we could down below. Back on the fantail we had a big old space with some tie-downs. We'd put a hundred tons of potatoes back there. A weapons carrier has lifters on it so it can be picked up and set aboard ship. Well, guess what? I stood up there and watched them guys look around all over the place, no other officers watching them, and they reached over and picked that weapons carrier up and set it onto the ship next to the potatoes, covered it with a big tarp. An hour after that we were backing out of dry dock so we could get out of Pearl Harbor before they put the gate up. They had cables down there to keep enemy submarines out of the harbor.

"When we got to Saipan, they set that weapons carrier off onto the dock, and everybody was riding around. I even went out in it for an hour or two. Some of the guys who pulled that stunt struck a deal with some of the guys on Saipan, military people. They liked that weapons carrier. They were moving to the war zone, and they didn't have anything like that.

"Our guys said, 'Well, what have you got to trade?' They said, 'We know where there are about four pallets of Iron City beer. Dozens of cases.' Done. 'Let's haul it down to the ship.' So they went on down to the ship, waited till the officer of the deck left his post, and they picked those pallets up, brought them aboard, and moved them to a walk-in cooler. Iron City beer was nasty-tasting stuff, but when we got to Ulithi after Iwo, it was really good, I'll tell you that. It was worth that weapons carrier.

"I pitied that pore little officer, though, having to walk all the way up through that shipyard, back to his commander saying, 'Guess what? I lost the weapons carrier.' It took us four days to drink up all the beer.

"I served on the USS *Terror*, a cruiser minelayer (CM-5). It was big, four hundred seventy-five feet long, with close to five hundred on board, including the admiral and all his staff. We were the flagship of the mine fleet. When I came on in Hawaii, I asked when they laid mines, and someone in the crew told me they had used it to lay mines at Casablanca early in the war but after that we were taking the battle to the enemy and we weren't laying mines anymore. They changed its function and moved the *Terror* to the

Pacific to service minesweepers because we were island jumping by then.

"We went with a large number of these little boats, minesweepers, to Iwo Jima six days before the invasion. They were only forty or fifty feet long, each served by a crew of ten. They were like PT boats [fast-moving patrol boats] except their job was to cut loose the mines that had been anchored off the invasion beaches.

"It was my first combat action. I was a water tender third class. I was usually down in the boiler room. Everybody had a station to go to in the battle. I was in the mess hall, high up, so I could see out. My job was to regulate, cut off, or open valves, down below hydraulically if there was bomb damage.

"A storm went by, and we got there early in the morning, woke up to a lush green island called Iwo Jima, except it wasn't lush green. It had been bombed to smithereens.

"Some of the minesweepers had wooden hulls so they could get close to the magnetic mines without setting them off. We had demagnetizers too. The *Terror*'s job was to take care of those boats, pump fuel into them, service them, help with repairs. They'd come back alongside of us with mattresses hanging out of holes that had been shot in the sides not too far above the waterline. Some of the holes were big, made by forty-millimeter artillery.

"We were like the old mother hen with a bunch of chicks out there. We had a big old wooden float, like a barge, on one side, and they'd pull over and tie up to that. It had ladders going up, and we had a crane that could reach over and go down. As soon as they came in, our guys in damage repair would go over the side and see what they needed and measure it all off. They'd string acetylene torches over the side and use them to cut pieces out of the ship so they could weld plate over the holes.

"There were mines in the invasion beaches besides those in the water. I heard a lot of explosions. We had some boats with flat bottoms that could get in close, and they had rows and rows of rockets on deck, pointed out, and they'd fire a row of them, walk them up and along the beach so they covered everywhere. When one boat would run out of rockets, another would come right in behind and take over, and they marched right up the beach, taking out mines as they worked their way north, starting from Suribachi.

"This went on for three days, and we got so much damage to our sweepers from artillery fire out of the bunkers that they put the invasion off three more days. It was supposed to start February 16. I didn't see the UDT [underwater demolition teams] guys, but I knew they were out there.

"They never managed to sink any of our sweepers, but by the end of the second day we had twenty-one killed on the small ships, and numerous wounded. We had to replenish some of the crews with people off our ship.

"We buried our dead at sea. We steamed to another volcano that had stinking smoke coming out of it, and we backed into a little cove between two reefs. I think we put an anchor down. The place we were working on deck was all covered with blood, so we washed it over the side with hoses, and when we did, that whole lagoon come up live with sharks. We shot them up real good, and they all disappeared.

"We heard later it had to do with shooting them through the liver, which exuded some kind of chemical that told the rest they were in danger, so they all left. I think that liver extract was used later to create a shark repellent to be given to pilots who could spread it out in the water when they were shot down. I don't know if it worked or not.

"We put the dead in body bags made out of real heavy canvas. We'd cut out a section, put a body on one side, then throw it over and sew the sides together. We used big old hook needles, like carpet hooks. You'd flop the canvas over the head and stitch the needle and string with pliers. We sewed a thirty-five-pound practice shell between their feet.

"We had a board rigged up, like a heavy piece of plywood. We put hinges on it and attached a lifeline. We had the flag over the body in the canvas, and we'd go through the whole service, and they'd say, 'Now we commend this body to the deep,' and we'd pick up the board, and the bag would slide straight out and down into the water. It would disappear in a hurry.

"We did it that night and left. The next morning we had to come back and do three more who had died during the night. That's why I think that volcano was something like thirty-eight miles south of Iwo Jima.

"The first day the Japanese didn't fire at our boats at all. The first day the Japanese thought they were decoys, didn't know what they were doing. They didn't want to give the location of their guns away by firing at us. But when the sweepers got in close enough by the second day, the Japanese would take a chance and shoot at them. They didn't want to fire because it would expose their gun positions to ships offshore, which could then blast them.

"How did the sweepers work? There's a cable under the bow that goes out at an angle, like a pyramid, and out at the end is a torpedo-looking device that's got a big old cutter in it. It's called a paravane. Your sweeper cable catches the cable holding the mine in place and slides on down to the paravane, which cuts the mine loose so it floats away or up to the surface, where you can fire at it and blow it up.

"They didn't shoot every one. Some drifted to beaches, where they were recovered and parts of them were taken to the translator, who could read when they were made and stuff like that. I saw some that were made in 1931. Some of them were three or four feet high, and when they'd drift ashore, some of them would bust one of their horns and blow themselves up.

"When the invasion flotilla came in the dark on the morning of the nineteenth we didn't leave; we just moved over a little ways, northeast off the Quarry, always on the move, always zigzagging. When they started in, I could look down the whole beach and see the waves of marines coming in. Some other pretty good-sized cruisers showed up too although when we arrived, it was just our ship and the minesweepers.

"On the fourth day there come an announcement that the flag was going up, and quite a few people come out on deck to see it. We headed for Saipan soon after that as fast as we could because we had so many wounded, and our doctors were working day and night on the wounded and the burned. We had people taking mirrors down so guys couldn't see how badly they were burned.

"The *Terror* made twenty-five or thirty knots, always zigzagging. We made it down there that night or two days later. There were so many wounded that we had them in our bunks. The one in my bunk had a leg wound from shrapnel. They operated on him the night before we got to Saipan. That piece of shrapnel, it was about the size of a cigarette, went in right behind his knee, and they took it out way down in his calf muscle.

"There was a big sick bay. I think we had three doctors, one a nerve specialist. They were operating day and night. Corpsmen were doing all they could to help plus evaluating the injured to see who needed surgery the most. If somebody wasn't wounded too bad, they'd come down looking for a place to put him. We probably took several hundred back to Saipan. Most of them were sailors in blue denims. I didn't see anybody in camouflage like the invasion marines wore. I figured they were all off the minesweepers.

"When we got to the dock in Saipan, it looked like a sea of white down there, all the medical people waiting for us, ambulances lined up.

"After our R and R with all the beer in the lagoon at Ulithi we went back to Saipan, picked up more supplies, and headed toward Okinawa, then moved south down along the Retto chain, south of Japan, to Kerama Retto, to wait for the seizure of Okinawa, getting ready for the invasion of mainland Japan or the China coast.

"We were hit by a kamikaze carrying one or two five-hundred-pound bombs early the morning of May 14, 1945. They liked to come in real low, in the sunrise, but he was a little early. We had smoke screens laid down, but the wind blows that smoke around, and he saw an opening, made a loop up in the smoke, and came back and hit us right in the after stack. It made a big gaping hole in the stack and went on down through the middle of the ship, exploding down inside.

"It killed all our doctors and corpsmen, took out the sick bay, part of the mess hall and the kitchen. The officers' quarters were right there, and all the ship's records, everything that would burn, was up there. Losing the records caused us a lot of trouble because every shot we ever had for whatever ailment, we had to take over. I'd have to look it up, but I think we had about fifty killed and over a hundred injured. One of the MIAs [missing in action] was not found until we got all the way back to San Francisco. We had to put cables on the stack to keep it from falling over and camouflaged the damage areas with canvas painted to look like the rest of the ship.

"I was about three decks down when the plane hit. There was a terrible compression like you were inside a big bin. A vertical pipe sheltered me from the worst of it, but the explosion vaulted me down the passageway thirty-five to forty feet like a bullet, taking off skin wherever it was close to the bone. It knocked me out. I had a helmet on, but it did not protect part of my neck. The pipe protected me except for the back of my head, and I still get junk out of there, must be paint or dirt or wood from something, I don't know what. They've looked at it a few times and don't see anything, but every once in a while it'll swell up and I'll get some junk out of it.

"It hit us around four a.m. and we fought the fire till almost nine. We put the dead in body bags, and they were buried ashore. A friend of mine, John J. Epping, was killed, and I unzipped his bag to make sure he had his dog tags with him.

"When somebody got killed, they took all the pictures, all the address books, and stuff and threw it in the garbage, because you might have a wife at home, and you got a girlfriend somewhere else, and you don't want them to get together. You don't want them to see the address book and all that stuff. But I salvaged a book out of the garbage, a little diary, showing when he left, starting in Hawaii, all the way to Iwo Jima and wherever we stopped.

"I thought I'd keep that because someday something might happen and someone might want it, and sure enough, long afterward—just two or three years ago—his brother wrote the people that put on the ship's reunion, asking to hear from anybody who knew the status of his brother John. So I sent him that diary, and he called me about two weeks later, and he was so happy I sent him that thing. Over fifty years later.

"We thought the kamikaze was a twin-engine Betty. There were two guys in it, and unbelievably their bodies were in better shape than some of the guys I saw. One was an old guy, real raggedy-dressed, and the other was younger, in a nice uniform, probably went along for the ride. They didn't get the treatment ours did, though. We just swept them over the side with the rest of the junk."

Jim Bush got out of the service in the summer of 1946. He and his wife, Patty, were married on June 9, 1950. They had two children, David, born in 1952, and Tammi Jo, in 1958. They lived in Ajo, Arizona, where Jim worked as an electrician for the Phelps Dodge Mining Company and later operated a sand and gravel company. He has served as a Santa's Helper, driving the sledful of toys, since 1946. He and Patty treasure their granddaughter, Tatiana, who was fifteen in 2006.

James V. Bush Jr. died in Phoenix, Arizona, November 3, 2007. He was eighty-one.

3

CORPORAL JAMES "SALTY" HATHAWAY

Amtrac Crew Chief
Tenth Amtrac Battalion, Fourth Marine Division

I saw the first flag. I didn't see the second. Someone said, "Those crazy damn marines are putting a flag up on Suribachi," and I turned and looked and seen it go up. The second flag went up several hours later, I understand. All hell broke loose when that flag went up too. The Japs just shelled the shit out of us.

James Hathaway, in uniform,
at age seventy-eight.

James Hathaway as a young marine.
The Bronze Star is pinned to his chest.

In the name of the President of the United States, the Commanding General, Fourth Marine Division, Fleet Marine Force, takes pleasure in awarding the Bronze Star Medal to Private First Class James S. Hathaway . . .

For heroic achievement in connection with operations against the enemy while serving as a crewman with an amphibian tractor company on Iwo Jima, Volcano Islands, on 20 February 1945. Although he and his crew had worked during the preceding twenty-four hours under enemy fire and without cessation, Private First Class Hathaway volunteered to transport an urgently needed load of ammunition to a front line infantry unit. He fully realized the danger of the mission, it [sic] being necessary to pass through mined areas and return to the beach in the dark, but he knew also that no other amphibian tractors were available for the task. He assisted in unloading the ammunition despite enemy fire in the area, then helped in loading casualties on board the tractor and started the hazardous return trip to the beach, where he left the casualties at an evacuation station. His initiative and courageous conduct were in keeping with the highest traditions of the United States Naval Service.

"I'm seventy-nine years old, I'll be eighty in a couple months. I enlisted in the Marine Corps at eighteen years of age in 1943 off a farm north of Rocky Mount, North Carolina. My dad had five hundred seventy-one acres. We plowed with mules and raised corn, cotton, and tobacco, but I never was a smoker or a drinker. I come off a tobacco farm and never took a cigarette. I went through the whole Marine Corps and never took a drink. It didn't do nothing for me.

"We had twenty-six mules, two horses, and a pony. We went to town in a horse and buggy. It was June or July and hot as the devil. I took a bus from Charleston, South Carolina, to Yemassee, where we were greeted by a corporal with a swagger stick, and we were told right then who our mothers and fathers were and who God was and everything else. I went on from there to Mainside, Parris Island, and was dropped off solo at the receiving barracks before daylight. Then we got the bucket and the haircuts, the whole nine yards, went in one end of the building, took a shower, and come out the other end buck naked. They issued us uniforms.

"Boot camp was twelve weeks. Our DI's [drill instructor's] name was McCarty, I believe. They used to beat us on the head with the swagger stick and boot us in the butt and all that good stuff. I often wondered then: What in the world has that boy James got himself into now? But I got through OK. We slept in Quonset huts. One time they had us down eating grass, and the commanding general of the base drove by and stopped and backed up and asked the drill instructor what was he doing. He said, 'Sir, they march like cattle, and I'm going to make them eat like cattle.' The commanding general said, 'Carry on,' and drove away.

"During our two weeks on the rifle range we slept in tents with the mosquitoes and sand fleas eating us all up. There was only one paved parade deck, and the rest of it was dirt. We drilled in sand. As we got better, we were allowed to get up on the parade deck.

"I understand we were the second or third platoon to go through with M1s. I shot Marksman the first time out. I couldn't find the target. The front sight of my rifle was off to one side or something. After I got it fixed, I shot Expert.

"We got out of boot camp mid-August. There was no fancy graduation. They gave us the eagle, globe, and anchor and shook hands with us when we left on the bus. I made PFC out of boot camp. When I come home on leave, my dad said some civilian people in cheap suits had been there checking on me at the farm and in town, with my schoolteachers and all. When I went back I got sent to Courthouse Bay Camp in Lejeune. This was an amphibious tank school at that time, amtracs, top secret.

"We were in a restricted area down there. We weren't allowed to talk about the amtracs or anything. Nobody even knew what it was, a tractor that floated even when it was full of men or equipment. We went though two or three months of training with Alligator amtracs, which had aluminum tracks and truck engines in them. I think we were the first or second group to go through because we knocked down all the trees and vegetation and even tore up a bunch of houses. The amtracs were painted orange so we wouldn't run into each other in the woods.

"The amtrac weighed sixteen tons loaded. It was a beautiful piece of equipment, cost thirty-two thousand dollars. It was eight or nine feet wide, nine or ten feet tall and about twenty-seven feet long. It was called the LVT, for landing vehicle, tracked. They kept improving them as the war went on. We had an LVT3 on Iwo. It was powered by a seven-cylinder aircraft engine and had a bilge pump that wouldn't quit. Later the LVT4 had twin Cadillac engines, but the LVT3 was faster.

"We finished training on one called a Water Buffalo, which could carry eighteen or twenty guys. It had two thirty-caliber machine guns and one fifty, and a tracking mount for one of the thirty calibers on the back. We got all kinds of training in ammo handling and demolition and then took a train across the country. The train had to break up and go across one of the rivers out there in a boat. Our company of one hundred twenty was formed in Camp Oceanside, California, where we took more advanced training.

"We had a corporal there, an Italian kid, who took a dislike to me and gave me every shit detail there was, partly because he knew I'd do a good job. He gave me a hard time continuously. My dad had warned me some Yankees were tough, so I took all I could from the guy and then got mad and knocked him down three or four times. After that the guys started to call me Salty. That stuck with me all through the war.

"There were twelve or fifteen amtracs in a platoon, with three men assigned to each one. They were planned as troop carriers at that time. The first seven or eight waves of troops in a landing were brought in by amtracs, before the Higgins boats. The amtracs would arrive on LSTs [landing ship, tanks], drive off and swim to shore, and go right up the beach.

"We went up to San Francisco to get ready to board our ship on Thanksgiving of 1943. I remember because we had three turkey dinners in a row, one in the train station, one on the train, and another when we got to San Francisco. We were there probably a week before we went aboard the heavy cruiser *Boston*, one hundred twenty of us. It was a beautiful ship, brand new, and had just come through the Panama Canal and up the coast. We had two destroyer escorts on the trip to Pearl Harbor, where we went aboard LCIs [landing craft, infantry] that took us over to Maui. They let us off in water waist deep. Our amtracs were already there, waiting for us on the beach. We fixed them up like we wanted them and trained there for several weeks. We set up in pup tents. We had a water tank, dirt and dust.

"We joined the Fourth Marine Division when they came over, went on maneuvers and did several practice landings with them on Maui. We'd go out and pick up troops off the cargo nets and bring them ashore in waves, like a real landing. We'd bring seventeen to twenty troops ashore in one amtrac, and there'd be maybe twenty amtracs in a wave. When we got to the big islands like Iwo and those places, there'd be a whole string of companies joined in one wave. The first waves would come two minutes apart, and then they would extend it to five-minute intervals, then seven, then fifteen. I happened to be in A Company, First Platoon, First Squad the whole dern war, which meant I was in the first wave in every dern landing we made."

[Roi and Namur are twin islands in the Kwajalein atoll of the Marshall Islands. Roi is 1,200 by 1,250 yards and Namur is 800 by 900 yards, neither a square mile in size. They were defended by about 3,000 Japanese. Following heavy bombing, the two islands were invaded by the Twenty-third and Twenty-fourth Regimental Combat Teams of the Fourth Marine Division on February 1, 1944. Marine casualties consisted of 190 dead and 547 wounded, while 264 Japanese were taken prisoner and 2,472 were killed. The Fourth Marine Division was the first to go directly into combat in the Pacific Theater from the United States and the first to capture Japanese-mandated territory—Iwo Jima—in the Pacific.]

"Our first landing was on Roi and Namur, and it was like hitting a sandbar, just a maneuver for us. Very few amtracs blowed up, and we didn't lose but one or two drivers. The Japs didn't know what we were. We rode up on the beach and let the troops out. We got shot at a few times, but it was not too bad on those islands. The amtrac people had it real easy for some reason. We took Roi in six hours and Namur in just about a day. We came back from there to Maui, an eighteen-day trip around February 21.

"Back in Maui, we went through another phase of training, more maneuvers, and then on June 15 we hit Saipan, which is sixteen miles long. That was a big operation for me; we got shot at a lot more and everything. The amtracs landed eight thousand marines in twenty minutes. I was the crew chief, Ed Kaminsky was the radio operator, and Goule ran the ramp. You did get scared, though. Anybody who said they weren't scared is a damned liar. My foot would start jumping up and down on the accelerator as we went in, and I had to hold it down with my hand on my knee. Guys would go berserk before we'd hit the beach, and Goule had to knock them out or tie them down. I remember going in at Saipan. They were just shelling the daylights out of us and I told Kaminsky to call the Navy and tell 'em to lift their fire, they're killing our own troops. And he come back and said 'That ain't Navy. That's Japs.'

"The first assault wave hit the beach and continued inland right up to edge of the airfield, and the second assault wave had shotguns and regular rifles. The infantry carried twelve-gauge pump shotguns with double-ought buckshot along with their M1s, so they wouldn't hit us up front. The shotgun fire wouldn't carry like an M1 slug, you see? Because we had just overrun the Jap defenses on the beach. At that time we had a little bit of armament on the amtracs, a quarter inch of steel plate up front. We just overran the defenses. I remember one time hitting a foxhole and just putting it on one track and spinning around and just screwing this Jap right out of the ground. He got hung in the tracks. We went on into the airport. When the second wave caught up with us, they throwed the shotguns away.

"We stayed with them at the airfield for two or three hours. Then we went back out for more troops and continued to ferry them in. We brought ammo up and wounded back. Saipan was a heavy-duty operation; it was more wounded and everything. I remember the third night an Army outfit, the Twenty-seventh Division, came ashore. I remember they relieved us, and we dropped back to the beach. We were getting hit all the time. We woke up the morning of July 2 on the front line. The Japs had a big banzai attack, and the Army had quit and run. Almost two battalions of the division came running through. They just weren't trained; they were just nothing. They threw down their weapons and ran.

"Someone passed the word on the radio that the damn Japs had killed the damn doggies. A whole lot of enemy were killed that night. It was bodies in every direction; we were just running the machine guns all night, killing Japs. I don't know. It looked to me like it was thousands of 'em. I may be exaggerating, but it was at least hundreds, lying around like cordwood. We burned up one machine-gun barrel and had a second one halfway burn up. The fifty caliber about burned out. We were on the edge of the water almost, and the amtracs were so full of holes they wouldn't float. We had no place to go. They almost broke through. We just kept killing them, throwing grenades and ever' dern thing. The Japs were all hopped up on sake. One had a rubber hose, and he was beating the amtrac with it. They had sticks with bayonets on them.

"We had flares in the air all the time. It was just like daylight almost. Amtracs in line blasting as the Japs came charging. The Marine amtrac people were in kind of a staggered line, a good fifteen or twenty amtracs. The Army guys ran past us right into the water, and the Japs came right after them, and the marines stood up there and met them with thirties and fifties and burned their barrels out. I was too damn busy to be scared, for some reason. You get a grim feeling over your body.

"The Twenty-seventh Army Division was green troops, a New York Guard outfit, is what I was told. We heard that General Smith, Lieutenant General Holland [Howlin' Mad] Smith, was chasing the Army General Ralph Smith with his forty-five, trying to kill him. That's a true story too. I think he shot at him two or three times but he never did get him. That Army general was relieved, and the Army guys were sent back to Maui and told they'd pull guard the rest of the war. [Two battalions of the 105th Regiment were evacuated.] I heard they court-martialed a hundred and some officers from the top man down in that outfit. General Cates was commanding general of the Fourth Marine Division. Next morning we pushed forward and recaptured the airport and went on from there.

"About the fourth day there was a big naval battle out there somewhere, and every ship in harbor left except for one LST. What happened was we got into a warehouse of sake and beer and Japanese whiskey, I guess, and loaded up the amtracs. We had been aboard an LST for thirty days or so and got to know these guys real well, so we took an amtrac load of that beer out to the ship and give it to the guys. They all got drunk. Every ship was going next morning for that big battle that got known as the Great Marianas Turkey Shoot except for one LST, and it was sitting out there all by itself. The whole crew was drunk.

"We went to visit them later on, went down to see the crew, and do you know the skipper of that ship came out with a forty-five pulled, and he stood on the ramp and said, 'I'll shoot the first son of a bitch that steps aboard this ship!'? That was after we got 'em all drunk. Little things like that happened during the war."

[Saipan was secured by July 9, nineteen days after the great turkey shoot. More than 3,400 Americans were killed while 13,100 were wounded. Enemy dead totaled 16,525.]

"After taking Tinian, we went back to Maui to refit, retrain, and take on new troops, and what made us so hot was that all the rank, corporals and sergeants, was being made back in the States, and we couldn't even get promoted. We'd get back to Hawaii, and I'd see a whole bunch of new faces, corporals and sergeants, green troops, shiny faces, you could just see them. You can tell how many times a man had been in combat by his actions, the way he sits, his looks, his appearance; it's just different. As a combat veteran you'd go to the mess hall on Maui and forget to wash your mess gear. You'd just hang it up in the tent, and all of sudden you'd look up and say, 'Damn, I got to go wash this mess gear,' and stuff like that. And everywhere you went you looked for a hole to dive in or someplace to get behind. You'd just get crazier and crazier.

"When we got back to Maui after Saipan, we struck out to find those Army guys. We were really bloodthirsty. We were going to get as many as we could, but they took 'em to another island so we couldn't get at them. The Seabees were down the beach from us, and they were out looking for them too. There was a few scraps, but they got rid of most of them pretty soon. The court-martials of those guys in the Twenty-seventh Division followed.

"We went through another phase of training on Maui, going to obstacle courses, machine gun school, throwing grenades. We even went to the rifle range. We had rifles on the amtracs. I'd picked up a thirty-caliber carbine on Saipan, and I unloaded a fifteen-round clip into an enemy soldier. and he kept coming. Then some guy raised up with an M1 and knocked him back about three feet. From that day on nobody would take a damn carbine rifle. It'd kill a man [if you hit a vital organ], but it wouldn't stop him. That one I shot was just like hamburg. I got his Jap rifle. My son has it in North Carolina.

"Going to Iwo, we were aboard ship before we found out where we were headed, just like Roi-Namur, Saipan, and Tinian. Nobody knew what was coming. The convoy, hundreds of ships, zigzagged continuously, changing direction every fifteen minutes. We stopped in the Bay of Guam; some of the convoy dropped off there. From there to Iwo took about ten days, so altogether we were thirty-some days aboard ship, didn't do a darn thing but sit on our butts.

"The three days of shelling went on as we were approaching. We had these TCS radio sets, and we'd take 'em up topside on the LST and listen to the Navy talking to its planes, so we knew pretty well what was going on. We just steamed straight in on D-day. We glimpsed the island out at sea; it was just a shadow.

"When they served steak and eggs, we knew that would be our last meal aboard ship. Every operation we went on they'd give us steak and eggs, and then you had all them dead marines with steak in them. General Clifton Cates gave us the godspeed farewell message over the ship intercoms. We had heard two Navy pilots had been captured and tied to poles on Iwo and the Japs ran by, cutting them with swords. General Cates said in his farewell speech, 'You know what went on ashore. Take no goddamn prisoners.' Those were his exact words. All the time I was on Iwo Jima I saw one prisoner, and a chaplain had him.

"We ran the amtracs single file off the LSTs at roughly eight o'clock, formed our waves, and went straight into the beach, I believe it was Blue One [various sections of the landing beach were described by color]. We had it all timed, precisely on schedule. A battleship sitting off the coast with anchors out bow and stern was lobbing sixteen-inch shells onto the island. You could actually see a sixteen-inch shell come out of the muzzles of those ships. I looked back, and I could see this big old brass thing coming out of the muzzle. The power of that shell would pick you right up out of the water, and the track would speed up on the amtrac. I understood the ships would back up twelve feet in the water when they let off a broadside.

"My wave split; my two guys and I went around the bow of my ship, and the amtrac on my left went around the stern, and when we rejoined, I was in the first assault wave. I was in A Company, First Platoon First Squad, the Tenth Amtrac Battalion. Every landing. [Here Hathaway laughed.] They just never did change it. A

Company goes first every time. We had quite a few killed. We lost more on Iwo Jima than we did Saipan. We had the new modified amtracs, LVT3s. They had aircraft engines, seven cylinders, air cooled engines. They made eight knots.

"The water was always rough from the bombardments going on, and the waves were bouncing you around. The Japanese tried to confuse the first wave by ordering us back but we had two Navajos, Isaac and Sam, in the headquarters platoon as radiomen. They didn't call them wind talkers then. We'd had orders that once we hit the line of departure, to go straight in, no one stop for anything, wounded, hurt, killed, anything, and here all of a sudden came this voice telling us to go back to the line of departure. But then Isaac came on, telling them in Navajo to repeat the last transmission, and the Jap didn't know what to say. He started speaking Japanese then, and we just kept going. We wouldn't have turned around anyway. I did let up on the gas, I said, 'Darn, this sounded kind of official,' but I didn't turn. I think one or two amtracs did swing around, but they caught right back up. Those Navajos were pretty good. They'd grunt two or three times, and it'd mean a whole sentence.

"It was real dangerous close to the beach. You had to kinda kick in the clutch and time yourself, wait for the wave to settle down. Every third wave was a big one. You popped the clutch and headed in with that one, went right onto the beach. The sandbank on Iwo Jima was so high that we couldn't get up very far, but we had protection.

"The amtracs we had on Saipan you had to go over the side, but the LVT3s had a ramp in back, and guys would stream off, cut around both sides, and charge up the beach. We'd have the machine gun going, and we also had daisy cutters, twenty-four rockets mounted on the back, all fired by electrical charge. They just flowed out. They'd go zoop. We had blisters, periscopes, sticking above the armor plate in front. The water would hit, and the periscope would fog up, and you'd have to go in with your head stuck up again.

"One of the boys had a camera. You weren't supposed to have them. It was against all kind of regulations, but he took some pictures. I got one or two of them here at the house.

"One time a Navy Corsair was strafing right above us. He evidently got hit as he went in. He circled around with two of his machine guns going, strafing our own troops. You could see him dead at the stick, all bent over, with his guns still firing. He hit the water between me and the amtrac next to me, threw water all over us. Darn thing almost drowned us.

"We were not too far from the base of Suribachi, maybe six hundred yards. We hit the beach and were supposed to go inland, but we couldn't get up the bank. The sand was too soft. So we just dropped our troops off and continued down the beach single file to our left, then went back out to sea while the second wave hit two or three minutes later. They had beachmasters who would direct us, and they had little boats off the beach, LCIs I guess they call 'em. They'd direct traffic. We'd come out, and they'd tell us which direction to go and what ship.

"Getting back aboard ship was a job in itself. The ramp would go down, and you had to back on, catch it with your tracks, and the bow of the amtrac would go under. You had to sit soaked in water and pop the clutch when the tracks caught the ramp.

"We made five or six trips that day, taking troops and whatever they needed in, hauling wounded back to the hospital ships. We lost quite a few of our own outfit, amtracs getting shelled or hitting land mines. My boat was all shot up. We could carry eight to ten wounded. The crewmen would help load and then hold up plasma bottles or do whatever was necessary. It was pretty messy, you know. Somewhere around the third day an eighty-eight shell hit near my amtrac when we were a couple thousand yards out in the ocean, spun it around, and it sank. We bailed out, of course. We had life preserver belts. You'd mash a button, and they would inflate. We figured the war was over for us; we were going aboard a ship. We were just all smiles; we were out of it, you know, we were going home. A small boat picked us up and took us out to another LST. And shit, we got out there and there was a damn brand-new amtrac sittin' there on the dern ship, waiting for us.

"On the third or fourth day I was on top of my amtrac, getting ready to get off and get a little rest; we had been running day and night. A kid digging a foxhole next to the amtrac hit a land mine with his shovel, or else a shell went off, but it blowed me through the air off the amtrac. When I come to, I was stooped down in a hole, I was numb, my teeth were loose, and my head was splitting. I threw up my hand and counted my fingers. Then I pulled the other hand up and run it over my other arm. I felt of my legs, and I started smiling then, you know, because both my legs were there. I just laid still until I finally come to all the way. The kid who'd been digging the hole wasn't around. It was either a mine or a shell, an eighty-eight. I think it was a mine, but I'm not sure. A piece of shrapnel had hit me in the back and cut my blouse. A corpsman put some Merthiolate and a bandage on it. I never even turned into sick bay. I didn't even know it left a scar until I got home after the war. My mother, I had my shirt off, she says, 'Why, son, where'd you get that scar on your back?' The other two guys from my amtrac were sleeping or resting out on the ship. Lots of times we'd go out by ourselves, just one guy, and bring in a load of ammo. I was on top fixing to get off. I was going to get under the amtrac or something because they were shelling us pretty heavy.

"There was no Purple Heart for that, but the three of us did get the Bronze Star award for action on Iwo Jima. The citation is wrong. It says we were the only amtrac around, but that wasn't true. There were others. It says I was a PFC, and that isn't right either. I was a corporal.

"But anyway, I was the first amtrac to get up the sand dunes and make a road. We called it Roosevelt Boulevard. We had a company of marines cut off at the one end of the island. We loaded up a bunch of ammunition and water and broke through the line to bring them supplies. We just drove right over them damn bastards, firing machine guns. It must have been about the fifth day. [The citation says February 20, the second day.] What was left of our company was surrounded, completely out of ammo. We had a dump established on the beach by then—ammo, food, water, and supplies—kept bringing it in continuously. We took on a load, then went up, through, and over the Jap defenses. We could see their land mines because all the sand had blown off, and we'd scoot around them with the amtrac. That volcanic ash was something else.

"Our top speed on land was twenty-eight miles an hour. We were running in second gear and hitting them with machine guns. We ran right over the top of them. They were firing back and could have got us with bazooka or mortar. We stayed with the marines a little while. They kept hollering at us, 'Get that damn amtrac out of here! You're drawing fire!' They filled us up with wounded. We had fifteen, I guess, some of them real seriously hurt. One or two of them died before we got back to the ship. We came back the same trail we went up. When we got in the ocean on the way to the hospital ship, I was holding one guy, and he died. His mouth come open, and the blood just shot right out and soaked me. I jumped out in the ocean water and washed off. It was pretty bad, but we got the most seriously wounded out.

"I saw the first flag. I didn't see the second. Someone said, 'Those crazy damn marines are putting a flag up on Sunibachi,' and I turned and looked and seen it go up. The second flag went up several hours later, I understand. All hell broke loose when that flag went up too. The Japs just shelled the shit out of us.

"I was there all thirty-six days and kept doing mainly the same thing the whole time. All three of us came back together, which was kind of remarkable because so many of them didn't, you know. I lost two or three of my real good buddies.

"We didn't get too excited toward the end because you knew it was phasing down. A couple B-29s came in with landing gear out before the fighting was even quit. Sometimes mortar would hit right in front of a plane as it was landing. The Army Air Corps, the Mustang fighters, came in. A bunch of them landed there. Those guys were a bunch of alcoholics. They'd come in so drunk they couldn't even get out of their planes. They carried the booze with 'em, I guess. They'd bounce three or four times while landing, and we'd debate if he was drunk and would he be able to walk when he got out of the plane.

"The A-bomb was quite a thrill for us. After Iwo we went back to Maui to train for the invasion of Japan. We were told we were going to hit the southern island of Kyushu and to be prepared to lose ninety-eight percent on the initial landing. It was quite a thrill when they told us that much. We had loaded up the ships at Maui when we heard they had surrendered. We had our amtracs aboard and ever'thing. There was celebration going on all over the place. Some guy opened up with a thirty-caliber machine gun right down the company street.

"I left the Marines when I returned to the States, but after ten months on the farm I told my dad, 'I know something better than this.' And I reenlisted in the Marine Corps, as a PFC. I had been a corporal when I got out. I came back in motor transport because of my experience with the amtracs. I checked in at Cherry Point, did tours overseas and different things, but I never became a drill instructor. I did go to Korea. We were more or less in combat, stationed right behind the infantry with the trucks and jeeps, doing maintenance and all.

"We were in the division move up near the Chosin, and I remember it snowed nearly a foot and we were sleeping out in it. Korea was so darn cold that guys were losing their feet and fingers. I put some sandbags on my feet, two or three of 'em, and tied them up around my ankles. I looked around, and everybody was doing it. It saved many a foot.

"I got discharged at Camp Lejeune in '63, opened a filling station. I later built a shop in Jacksonville. I had ten or twelve mechanics working for me. I retired again twenty years later. My second wife, Inez, and I got married down here in Florida seventeen, eighteen years ago. I have a boy and a girl from my first marriage. The boy, James Alfred, is in his fifties. He's in real estate, up near Pinehurst, North Carolina. My daughter, Judy Yvonne, is a pilot, a captain with Hawaii Airlines.

"I stayed in touch over the years, seeing the guys at different times, anniversaries and the like. When you go to reunions, it's sort of amazing to see all them old guys from Iwo or Saipan messed up in their feet and legs, but when the 'Marine Corps Hymn' is played, they all get up."

4

CAPTAIN FRED HAYNES

Operations Officer
Twenty-eighth Marines, Fifth Marine Division

Some days, if we made one hundred yards, we were really doing it. On our side we had to cross corridors, and when you do that, you get enfiladed. At Iwo it was from the back, the front, and both sides. That's why we lost so many people in the north end, particularly in fighting for Hill 362. We attacked every goddamn morning.

Fred Haynes holds a photo of the flag raising, signed by members of his outfit. His right hand points to his fellow Texan Harlon Block. Haynes is the author of *The Lions of Iwo Jima*, the story of Combat Team 28 on Iwo Jima.

Young Captain Fred Haynes takes a cigarette break on Iwo Jima, March 3, 1945. The photo was taken during the attack on Hill 362A and the taking of Nishi Ridge. His Bronze Star citation speaks of his "outstanding service" in helping plan the invasion and for "coordinating the regiment's ship-to-shore movement," adding that he frequently "braved heavy enemy fire to obtain valuable tactical information" on terrain over which his regiment was to attack.

Fred Haynes, who was eighty-five in 2006, was a captain and operations officer during the Iwo Jima campaign. He later became a general. When I interviewed him in January 2006, he was one of three from the battle who had become a general and was still alive. As an operations officer during the battle, he was involved in day-to-day planning and indeed devised during the battle a strategy that may have saved a great many lives. Haynes joined the Twenty-eighth Regiment out of Quantico and was never wounded, though he served in three different wars. He retired a major general in 1977, after having commanded the Second Marine Division at Camp Lejeune, North Carolina, and the Third on Okinawa. In 1958–59 he founded the Combat Veterans of Iwo Jima, with a membership of about seven thousand veterans and their families. A little-known blood disorder, hemolytic uremia, hospitalized him from December 2003 to May 2004. He was unable to walk for a year and half afterward. With his balance uncertain when he did get back on his feet, he fell and suffered compression fractures of three thoracic vertebrae, leaving him unable to stand up straight. He was strong and active, nonetheless, and got around as well as most on the return to Iwo Jima on March 8, 2006. I was on that trip as well.

Captain Fred Haynes received a Bronze Star for his service on Iwo Jima even though in all thirty-six days of the battle, he never fired a shot. "I carried an M1 rifle because I wanted to look as much like a private as I could; the Japanese were very careful about targeting officers. They would bang away at 'em very quickly. I was on Hill 362 with Lieutenant Colonel R. H. Williams at the peak of that battle early in March. I was right on top of the hill and a Japanese ran out of a cave intent on doing bodily harm to us. Williams's runner, Yates, carried a thirty-eight-caliber revolver in a shoulder holster. Where he got it, I have no idea.

"Anyway, I went to shoot this Japanese, pulled the trigger, and nothing happened. So Yates pulled out his thirty-eight and killed him. The body was out in front of the hill. We had another runner with us, and he wanted to shoot this corpse. I gave him my rifle, and he was starting to aim it when Williams told him—and this was an indicator of how we indoctrinated people—Williams said, 'God damn it, you don't shoot corpses anytime! So put it down.' So he did. Then I checked the weapon. There was no ammunition in it. I had gone all the way to that point in the battle without ammunition.

"I came on active duty with the Marines not long after Pearl Harbor. I had been doing graduate work at Southern Methodist University for a master's in the new science of limnology, the study of inland waterways, now a well-known environmental science. I had actually graduated, in June of 1941, and later that year, probably December, I was doing some research in the library stacks and I saw a book called _Fix Bayonets!_ by John Thomason. He was a captain in the Fifth Marines at Belleau Wood and Château Thierry. The book is a classic, supergood. I took it off the shelf and read it. I made up my mind that if I had to go to war, I'd be a marine." [Colonel Charles Waterhouse (Chapter 12) was similarly inspired by _Fix Bayonets!_]

"Two Marine officers came through our campus to sign up potential graduates. I got on their list and was called to active duty the first of February 1942. I went to Quantico with three guys from Texas Christian University. All of us had played football. I played freshman ball at SMU before the coach urged me to give it up, and I became a track athlete. I played center and linebacker, and I only weighed one sixty-three. Our SMU team played Stanford in the Rose Bowl January 2, 1941. A lot of guys with significant football backgrounds fought at Iwo Jima. Our regimental commander, Colonel Harry Liversedge, had been an All-

American tackle at the University of California at Berkeley. Liversedge was one of these guys like Cheney [Lieutenant Colonel Chandler] Johnson. Liversedge always wore his helmet, and he never carried a knapsack. He rarely used leggings. After D-day he took his leggings off. He wore a tank officer's shoulder holster and carried a forty-five. He was one of those guys you need on the battlefield. He was a big man. He weighed about two fifty-five, two sixty. He was six-three or six-four. Even for those days he was pretty big. He had a kind of a loping stride. We called him Harry the Horse. He was a relatively quiet man.

"Combat Team Twenty-eight consisted of three infantry battalions, a weapons company, a headquarters company, and the Charlie companies of each of the combat support units, the pioneers, the tanks, the medics and the engineers, and usually we had the Third Battalion of the Thirteenth Marine Regiment, which was an artillery support unit. So we had about four thousand men. We walked off the island with about six hundred when the battle was over.

"Combat Team Twenty-eight landed on Green Beach at H hour. Our initial mission was to cross the narrow neck, about seven football fields wide [seven hundred yards], as rapidly as we could, then turn south to assault and seize Suribachi. I was responsible for making sure our boat waves were properly organized at the line of departure and dispatched on time to make the assault at nine o'clock. The first waves, the amtrac waves, were followed by, as I remember, two waves of Higgins boats, known as LCVPs [landing craft, vehicle, personnel]. Those were the organized waves. The Navy had patrol craft at both ends of the seaward line of departure, four thousand yards off Green Beach, and we had a ship-to-shore communications net operating from the command ship. It would indicate when each wave was to be at the line of departure and then the time, like at nine-five, nine-ten, and so forth, that the waves were to leave for the various beaches.

"There were probably seven waves ahead of me when I landed. I went ashore about nine-fifty with Colonel Bob Williams, who was the regimental executive officer. The last scheduled wave landed about nine-thirty.

"The Fourth Division was on our right, and on my right was the Twenty-seventh Marines. They had two battalions abreast. We landed in a column of battalions. The first battalion had the immediate mission of getting across the narrow neck. We had an excellent naval gunfire plan, really superior, and we pushed our troops up against the naval gunfire. We even had a few casualties from the gunfire, but not many. The combination of our previous training and the high caliber of the people we had in the First Battalion enabled us to cross this narrow seven-hundred-yard neck in about an hour and thirty minutes. They really smashed it.

"Back in California and Hawaii, when we were training, only about ten of us knew we were going to attack Iwo and Suribachi. We did amphibious landings at Pendleton and San Clemente, and when we got to Hawaii, we went through the whole cycle again before we left for Iwo. We picked a bubble on the slopes of Mauna Kea about the same height as Suribachi. We took engineer tape, used it to delineate lines where mines had been cleared, and formed the end of Iwo around that bubble. We would line up our troop units by boat team and walk them at the same speed, roughly about three miles an hour, and when they came to this tape, each boat team would deploy and follow the maneuver to get across the island. And then the Second Battalion would move in on the left. We had excellent, totally realistic training, and while the youngsters didn't know where we were headed, they knew damn well they were going to do something like that. We were just going to go hell-for-leather straight across. We thought the First Battalion was practically ruined by the time they crossed the island. And of course the confusion on the beach as the troops moved inland was incredible. This was far worse than anything I ever experienced in three different wars. It took us about three or four days to figure out how many we had lost. I think we lost like three hundred men out of thirty-two hundred in the regiment on D-day. I'm one of the few people who lived through this battle without a wound and who started from scratch with the formation of the regiment and the combat team and continued with it through the occupation of Japan.

"Kuribayashi, the Japanese commander, was a really smart general. He waited until our units got on the beach, including Williams and Liversedge, the commander of Combat Team Twenty-eight. Within minutes, Kuribayashi put all his artillery and his heavy mortars on these beaches. It was chaos.

"But we got in and formed a command group on the beach with Liversedge and Williams. In the very late afternoon—and I'll never understand this—Liversedge said, 'You know, we'll have to move to a better place where we can command this unit.' So about one hundred of us, communicators and all, stood up and walked across the neck, almost halfway, to where we could see both beaches, and not a soul was hit.

"It was not quite dusk. And the next morning the Japanese pinpointed us and dropped a mortar barrage on our command group, killed our regimental surgeon, and blew the legs off one of our uniformed correspondents.

"I'd never been in battle before, and I didn't know whether I'd panic or what would happen, but I found out quickly that I didn't flap very easily. About ten-thirty we felt that it was absolutely essential to get our Third Battalion, which was being held back as a division reserve, back in under our control because a gap in the line had developed. The First had crossed the island, the Second had turned left, and casualties were very heavy. There was a lot of confusion, and this gap had opened between the right flank of the Second and the left flank of the First.

"We told General [Major General Keller] Rockey, the commander of the Fifth, it was absolutely essential to get the Third in, so we started landing them, about ten-forty, and they came and filled in the gap. By the close of D-day we had all three infantry battalions, all of our thirty-seven-millimeter guns and all our seventy-five-millimeter half-tracks, with the exception of one thirty-seven that had been blown up and sunk coming in.

"The weasels, small tracked vehicles, were the prime movers for the thirty-seven-millimeter guns. The Navy would not allow us to put a weasel and a gun in the same boat because they said it would overload it. Colonel Liversedge wanted to land eight thirty-sevens in the scheduled waves. We persuaded the Navy to let us overload the landing craft, so we devised a means of putting the gun on top of the weasel so we were able to double the number of thirty-seven millimeters that we got ashore in the initial waves.

"The seventy-five-millimeter half-tracks were good-sized weapons, and we had trouble getting them off the beach. We got a couple bulldozers and were able to move the half-tracks and a couple tanks that had got stuck. I've never seen anything like that black sand since. It was the consistency of percolator-grain coffee, and you'd sink up above your ankles in it. There were three terraces, or three levels of sand, on the beach. We got steel mats put down by the close of D-day, but the beach continued to be just utter confusion.

"The beachmaster for the division was a Navy commander who later became the first violinist of the San Diego Symphony. He was really an interesting guy. He's dead now, but he was terrific. He was a no-bullshit type, and he got it done, but how he did it I'll never know. Our supply system was a little bit different than it had been earlier in the war. We pushed everything up. We didn't wait for somebody to say, 'I need more ammunition.' We pushed ammunition based on rough calculations, straight on up to the battalions as quickly as we could.

"Each amphibian tractor carried a predetermined packet of essentials, like a crate of grenades, two boxes of sixty-millimeter ammo and two boxes of eighty-one and about four boxes of machine-gun belted ammunition. The minute that amtrac got above the waterline, their instructions were to throw this stuff out on the beach, which they did. And that saved our butt on that first night and the next day because the marines all knew they could go back down there and get whatever they needed and get their butts back up there.

"We were able to dig foxholes about two feet deep. This was the middle of the winter, in February, and it was in the northern Pacific and it could have been very, very uncomfortable, but the whole island was a volcano, and once you got down six or eight inches, the temperature was very pleasant. Many of us would dig a little hole and put a can of C rations in it, and next morning you'd open it up and you'd have warm beans.

"There was no natural water on the island, and we were quite lucky because our Navy made water aboard ship. The Japanese only had what little they could catch, and it didn't rain very much. By the time we were about a third of the way up the island, they were getting a hard biscuit a day and about a cup of water, terrible water. In my judgment, the Japanese officers were criminal in continuing this battle; they tortured their own men. These poor bastards got a biscuit and a cup of water a day, and they had to work underground in temperatures of one hundred ten to one hundred twenty degrees. As letters from Kuribayashi pointed out, they'd work maybe ten or fifteen minutes, and then they'd have to get out. Otherwise they'd collapse from heat exhaustion.

"They were going to die anyhow, and he told them, 'Look, guys, I want you to kill ten Americans before you die.' That was the order. And it looked like for a little while like they might be able to do that. It was the only battle in which we lost more than they did. They lost about twenty-one thousand and we had more than six thousand dead, nineteen thousand wounded.

"Prior to the landings, we had asked for ten days of bombardment, but the Navy said they couldn't do that. We said, 'Well, give us five.' They couldn't do that. So they gave us three, but the naval bombardment was what got us ashore and across the narrow neck. It saved our butt. The Navy guys were very courageous, and they came in close in gunboats, snuggled right up against the beach, firing directly into the caves on Suribachi. Each of our battalions had a destroyer in support, and the regimental combat team had a cruiser in support. The division had a battleship. There were actually two battleships, five cruisers, and nine or ten destroyers in overall support. And it was effective in the southern third of the island; it was less effective up by the Quarry to the north and on the ridgelines. Naval gunfire is a flat trajectory weapon and difficult to use in many places. About all you could use on the ridges and hollows was artillery and mortars. Artillery tubes began to wear out when Combat Team Twenty-eight started to fight in the north end of the island. We ordered new tubes, and one of the unfortunate incidents of the war was losing those tubes. They were being delivered by air from Guam, and the wind shifted with the first batch, and we sat there and watched the tubes parachute right in the water. So we had to deal with inaccurate artillery tubes.

"Many of us thought Cheney Johnson, who commanded the Second Battalion, was probably killed by our own artillery. He was blown to smithereens. I think all they found was a piece of his torso and his shoes. Eventually we got new tubes, and the artillery became more accurate. Cheney wore a combat fatigue hat. He never wore his helmet. My personal view is that Johnson tripped the detonator on a U.S. aerial bomb dud the Japanese had rigged just north of Hill 362. Captain Naylor, the F Company CO, had warned Johnson not to go into the ravine, but he did and met his demise.

"But you need a few guys like Johnson, who sort of wander around the battlefield without their helmets and get things done. They become an inspiration to the troops. That was true of Liversedge, who was our combat team commander, and of Williams, who was his exec, and Johnson.

"Suribachi was captured on the fifth day. We landed on the nineteenth of February, and the flag went up on the twenty-third. The first flag went up at ten-twenty a.m. The second and most famous one went up about two that afternoon. We didn't pay much attention to the second one because you know, we were all busy, fighting the war, and the big impact was the first flag. You could barely see it, just a little tiny thing. Major Oscar Peatross—I was his deputy—and Williams and I went up the mountain shortly after that first flag was raised, when the second patrol was getting ready to come up."

From the top of Suribachi, Haynes and his group got their first view across the battlefields.

"We saw the mess on the beach and what we had ahead of us. You could see the real challenge was going to come once we got past the airfields, where we had one hell of a fight. That photo of me was shot while we were taking Hill 362. We had more casualties in three days taking 362 and Nishi Ridge than we had taking Suribachi. We lost two hundred fifty men a day up here. That's more than a rifle company a day, *boom boom boom.*"

[Haynes described the landscape around Hill 362 Able in an article for the *Marine Corps Gazette* in 1953: "Northern Iwo was a treeless wilderness of cave-studded, jagged, frequently ill-defined compartments, radiating from a central plateau toward the coastal cliffs. The terrain around Hill 362 constituted the right (west) one third of the main cross-island position. It dominated the western side of the island south to Suribachi."]

"That was the meanest fighting because whereas we could get naval gunfire into vertical sections where all the caves were, here you couldn't do it. We had to depend on infantry guts, just getting up to these places and then cross them.

"The battle became a slogging thing, almost a depressing proposition, because there had been all the excitement and progress: We took the mountain and put a flag up, and when we went into the line, we fought on the left flank. Progress from midway on was just tiny. Some days, if we made one hundred yards, we were really doing it. On our side we had to cross corridors, and when you do that, you get enfiladed. At Iwo it was from the back, the front, and both sides. That's why we lost so many people in the north end, particularly in fighting for Hill 362. We attacked every goddamn morning. We'd jump off around seven-thirty or eight o'clock. Wherever Williams went he always took me. In the evenings at the end of each day it was our responsibility to make sure our lines were tied in, particularly with the Fifth Division units on our right.

"I went up to our OPs [observations posts] frequently, and I could see what we were faced with. The proposition I made to Colonel Williams and Liversedge was we should try to form a horseshoe, so we could go down these corridors instead of across and avoid the enfilades. So Colonel Liversedge said, 'OK, get your-self an airplane and go look.'

"So I went to Airfield No. 1 and asked a pilot of a grasshopper, one of these little Piper Cubs, to fly me down the corridors and then back up the corridors from the sea. I told both colonels what I had seen made it seem right. The idea was to hold the line steady and swing the right-flank units around to positions from which we could attack down the corridors.

"Then you're going the length of the corridor instead of across it. And when you did that, instead of going where you got fire from the flanks, like in the case of 362, where we lost a huge number of casualties by fire from the rear because these bastards had caves up here on the south side, and then they had these interlocking caves, underground tunnels, and they came out on this side and they could shoot you in the back. So if you came over the top, you not only got hit from the back and the front, but you got the sides also. There were probably fifteen or twenty of these corridors, each six hundred to seven hundred meters long. So the aim was to go up them instead of across. Then you could put machine guns and observation over on both sides, and you could shoot this way and that way, and it was a lot easier: set up interlocking fields of fire and close off the caves. And that was what we did ultimately. There's no way you could tell for sure how many casualties we reduced, but whereas we had huge casu-alties initially, once we started that maneuver, the numbers dropped off.

"I had no frame of reference from past experience. Nobody did for this kind of thing. This was really the first time that any of our officers and men had been in anything like this. In fact, nobody did after that either, even though Okinawa was a tough place. Very few Japanese surrendered on Iwo. My Combat Team Twenty-eight captured a total of sixteen prisoners in the thirty-six-day campaign, and all but two or three had been wounded or were physically incapacitated from lack of food and water."

Why were there so few? Were captured Japanese simply shot?

"We conducted an extensive indoctrination program prior to Iwo in which we made a strong point of the need to take captives. This had to be done with great care because the Japanese were very canny: They'd put hand grenades under bodies of their own people so that when you moved them, the grenades would go off; they also booby-trapped artillery shells, kind of like these guys the jihadists are doing in Iraq. So we urged the men to be very careful in how they took people. Nearly everyone we captured begged to be shot. They begged to be killed.

"During the interrogation of one prisoner, he said, 'You know, as far as the Japanese are concerned, I'm dead.' Which was another way of saying, 'I can't come out of the woodwork. I've got to be very careful.' It was hard to find any POW who would talk. But I well remember an instance in which a Japanese was buried up to his neck in debris, from an artillery round, probably, and he was alive. One of our Japanese-language officers gave this guy a cigarette and then very gingerly removed the dirt from around him. He confirmed some of the order of battle information we already had.

"The most useful intelligence, after we landed, came mainly from our own OPs, our aerial observers, and from documents that we found in a couple of caves in Suribachi. So we had a pretty good idea of what the order of battle was. We also had two excellent interrogators, who had been to the Japanese-language school, and we had a third, John Lloyd, who had been raised in a missionary family on Honshu. He knew Japanese street language.

"By the time we finished 362, we were not Combat Team Twenty-eight anymore. Our leadership was gone, we had only a couple company commanders left, most of our lieutenants had been either killed or wounded, many of our NCOs had been killed or wounded, and I liked to say we walked by faith. Casualties in the companies of the Twenty-eighth were running well above fifty percent by the evening of March 1. We just believed in the guy on our right and the guy on our left, and we had been told to do it, and we were gonna do it, do it to the end."

[Haynes has written his own account of Combat Team Twenty-eight's ordeal, *The Lions of Iwo Jima*, published by Henry Holt.]

"Yates, the runner who killed the Japanese when my rifle didn't fire, later had his leg broken by sniper fire and had to be evacuated. He had had this damn little black and white terrier, a mascot he called Tige, short for Tiger. He smuggled him aboard ship to go to Hawaii and then smuggled him aboard ship to Iwo. Yates was primarily a runner for Williams, and the night before D-day I was in the wardroom. I couldn't sleep, and neither could Williams. He said to me, 'What the hell are we going to do about Yates's dog? We can't take him ashore.'

"And I said, 'Well, you know the Navy kids will take care of him, so we can tell Yates to leave him aboard.' But I remember saying to Williams, 'You know he's not about to do that. He'll smuggle him somehow.' And he did. He put the dog in his knapsack and took him ashore. Later, after Yates was wounded and evacuated, we got one of the communicators to take care of Tige, and he lived through the battle. We decorated him with an Asiatic-Pacific Campaign Medal with one star, put it on his collar when we got back to Hawaii.

"What was the Japanese leadership like? The commander at Iwo, Tadamichi Kuribayashi, had been an attaché in the United States. He was also a cavalryman, and he wrote a song to the horse cavalry. Both he and Lieutenant Colonel Takeichi Baron Nishi, who commanded a Japanese tank unit at Iwo, at various times had indicated that the Japanese were dumb as hell to fight America. Both knew they couldn't beat us. But nobody paid any attention to them. So Kuribayashi ultimately committed hara-kiri toward the end of March. We know this mainly from intercepted communications.

"He sent a message on the fourteenth telling the emperor that he was sorry but he didn't think he could hold Iwo. We're not sure of this, but we have fairly good evidence of Kuribayashi's death from a Major Horie, who was on nearby Chichi Jima during the battle for Iwo. He thought Kuribayashi stuck himself in the gut with a knife and had his aide chop his head off.

"Nishi dug all of his tanks in and used them as pillboxes on Iwo. Between the fifteenth and the twentieth of March, he got hit in the leg and then committed seppuku. We never found his body. These are things that we found out from the very few Japanese who lived holed up in caves.

"Kuribayashi's eldest son is still alive. His name is Taro, and he is a member of the Upper House in the Japanese Diet. Kuribayashi had two daughters, one of whom died of typhoid in Tokyo during a B-29 raid there, and the other became a movie star, believe it or not. His grandson is in the foreign service of Japan."

What happened to the island after the battle? It provided an emergency landing strip for crippled B-29s returning from attacks on the mainland, for one thing. Haynes described another purpose.

"Iwo Jima became a critical navigation point for the atom bomb attacks on Nagasaki and Hiroshima. Colonel Paul Tibbets, who was in charge of both bombings, had Charles W. Sweeney, the pilot for the Nagasaki bombing, go to Iwo and dig a bomb transfer pit near Suribachi, down at the end of the runway. This was so that if Tibbets's plane, the *Enola Gay*, had trouble, she'd be able to get back to Iwo, come over the transfer pit, and lower the bomb into the pit, so he could get another B-29, pick it up, and go finish the mission.

"Second, three B-29s followed Tibbets. One, McKnight's *Top Secret*, landed at Iwo as a standby aircraft in case the *Enola Gay* had trouble en route. Chuck Sweeney in the *Great Artiste* and George Marquardt in *Number 91* flew the entire mission with Tibbets from the Marianas, and they used Iwo as a navigation point. After Tibbets made the drop, they were the ones who did the photography and the radiation checks. And of course Sweeney then turned around and three days later flew the second A-bomb to Nagasaki.

"What gives the battle for Iwo Jima such lasting significance? First of all, it was the bloodiest and most difficult of any battle that the Marines fought, ever. Even though Okinawa was greater in terms of casualties, it was a battle where three Marine divisions and several Army units participated. And the Iwo battle had enormous significance nationwide and worldwide because of the photo of the flag raising taken by Joe Rosenthal. It was a huge boost to morale back in the U.S. People were getting weary of the war. The European war they were pretty sure was going to come out OK, but here was Iwo, a little tiny goddamn island, eight and half square miles. Tarawa had been a tiny island, and it had been terribly costly. Peleliu had been costly. The Marianas had been costly. Guam had been costly. The war tolerance in the U.S. was pretty low, so this was a huge boost to the morale in the U.S. The photo epitomized courage, cooperation, patriotism, working together. It had a Navy corpsman in it. You remember, there were five marines and one Navy guy.

"A second feature was this: You can't identify the flag raisers. You can only see a little part of James Bradley's face, hardly enough to recognize him. The others are hidden, and they could all have been unknown if Roosevelt hadn't said you got to bring them back. We didn't know who they were. This was not a posed picture, and it was so symbolic because of where these marines came from.

"The guy putting the flag in the ground is Harlon Block, another high school football player from Texas, who joined the Marines with all the senior members of his ball team. Bradley was a rural kid from Wisconsin. Ira Hayes was a Pima Indian from one of the poorest tribes. Strank was probably the best of all the group. He was a sergeant, an immigrant who came across as a baby with his parents from Czechoslovakia. His dad was a coal miner, and Strank became a coal miner until he joined the Marines. He was killed, of course. And Gagnon was a Canuck from New Hampshire or Vermont. He's the one you can't see. You can see a hand, I guess. It was a representation of America. The only thing not there is a black. We didn't have black Marines in combat.

"We had a black DUKW company [see page 255] that was Army, and we had ammunition and depot companies, most of them black, on the shore party, and they did a lot of the digging of the graves. They were in that last fight, and Harry Martin was given a Medal of Honor. He was killed there."

Iwo Jima is the signature battle of the Marine Corps because it epitomizes keeping going in the face of fatigue and an enemy who fought to the death. It epitomizes the Marine Corps' esprit, which is a lot like love. It's impalpable. You cannot touch it. You cannot exactly get your mind round it, but you certainly know it when it's there. Marines trust one another. You have this animating spirit, this belief in the guy on your right and the guy on your left. They've all been through a similar kind of training, and it's tough training done by people who have been in some pretty tight spots. You understand that these guys know their job, and they will cover you and you them. It's a belief, too, that you can't beat us because we're in it until the end, and we're in it together as Marines. You may knock a few of us off, but if you do, watch out. If you kill Marines, one thing is for sure, there will be other Marines coming along soon, and they will keep coming until they find you.*

After World War II Haynes rose to the rank of major, serving as executive officer of an infantry battalion in Korea. As a colonel he became military secretary to the commandant in 1968. After being promoted to major general, he was given command of the Second Marine Division on the East Coast and, in 1973, took command of the Third Division in the western Pacific.

"Headquarters had moved from Vietnam to Okinawa, and we did the evacuation of Phnom Penh. Later I was given command at Camp Lejeune, North Carolina, and went from there to Washington for my last tour of active duty. I retired January 1, 1977."

Following retirement, Fred Haynes joined an aerospace firm, and for several years he was a military commentator for CBS News in New York. He is chairman emeritus of the American Friends of Turkey, which later became the American Turkish Council. He also is a member of the Council of Foreign Relations. He and his wife, Bonnie, a TV producer, have four children between them from prior marriages.

* Fred Haynes speaking in *American Spartans* by James A. Warren.

5

CORPORAL HERSHEL WOODROW "WOODY" WILLIAMS

Medal of Honor
Twenty-first Marines, Third Marine Division

Our objective was the first airfield. We didn't hardly move for a day or so. There were bodies everywhere, absolutely, stacked up like cordwood, just unbelievable.

Woody Williams at home in Ona, West Virginia, February 24, 2006.
Photo by L. Wayne Sheets

Hershel Woodrow Williams displays his Medal of Honor, awarded by President Harry Truman on December 5, 1945.

Woody Williams spoke to me at length from his home in Ona,
West Virginia, in early January of 2006. Eighty-two at the
time, he said he would never go back to Iwo Jima. "I guess it's
an idiosyncrasy. We paid a terrible price for that thing, and if
we'd have kept it, I'd have gone back on the first invitation. It
was a mistake to give it back to the Japanese. We paid a terri-
ble price, eighteen thousand wounded plus sixty-eight hun-
dred killed, and we should have kept it, as a memorial, if
nothing else. Now, I just don't want to make that association.
I want to remember it as it was. I know it doesn't look any-
thing like it did then. I have no desire to go back."

"I weighed three pounds when I was born October 2, 1923. I
don't know how I made it. I was the last and smallest of eleven
children. I got all the hand-me-downs. Only four boys survived.
The flu got them. My folks were in the dairy business, and when I
reached five years of age, I became subjected to it. This was long
before the machines came in, and we milked by hand. My job was
to get out to the barn around five a.m., with a bucket of soapy
water so I could wash the cows' teats before the others got there.
We milked thirty to thirty-five cows on a sixty-eight-acre farm.
We were about seven miles out of a town called Fairmont, West
Virginia, and all our business was there, so each morning my
father or my brothers would take the pickup truck, a Model A
Ford, and we would head to town and make house-to-house
deliveries.

"We bottled the milk on the farm, in pints and quarts, and of
course we had a separator, so if you wanted a quart of pure cream,
we could give that to you too. Our milk sold for seven cents a
quart. My job, along with a couple of my brothers, was to ride on
the running board and my father would yell out, 'One quart of
milk!' or a dozen eggs or a pound of butter; we'd grab it and run it

to the customer's door, gather up the empty milk bottles, and run back to the truck.

"I went to grade school in a little country community called Quiet Dell in Marion County. It started out as one room, but they added a second one eventually, so you'd go from first to fourth grade in one room and then from fifth to eighth in the other.

"Then you'd have to go to high school in Fairmont, and of course there was no bus service or anything, so you got to school however you could. The morning milk deliveries made it easy for those of us in high school. We also had evening deliveries, and they'd pick us up and bring us home. Any sports or extracurricular activity was completely out of the picture for us. There was too much to do at home.

"My father's name was Lloyd Dennis. He died when I was nine years old. My mother was named Lurenna, and everybody called her Rennie. I don't know her background. Maybe we just had some unusual names. One of my brothers was named Nora, and I don't think I've ever met another man with the name Nora.

"Of course there was very little money, but we would usually get a dime on Saturday, and we would go to town if we weren't putting up hay or didn't have something else to do. They wouldn't take us, so we'd either walk or hitchhike. A nickel would buy an ice-cream cone, and a nickel would get you in the movies.

"I did not graduate from high school. My brother next to me dropped out and went into the Civilian Conservation Corps in the late thirties. He was making about twenty-one dollars a month. That was a lot of money then, so I decided I wanted to do the same thing. I dropped out of high school in the eleventh grade and went to the CCC. I had the hope they would send me where my brother was, but they sent me to another city, Morgantown. I stayed there ninety days and then they shipped that whole group of us all the way to Whitehall, Montana. I thought I was clear out of the world.

"We were building jack fences—barbed-wire fences with a post like a tent pole notched at the top. We put barbed wire on each side of them. The purpose was to keep animals off the government reservations. My job was hauling men to the forest who did the cutting and then eventually hauling those pine trees to the mill, where they would be creosoted and notched and turned into fence posts.

"I was there when Pearl Harbor happened December 7, 1941. A lot of the men enlisted right away. I was still coming up to my eighteenth birthday. Of course the Army was in charge of the CCC. They furnished the uniforms, did all the medical treatment, did all the chow. We worked under civilians off the base, contract people who supervised the road building or fences or whatever. So a lot of these CCC fellows went straight into the Army right after Pearl Harbor was hit. I wasn't eighteen yet, so I requested my discharge from the CCs and came home. I wanted to go in the Marine Corps. I did not want to go in the Army.

"Why? [Williams laughs at the memory.] During the time I was twelve or thirteen, we had two fellas that had gone into the Marine Corps from Quiet Dell. Of course ever'body knew ever'body, and most people were related. I had one aunt and five uncles in the area and first cousins by the dozens. But these two guys had gone on active duty in the Marine Corps—at that time you had to enlist for six years—and they would get a thirty-day furlough once a year. They would come home in their dress blues. The Marine Corps was trying to make a name for itself so it could attract people. These two guys were tall, very polite, just really squared away, with spit-shined shoes and all that stuff. We kids would hang around and go with them wherever they would let us. They'd tell us these great big wild stories, probably most of them not true. It was good entertainment anyway.

"But I decided, apparently in my subconscious, if I ever became a military person, that was what I was going to be. That's all I knew. We didn't see any other military people.

"I went home to enlist in Fairmont right after my eighteenth birthday in October 1942. My mother did not want to sign for me. My father was already deceased, and I was the last of the Mohicans. I was still the baby. You know how that is.

"But I went to enlist anyway, to the Marine Corps office in Fairmont, sometime in November. I filled out a piece of paper and took it up to the marine sitting at the desk, and I handed that paper to him, and he kind of looked me up and down and said, 'We can't take you.'

"He hadn't even looked at my papers. I said, 'How come?' He said, 'You're not tall enough. You've got to be five feet eight or better. We can't take ya.' So I went home. I decided if I couldn't go in the Marine Corps, I wasn't going anywhere.

"So I went home and back to farming. But then, after the first of the year in 1943, the Marine Corps did away with that height requirement and began taking little runts like me. I was five feet six, and weighed one hundred thirty-five pounds. But I was muscular. I'd worked on a farm all my life.

"That recruiting sergeant had kept my paper, and he looked me up and then, in May of '43, I went in. I had really enlisted before that, but they put me on a waiting list because so many people were going in that Parris Island couldn't handle them all. So when my number came up, they sent me to Charleston to catch a train. I thought we were going to Parris Island, but they couldn't handle any more recruits. They had big tent cities, and guys who were there told me there was mud clear to your hip pockets. Anyway, they started a troop train down in Georgia or Florida and came up through the southern states, picking up people. They picked up six of us in Charleston, and we went all the way to California. So I'm a Hollywood marine.

"Training was tough. There were times I was laying out there in the mud or dust, dirty, thirsty, and bone weary, and I thought I might not get through it, but I never thought about quitting. They could kill me, but I wasn't going to quit.

"After basic, I went to a place called Jacques Farm, a tank farm at Camp Pendleton where they taught advanced infantry training with tanks. I didn't get into demolition until I went overseas."

A ten-day furlough did not give him enough time to go home following training, so Williams wrote his sweetheart, Ruby Meredith, that their wedding would have to wait until after the war. "I wouldn't marry her," he said, in an earlier interview with West Virginia writer Wayne Sheets. "I did not know if I'd be coming back, and I didn't want to saddle her with that kind of burden." He also told Sheets how he devised a way to evade the censors and let Ruby know where he was, by employing the first letter of each paragraph to spell out his location. His first overseas base was New Caledonia. "By the time I'd written enough to disguise my code, I'd written a letter the size of the Sears, Roebuck catalog. And my next assignment was Guadalcanal." He learned later from a censor that many other servicemen had used the same system.

"They shipped us to New Caledonia as a replacement group, where hundreds of marines were sorted out and sent to the various divisions as replacements. I got sent to Guadalcanal to join the Twenty-first Marines, Third Marine Division, which at that moment was on Bougainville.

"The First Division had captured Guadalcanal. Bougainville was the first campaign of the Third. They'd been to New Zealand, shipped to Guadalcanal, and now they were up in Bougainville. We were going to go up there, but those guys did us a favor and secured the island before we could leave. We joined them when they came back to the Canal, and that's when I got into flamethrower demolition. We trained there till June of 1944.

"I was a Browning automatic rifleman previously, before they sent me to this demolition flamethrower school. The guy who took my place on the BAR got killed when we got to Guam. So if I had stayed with the BAR, you wouldn't be talking to me, unless you got a line direct to heaven. We had a banzai one night, and they overran his outpost and got him.

"We went to Guam July of '44. It was our first action, jungle-type fighting after we got off the beach. The jungles were very thick. You just had to beat or cut your way through. You didn't see the enemy until after you killed him. But one of the memorable things, there were thousands of frogs on Guam. It rained a lot on Guam, and the shell craters were full of water, and there would just be hundreds of frogs in those shell craters. At night those things would move, and of course, to a scared marine, he thought it was a Japanese. I expect we wasted more ammunition on frogs than we did on the Japanese. Whatever noise happened, we shot at it.

"When we hit the beach, we picked up our flamethrowers, but we didn't need them after the initial invasion, so they stayed in Headquarters Company. You were a rifleman again. We had M1s. They issued me a forty-five, which I carried on my hip, and a carbine, but as soon as I could find an M1 that somebody had dropped or lost or belonged to a guy who had been wounded, I threw the carbine away and got me that M1. I couldn't hit the side of house with that carbine. I didn't like it. I'd always pick up an M1 and take that with me."

Along with maneuvering the flamethrower, demolitions consisted of learning how to set fuses and fling satchel charges.

"We also used a lot of pole charges, about a ten-foot two-by-two piece of lumber or anything else you could find. Marines always improvise some way. If you haven't got it, you make it or steal it. Instead of carrying the satchel, you'd tape or fashion or tie the satchel charge to the end of a pole so that once you burned out a pillbox, then you could run up and stick the pole charge through the aperture of the pillbox and blow it up rather than have to go up there and try to stuff a satchel charge in there by hand. Or you'd take a pole charge and stick it down a cave. You were more accurate that way than you were just throwing it.

"Most of the explosive was composition C2. We did use a lot of quarter-pound blocks of TNT when we didn't have C2, which was very secure. You could shoot through a composition C2 and it wouldn't go off. A blasting cap fastened to the C2 would make it go off. The fuse set off the blasting cap.

"They issued the flamethrower operator an assistant because somebody has to carry all his gear. He can't carry a pack and ammunition and all that other stuff. The fellow who became my assistant was from Floyd, Montana. With my having been in Montana, we had a little rapport with each other. He was six feet six. Now I'm five-six and he's six-six, and he carried everything I couldn't: my canteen, my roll pack, and everything else. His name was Vernon Waters, and he was my assistant when we got to Guam. He was still my assistant on Iwo, and we lost him there.

"We stayed at Guam after capturing it and continued to train for jungle-type warfare. Then we got notice we were going some-place new. The whole division was boarding ship. Once we got aboard, they brought out this mock-up on a piece of board that showed the island of Iwo Jima. Looked like a pork chop. That's when they told us where we were going.

"The Fourth and Fifth Division would be the primary force. We were in reserve. We'd probably never even get off ship, we'd probably be gone for four or five days, and then we would come back to Guam. Well, you know intelligence, ha. It's not always good intelligence."

"The Fourth and Fifth went ashore February 19 [Williams told Wayne Sheets]. On the twentieth somebody decided more marines were needed. At three in the morning of February 20, we off-loaded onto Higgins boats. My scariest moment was getting off that ship by rope ladder. There was no light and we were carry-ing a backpack that weighed sixty or seventy pounds, and we had to go down that rope ladder forty or fifty feet. I knew if I fell into the water it would be the end of me. I couldn't swim.

"We stayed in the Higgins boats and amtracs all day long. Everybody was sick, either from seasickness or because the guy next to you vomited all over you. Conditions were beyond description. There was no room for us on the beach. Units there were pinned down, suffering unbelievable losses, and couldn't move inland. About ten that night they took us back aboard our ship. They gave us some food and everyone collapsed and slept wherever they were. At three the next morning we did it all over again, aiming for Red Beach."

"Fortunately most of the group I was with were in amtracs [Williams told me]. They hit the beach and stopped because those things couldn't go in that volcanic sand. They just bogged down. You got off when the front ramp dropped. Trying to walk or run in that volcanic ash was like trying to move on a floor covered with BBs. You couldn't get any traction, and there was no cover. The enemy was firing straight across the ground, and there was nothing to stop the bullets. If you tried to dig a hole, the sides caved in. The only protection was shell holes that had been blasted in the ash. There'd be six or ten guys in each crater."

Williams said he did not know how he conquered his fear. "I had a job to do, and I suppose I got so wrapped up in it I didn't have time to think. I knew deep down there was a power greater than I was. I didn't know what it was, but I prayed to it lots of times. Many years after I left the Marine Corps I came to realize that power was God Almighty and that He alone had the power to save a life—mine. When I was going after the pillboxes, I absolutely thought that I would die."

Williams's C Company, First Battalion, Twenty-first Marines, consisted of 279 men when it hit the beach on February 21. By March 5, thirteen days later, only 17 were left.

"Because of the tremendous losses in men and equipment suffered by the Fourth and Fifth Divisions, our division became the spearhead. Our job was to punch a hole in the Japs' line of defense, mostly pillboxes, so the tanks and personnel carriers could come ashore and start inland.

"Our objective was the first airfield. We didn't hardly move for a day or so. There were bodies everywhere, absolutely, stacked up like cordwood, just unbelievable. And the airfield of course had been bombed and strafed and bombed until there was nothing left except shell craters and the pillboxes I got involved in. Somebody reported later there were about eight hundred of them in the area where we were headed. Those pillboxes had a deadly field of fire over that airfield. You'd just run from one shell crater to another, and if you made it, you felt pretty lucky. That's all the protection you had.

"Then, on the twenty-third, of course, the flag went up. We were still on the beach at that point. I didn't know what was going on. I guess I had my head under the sand about as far as it'd go. People around me started yelling and screaming and jumping up and down and firing their weapons, and for a few seconds I couldn't tell what in the world was going on. And then I looked up and saw Old Glory flying above Mount Suribachi, so I just joined and fired mine too. I jumped up and down and screamed.

"It was about that time the CO asked me if I thought I could do anything with the pillboxes that had us stymied. I was in Headquarters Company, C Company, and when I hit the beach, I had six flamethrower and demolition people with me. Each had an assistant like Waters, so there were twelve of us. But by the twenty-third they'd either all been killed or wounded, and we hadn't used a flamethrower up until that point. My job primarily was to keep them supplied with demolition and flamethrowers as they needed them.

"I had not had any occasion up until then to use any demolition or flamethrowers. Since I was a corporal and all the other guys were PFCs or privates, I'm the man in charge, and I was acting sergeant. We were all called to a meeting in a big shell crater. We had tried and tried to get across that airfield and get through those pillboxes, but we had been kicked back every time. Pillboxes surrounded the airfield, and they were self-protecting with what I call interlocking fields of fire; you couldn't get to one without exposing yourself to the others.

"So the CO, Captain Beck, asked if I thought I could do anything about some of those pillboxes. Somebody else said later I told him, 'I'll try.' I have no idea what I said. So he assigned me two BAR men and two riflemen, and I picked up the flamethrowers and started knocking some of them out. The BAR and riflemen would cover me as I went from crater to crater, until I reached the point where I had to crawl. You could only run from one place to another for so long, and when you get so close, you got to get down and crawl on your belly. If you raise up, somebody's going to get you.

"We were using a mixture of high-octane gasoline and diesel fuel, so if you fired the thing into the air and you had any air blowing toward you, it'd burn all the hair off your arms and eyebrows. It would kick back at you, so we fired it in two- or three-second bursts and rolled the flame on the ground. It would roll across the ground, twenty to twenty-five yards depending on terrain, and right into a pillbox.

"We had quit using what we now call napalm; back in those days it was called phosphorus gel because it had phosphorus in it and it stuck to whatever it hit. But it was a single stream. You only had about seven seconds of fuel, and you'd fire it, and by the time you got on target you've already shot up everything you had. We didn't like it.

"The guy in charge and the rest of us came up with this mixture of diesel fuel and high-octane gasoline. It burned about thirty-four hundred degrees Fahrenheit, and it wouldn't burn a body up, but it would catch your clothes all on fire and take all the oxygen out of the air. That's what he [the enemy] died of: suffocation.

"You had to get within about twenty yards of a pillbox, with machine-gun bullets kicking up around and everything else. I don't know how I lived; I have no idea. I was just reading this morning somewhere in an interview that I had where I mentioned these thoughts come and go, and some of what happened that day I never have remembered. But at one point I do remember I was in a ditch. They had ditches that connected so they could go from one pillbox to another and still stay below. I was crawling up one of those ditches, and they were shooting at me with a Nambu [Japanese machine gun], and the bullets were ricocheting off my flamethrower.

"It was just like a jackhammer, you know, *drrrrrrrrrrr*. I guess I had enough sense to know if I backed up, I'm going to get in trouble. So I went forward, and when I got forward, I was at a point where he couldn't lower his guns far enough down to get me, so I got him. He was in a pillbox. You had to hit the aperture. The fireball is probably twenty foot in diameter, so it's a great big ball of flame. It would roll clear over the pillbox, but a lot would penetrate the aperture, giving you time to get up there and throw a satchel charge or a pole charge and blow the pillbox up.

"I've jokingly said over the years those marines back at headquarters apparently didn't like me because not a one of them ever volunteered to bring me a full flamethrower. I had to go back and get them myself, each time. When it's empty, you just roll out of it and git, go back and get you another flamethrower, and go back again.

"I got seven pillboxes with six flamethrowers. How many in each one? I have no idea. I guarantee you I wasn't counting, but somebody reported in some piece of literature that there were twenty-one Japanese in those seven pillboxes. I never got a scratch that day. One time the men in one pillbox came out and came running straight at me. I don't know whether they had run out of ammunition or whether they had decided that as a group they could get me. As they came running toward me with their rifles and bayonets poised, they ran straight into the fire from my flamethrower. As if in slow motion they just fell down.

"I was out there alone: Waters was back taking care of the flamethrowers, and the riflemen were laying down fire. One of the four was my pole charge man, so once I got the thing burned out, he would grab a pole charge and run forward with that and blow the thing up. He survived. His name was Schlager; I don't remember his first name.

"That was February 23, exactly the same day the flag went up. I lost two marines there that day who were giving me protection, and when I wear the Medal of Honor, which I do on many special occasions, and I'm giving a talk, I make a point that the medal really does not belong to me. It really belongs to those guys because they gave their lives. I do not recall their names.

"I got wounded March 6, a leg wound from shrapnel. I've always said it was a piece of our own; I still have it. I was really behaving myself at the point. I was in a foxhole that somebody else had dug. It was very shallow, and I couldn't get my body in it. I got my upper body in, but my knees were doubled up in the air and a piece of shrapnel come along and caught me just above the left knee. I called for a corpsman because I didn't know how really severe it was. He came and pulled the shrapnel out and gave it to me. He bandaged me up, gave me some morphine and put sulfa on it and said, 'I'm going to write a ticket and get you safely back.' And I said, 'I'm not going back.' At that point, Vernon was still living. I said, 'I'm not going back.' And he said, 'Well, I put a ticket on you, you have to go back.' And I said, 'You better take it off me, or I'll just tear it off. I'm not going.'

"So he said, 'OK, if you're that stupid.' He just let me go, and a few hours after that Vernon was out in front of me—he was also just a rifleman at that point—and the Japanese fired what they called a knee mortar. It came over a ridgeline and hit him smack-dab in the center of the helmet, never knew what hit him.

"After we got through the pillbox area, I was more of a rifleman than a flamethrower for the rest of the campaign. The next big flamethrower operation was right at the end, probably the thirty-fourth day. We had reached the other shore, and we were down in beach area securing the place, and they captured a Japanese who supposedly said there was a cave containing three hundred Japanese. It was on the side of a hill that went down to the ocean.

"My CO asked me to seal that cave. As a rifleman I'm still carrying two satchel charges on each shoulder. They were like satchels that you would carry to school, canvas bags with a strap on it and you'd just hang 'em over your shoulder and take off. They weighed eight pounds each. There were eight blocks of composition C2 in each one. They gave me some rifle protection so I could advance, throw the satchel charges in, and blow it up. It was a huge hole. Big.

"They got to shooting, and I'm getting my satchel charge, and I put only a ten-second fuse on it because I wanted it to explode pretty quickly because I don't want them to throw it back at me. So I ran up to the cave and threw the thing like you were throwing a softball, a big underhand throw. I sailed that thing into the entrance of the cave and ran back on the beach, and just as I hit the deck, I heard a pop. And it didn't explode. The cap went off, but it had drawn dampness and didn't have enough power to set the explosive off. So I prepared the second one, and we went through it a second time. I threw it in there and ran back as hard as I could run, and I didn't even get to the deck that time because I had shortened the fuse a little bit and it popped. So I knew I had to have some new caps.

"The CO sent me back to headquarters for a new box of caps, and I came back and prepared a third charge. I went up there and throwed it in, and boy, when it went off that time, it set the other charges off, just lifted the side of that hill off the mountain and sealed the cave. We never knew whether there was anybody in there or not."

The island was declared secure on March 27.

"We came off Iwo April 1 and went back to Guam. When we got back, the interesting thing, at least to me, was they had changed the whole method of training. We had been jungle fighting before; now we're going to go street fighting.

"Scuttlebutt was running around we're going to Tokyo. They'd built up some false-front buildings with windows and doors in them and a street between two houses. They were training us how to get through a window, how to go through a door, how to approach a house, that kind of stuff. We knew we were going to a city, we didn't know where, so the dropping of the atom bomb ending the war was a big relief.

"You know, your averages do run out and with two hundred fifty thousand civilians the Japanese had trained, women, children twelve and up, with every kind of a weapon you could think of, an ax or sharpened bamboo or whatever; they were going to fight us to the last person, so I'm not sure my number wouldn't have come up.

"I was on Guam when I was ordered back. The first sergeant said General Erskine had requested my presence in his office, and of course, as a lowly corporal, you go quickly. He congratulated me. I was going to be sent back and recommended for a medal. He never did tell me it was the Medal of Honor, and even if he had, I don't think it would have meant a thing. I didn't know it existed."

Williams was flown to Hawaii, where he was given a seat on a planeload of prisoners of war returning from camps in Japan. A seat came open when one of the prisoners died.

"Those people did not even look human. I'll never forget that as long as I live. It was just unbelievable, the condition of those marines, right out of prison camps in Japan. Some of them had weighed one hundred sixty or one hundred eighty pounds, and now they were down to eighty or ninety pounds. They just looked like a skeleton with skin drawn over it."

He went home from San Francisco by train to Fairmont, where he picked up his mother, Rennie, and his girl, Ruby, and went on to the White House, where he and twelve other veterans—three Navy and the rest of them marines—received the Medal of

Honor out on the lawn from President Harry Truman on October 5, 1945.

"There were at least four from Iwo, myself and Jack Lucas and George Wahlen, a corpsman [Chapter 16]. They're still living. Of course my mother wasn't scared, but I was. I think I was more scared there than I was on Iwo."

Woody and Ruby got married twelve days after he received the medal. They were to have two daughters and five grandsons. He left the corps that November and in January went to work for the Veterans Administration, where he stayed thirty-three years, looking after veterans from West Virginia.

"In 19 and 62 my life changed because God took hold of me and turned me and headed me in some other direction, and I became a lay speaker for the Methodist Church. If a preacher is on vacation or gets ill, we replace him."

He became chaplain of the Congressional Medal of Honor Society in 1986, replacing Desmond Doss, and served into 2005, when Woody stepped down.

He was active throughout in the Marine Corps League, serving as commandant and in other capacities. He also served the Veterans of Foreign Wars and the American Legion and helped raise money for scholarships for the children of slain marines or league members who had died.

Woody also raised and trained horses for thirty years, first Morgans and then American saddlebred. A grandson took over when Williams grew too old to continue.

"West Virginia has the record of having more people per capita serve in the armed forces than any other state. It's always been a very patriotic group of people. For whatever reason, few West Virginians were involved in the Civil War. The line goes right through us, North and South. But patriotism has always been one of the high-water marks of West Virginia. Many cities put on tremendous parades for Veterans Day and Armed Forces Day. Every year I'm invited to speak.

"In fact, dating from the Civil War, West Virginia has had sixty-eight of her sons receive the Medal of Honor. I'm the last one left. If I could write my own epitaph, it would probably say, 'Here lies Woody Williams, who loved people and the United States of America.'"

Medal of Honor citation

For conspicuous gallantry and intrepidity at the risk of his life above and beyond the call of duty as demolition sergeant serving with the First Battalion, Twenty-first Marines, Third Marine Division, in action against enemy Japanese forces on Iwo Jima, Volcano Islands, on 23 February 1945. Quick to volunteer his services when our tanks were maneuvering vainly to open a lane for the infantry through the network of reinforced concrete pillboxes, buried mines, and black volcanic sands, Corporal Williams daringly went forward alone to attempt the reduction of devastating machinegun fire from the unyielding positions. Covered only by four riflemen, he fought desperately for four hours under terrific enemy small-arms fire and repeatedly returned to his own lines to prepare demolition charges and obtain serviced flamethrowers, struggling back, frequently to the rear of hostile emplacements, to wipe out one position after another. On one occasion he daringly mounted a pillbox to insert the nozzle of his flamethrower through the air vent, killing the occupants, and silencing the guns; on another he grimly charged enemy riflemen who attempted to stop him with bayonets and destroyed them with a burst of flame from his weapon. His unyielding determination and extraordinary heroism in the face of ruthless enemy resistance were directly instrumental in neutralizing one of the most fanatically defended Japanese strong points encountered by his regiment, and aided vitally in enabling his company to reach its objective. Corporal Williams' aggressive fighting spirit and valiant devotion to duty throughout this fiercely contested action sustain and enhance the highest traditions of the United States Naval Service.

Harry S. Truman
President of the United States

A lone marine is silhouetted against smoke from the dynamite used to close caves
shielding Japanese soldiers. The fight for the rocky outcroppings
of the Quarry took place in settings like this.
AP Wide World Photo, from the U.S. Navy

PART TWO

Iron Mike's Posse

I met Glenn Buzzard, Domenick Tutalo, and Pete Santoro at a drill instructor's reunion in 2004, when I went down to Parris Island, South Carolina, to do research for a book about the place. That was where I met Iron Mike Mervosh, a veteran of Iwo Jima who had also served two tours as a drill instructor at Parris Island. Neither Glenn nor Domenick nor Pete had served on the drill field, so why were they there? They all had been in the Fourth Marine Division, had served at Iwo Jima, and had known Mervosh back then, so the drill instructors' reunion offered them a chance to get together as well. Mike lived in California, Glenn in Ohio, Domenick in New Jersey, and Pete in Massachusetts. They doted on Mike, who was profiled in *The Few and the Proud*, a book about drill instructors that grew out of my visits to Parris Island and the Marine Corps Recruit Depot in San Diego, the two places where marine recruits are trained.

Mervosh saw combat in three wars, holding every enlisted rank from private to sergeant major over a thirty-five-year career. He was the Fourth Division middleweight champion until wounds suffered on Saipan and Iwo Jima ended his boxing career. He holds Navy commendation medals for action on Iwo Jima, in Korea, and in Vietnam, a Bronze Star for action in Korea, and three Purple Hearts. He served more than nineteen years as a sergeant major in battalion, regiment, brigade, station, base, and division. His last assignment before retiring on September 1, 1977, was Fleet Marine Force Pacific Sergeant Major—the largest field command in the Marine Corps—over eighty thousand marines.

I found Buzzard, Tutalo, and Santoro to be sensitive, self-effacing, thoughtful men whose stories deserved to be told. They're not really a posse, of course. They're just three old pals, each of whom knew Mike on Iwo Jima and who got acquainted and became friends as a result of attending reunions in the years long after the war.

6

CORPORAL GLENN BUZZARD

Machine Gunner
Twenty-fourth Marines, Fourth Marine Division
Two Purple Hearts

I didn't have to shave. I wasn't old enough.

Standing in the yard of his Ohio home in August 2005, Glenn Buzzard holds his dress uniform in one hand and, in the other, the thirty-eight-caliber pistol his brother Erett sent him. He purchased his dress uniform when he graduated from boot camp in 1942.

The decorations on young Glenn Buzzard's blouse include a Purple Heart with one gold star, signifying two recognitions. In the center is a presidential unit citation with a star, again indicating two citations, and an Asiatic-Pacific Campaign ribbon with three stars, signifying four battles. On the left shoulder is the Fourth Marine Division patch, the ruptured duck, an eagle in a circle, signifying combat experience.

I spoke with Glenn Buzzard several times over a period of months. We met at a few different reunions, and I visited him and his wife, Needra, at their home in Ohio. One time he told me how Pretty Boy Floyd, the notorious bank robber and killer, had been shot to death on October 22, 1934, by the authorities on the farm across the road from his father's place in East Liverpool, Ohio, just two months before Glenn himself came there to live with his dad. "His [Floyd's] car had run out of gas, and he walked a short distance and came up and asked this older couple for a meal. Back in them days they would feed you." Floyd wanted a ride to Columbiana and was talking to the couple about it when the authorities "got wind of where he was at and surrounded the place," Glenn recalled. "He went out the window and down past the corncrib and the barn, and that's why them two buildings were all shot up. And then he got out into the field, and they finally hit him and got him down, and then, according to what I hear, they didn't give him any sort of a chance, just kept shooting at him while he was laying there on the ground. They wasn't going to take any chances. My dad was home, working, and he heard gunfire and a hell of a commotion. By the time he got over there they wouldn't let nobody around, naturally, but then they brought his body right up to the edge of the road to be picked up. They drug it up there, and he was laying there on the ground, my dad said, riddled with tommy guns. He was a modern-day Robin Hood is the way it's been put. He had killed people, no question."

Glenn Buzzard was born in Chester, West Virginia, on December 15, 1925. His mother died in childbirth just before he turned five. There were two other boys, and his father was a bit of a hell-raiser, as Glenn put it, so "an old maid" named Nancy Lee Conkel took him home to live with her in Canonsburg, Pennsylvania, in the spring of 1931. His older brothers, Arnett and Erett, were taken in by others. "People didn't keep track," Glenn recalls. "Today you couldn't get away with that, but back in them days people farmed kids out and everybody was happy. Nobody stuck their nose in it. I know it's farfetched. The Depression was on, and Dad had to move out of his farm. Dad was a wild fella. He'd get out and get in fights. He was pretty rowdy. He had moonshine. But he never mistreated us kids.

"Nancy had a place across from my dad's, but she just came down in the summertime. She had a big old Buick, big wooden steering wheel on it. She was just a little person; she'd sit and look out through the steering wheel. She and my dad knew each other; maybe he farmed some of her property. They was just friends. She was a businessperson, as they called her, and never had been married.

"My mother died in November when I was four, and I turned five December 15. Because he knew the authorities would be coming out in connection with her death, Dad got rid of the moonshine still he kept upstairs. He kicked out the back of the gable end of the house and dumped everything, sour mash and all, out there to the chickens and the pigs and the ducks. He had to dismantle the whole still. I don't remember that personally, but my brother Arnett is eighty-seven this February [2007]. He's still got a real good mind, and I went out of my way to ask him questions. He said the pigs were wallowing around drunk.

"I was with Nancy till I was thirteen, about eight years. I'd come down in summertime and stay for a week with my dad or with her relatives in Chester. I went to school in Canonsburg. She was associated with the WD Wade Company and sold women's clothes out of the back of her car. She would go to Pittsburgh and buy the stuff wholesale. I remember she had big suitcases full of jewelry, men's jewelry: watch fobs—those were a big seller—stickpins, sleeve garters. That's how she made a living. She'd buy everything by the dozen and go door to door, sell one at a time. She had magazines, books, and cloth samples. Corsets was a big one back then.

"I delivered stuff for her after school, and on weekends I'd run clear across town. She kept her table completely set for eight people at all times, knives and forks and everything laying just so, and what she done she lay back one corner of it and we eat there every day. On Sunday I had to go to church. I wasn't allowed out to play because it was the Sabbath. She was strict about that.

"Long dresses was in, naturally, and she went up a stepladder to get up into the cupboard—I think it was my birthday in December—and she got her heel in her dress and pulled herself off that ladder. She went to the hospital, probably there for a couple weeks. I was home alone going to school.

"Canonsburg wasn't a big town. Everybody knew everybody. You didn't lock your doors or nothing. There was only two police. Attis was the chief, and Haney was his assistant. He was a little short fella and wore those knicker pants with big black leather boots, and he rode that motorcycle all over town. Down below Canonsburg was a children's home, Morganza.

"Haney come out on his motorcycle and said, 'You know they're coming to get you in the morning, to take you to Morganza. Don't you have a father somewhere?' I said, 'Yeah. Down in Chester, West Virginia.' So he took me and my dog Spanky back down to the station and put me to bed up on the fire truck on them hoses, and then he called Chester and got Doc Lyons, the chief of police in Chester. It was the dead of winter, and Doc Lyons walked up Middle Run Road to Cunningham's house. He knew Cunningham and my dad knew each other. My dad was at work in Weirton, West Virginia, in the mill, but Leonard Cunningham was a good friend of my brother Junior, and he says, 'I'll go get him. I know where it is.' So he did, in the middle of the night. He brought me down there, and I went right with my dad. It sounds complicated, but that was how things played out.

"I was in eighth grade, and my dad had remarried and had three more children, and me and my stepbrother would ride this red horse, a gelding named Charley, to Clarkson school and then tie its head up so it couldn't bend down to eat and let it loose. It would go back to the farm, and Dad would work it all day. Then we'd walk home, four or five miles, after school.

"I quit school at fifteen and went to work in a pottery, carrying molds. I was running around, and I got my first car, a Model A Ford truck. It would pull Logan's hill in high gear. That's how you could tell if it was a good vehicle. I didn't have to double clutch to get over neither. I gave one hundred fifty dollars for it.

"Everybody older than me was going to the service, and I was partying and getting in at two o'clock and having to go to work at six, and I got tired of that. So one day I just went to Pittsburgh and enlisted. There was a local football player who joined the Marines and got shot up on Guadalcanal. I suppose that had some influence on my decision to join the Marines. Anyway, I took my old Ford truck and went to Pittsburgh, found the post office building, enlisted on Monday, and they said come back up on Tuesday with my birth certificate and paper signed by my dad and the chief of police, and you'll go right straight to Parris Island. It was August of '42. My age, which was sixteen, never come up. Monday they gave me some physical and stuff and everything seemed be OK. Only thing was, I was humiliated to death because I never wore undershorts.

"The only time my age came into play, I was in boot camp on Parris Island, and the drill instructor, his room was right at the end of our big long wooden barracks, he called me into his room. I'm sure he wasn't too polite about it, but anyway, he just said, 'Do you want to get out of the Marine Corps?' I said, 'No.' He said, 'OK, go back to your bunk.' I suppose they had to ask that question to keep it legal, because somebody had found it out.

"I started boot camp in August, took the train to Yemassee. We got off there, got in them trucks. It was dark, like they always say, dead of night. You had to stand up on the trucks. Once they got you in, it was so crowded you didn't need worry about falling over. Boot camp didn't bother me much. I didn't have to shave. I wasn't

old enough. I was underage, but also, having the farm background, I was probably in better shape than most of them there. I
was six foot, and I weighed one hundred forty-four pounds. I
probably knew more for my age than most kids that had a mother
and father did. We had a lot of boys from New York and West Virginia. They didn't get along at all. There was always a lot of trouble
in our platoon. Consequently, when two guys got into a fuss, we
all had to pay for it.

"When we got out of boot camp, we went straight to New River.
We had rifles at Parris Island, but we did not get to fire them until
we got to New River at Hadnot Point, all part of Camp Lejeune
now. We trained with Springfields at Parris Island, but when we
went to the range they gave us M1s. We lived in tents.

"We trained and trained, and they built us up, and when they
had enough people, they called us the First Separate Battalion.
Mike Mervosh was in it too. We got six days' furlough, and when
we came back, they put us on a troop train to Camp Pendleton.
Then they brought other outfits in, and in the spring of '43 we
became the Fourth Marine Division.

"When they had enough battalions, they'd make a regiment
and then it takes three regiments to make a division. The Twenty-
third, Twenty-fourth, and Twenty-fifth regiments became the
Fourth Marine Division. [A platoon contained about 45 men, a
company had 250, a battalion contained 1,100, and a regiment
accounted for 3,300, or three battalions. There were 20,000 men
in a division.] Plus there were headquarters companies, artillery,
mortars. We were in machine guns. We didn't even train with the
riflemen until we went on maneuvers; then we fit in because that
was the way you were going to fight.

"That's how I got to know people in A Company, B Company,
and C Company. We had three platoons in D Company, which
was a weapons company. They would take the First Platoon in D
Company, put it with A Company, machine guns. Second Platoon,
B Company. I was in the Third Platoon, and we'd go to C Company. Next time we went out they'd maybe put us in a different

company. That's how I got to know those guys. But after Roi-Namur they got so low on officers they couldn't shift us around. So they changed that. Put First Platoon in A Company and so on. I was in C Company from then on.

"You had four squads in a platoon, two sections, a gun in each squad, so that's four heavy water-cooled machine guns and four light machine guns. You used the light air-cooled machine gun in the daytime; then at night you set up your air- and your water-cooled machine gun and you'd cross your fire, set up interlocking fields of fire in a solid wall right down the line. The heavies had a big water case. We trained with them a lot. We had carts to pull them on. The gun weighed ninety-one pounds, and we used it strictly at night. It was always right behind you on a jeep or something. We carried the air-cooled guns and had Browning automatic rifles, the next best firepower. You needed firepower. That was the name of the game.

"The BAR was lighter than our light machine gun, but it was a damn good weapon. It was part of the rifle platoon. They let us fire the machine gun from the hip. It would work, and I did it. You had to have an asbestos glove which they gave you. We'd tape that asbestos glove right on that barrel, and then we wouldn't lose it. Then you'd put an ammunition belt around your neck and tie it on to that gun. The worst thing was you couldn't put a whole belt through it because you couldn't control the belt feeding into it, so you cut the belts, which were canvas. The fifty calibers had metal belts. We cut it to maybe thirty shots. You only fired when you really needed it.

"I was a machine gunner all the way through. I never carried anything else. We had side weapons. They tried shotguns, and they tried carbines. The shotgun was a good weapon because it scattered, especially in jungle, but was hard to keep clean, and the shells were paper, so when they'd get wet, they'd swell up and wouldn't go in the chamber. When I became a machine gunner, I needed a sidearm. They came out with forty-fives, but they didn't have enough, so they give them to the squad leaders. Junior, my brother Erett, sent me a thirty-eight through the mail along with a Bible. The thirty-eight had no grips. It was up in the attic, just layin' up there, a six-shot Smith and Wesson. I knew it was there, and I asked him for it. I was on liberty somewhere, and I bought an old black holster for it. I had to get special permission to carry it. You peart near had to be in combat because I couldn't wear it with my dress uniform any way, shape, or form. I must have bought the ammo for it in Hawaii. They were lead bullets, which would splatter, which was good. It didn't have no handle grips, and I made a pair of wooden ones and taped them on. I carried it through all my campaigns.

"The first time I used it was in Saipan, on a banzai attack when a Japanese tripped over my machine gun in the dark. Needless to say, somebody killed him. I don't know whether I did or not. I fired at him with that thirty-eight. I know I had it going at him because it was close quarters. I couldn't get the machine gun on him, but whether I or somebody else did it, I kinda thought maybe I did it, but then it's nothing to brag about, taking a man's life. They was there just like we were, probably didn't know any more than we did. Anyway, that's life, that's the way wars are. People that know everything ain't in the war. They're sittin' back somewhere.

"I was wounded later that night in a mortar attack. Somebody took the thirty-eight off me because I had to go back to the beach next day on an ammunition truck to get patched up. It was in my back and shoulder blade area, but it was pretty well cauterized. Adrian DeWitt from New York somewhere pulled that shrapnel out. It was long, about an eight-inch sliver, and it was spent to a good degree. Otherwise it would have took my shoulder off. Another thing saved me on that one was my poncho. It was all tore up, so it took a lot of the shrapnel down in the kidney area. But I did get my thirty-eight back.

"For the trip to Iwo we boarded ship at Maui, had maneuvers at one of the other islands, then went to sea again. Then we went to Guam but didn't get off. Finally they told us where we were going.

"It was pretty devastating when we landed that morning, February 19, 1945. My first thought was: Why the hell didn't they know the island was this way, because of the sand and stuff like that? We wasn't just fighting the Japanese; we was fighting the elements, the island itself, the make of the island, worse than anything else. The devastation was terrible, bodies everywhere. They put nine thousand marines ashore the first day. You can figure it out yourself, nine thousand guys, and they weren't more than three hundred feet off the beach. They couldn't get far. It was devastating, just carnage everywhere.

"Not knowing about that sand was a big failure by our intelligence people. The other was they didn't realize the Japanese people could go underground that far. The effect of the bombing was almost nil. We thought it was doing a hell of a job, wiping them out every time we dropped a bomb, but we weren't.

"We landed up at the boat basin, as far away from Suribachi as you could get, in about the third wave. Everything didn't go according to Hoyle. They were trying to get nine thousand people on there in eight or ten hours. I'm not trying to take any glory from any wave. I was not in the first, but when I got there, the first wave was laying right there, waiting for us. Bodies everywhere; equipment couldn't move. The main thing was to get out of that boat and get the hell off that beach, three hundred feet in if you could. You're still right out in the open. It wasn't any safer, with every firing mechanism pointed at that beach. Nine thousand people they said put ashore the first day. That's a hell of a lot of people; it was elbow to elbow."

Why wasn't the landing force annihilated?

"Just sheer determination, I guess, or maybe they didn't have the ammunition to expend on a full-blown assault. Maybe they were conserving ammo, but I don't see any reason why they couldn't have blowed us clear off that beach. Only thing is we just overwhelmed them, I suppose, bodily. It boiled right down to the individual person. The company commander wasn't telling him what to do; the first sergeant wasn't telling him what to do. If Kuribayashi'd had more weapons than we had, we probably wouldn't have made it. But say eight or ten of you came to a hole in the ground and it was a pillbox, and if you was getting trouble with it, you congregated on it and took it out. You couldn't call for tanks, couldn't call for rockets. It was just sheer determination, small-arms initiative.

"The Quarry had guns sticking out of it, and the friendly fire damage was about the worst I ever seen. They were trying to get at them guns and they'd call in an air strike, and our kids would just roll dead off them hills because the planes hit short. We had front-line panels, but things got mixed up, you know what I mean? It was right out in the open, just like a theater, and we was off to the left and a little bit inland, and we could look right around. When we first went in, the Japanese guns were right above us, but they were six-inch guns, not for use on us but mostly to shoot the boats. They had plenty of other stuff. They didn't even have to point a gun. All they had to do was pull the trigger because it was all zeroed in. So the Japanese'd send up some guys, and they'd go pull triggers, and then the guys'd disappear. Then they'd send up some more because they had the people there, and it was all under cover. Most of the guns were in caves, and they slide right up to the opening, fire, then slide back. They'd put camouflage over them, brush, netting, whatever they had.

"The strafing planes hit the marines. A frontline panel is an orange plastic sheet you can roll up. One guy in every squad had to have one, and when they'd call to put out the frontline panel, an air strike was coming in, it was up to that one guy to run out there as far as he could beyond the front line out in no-man's-land. It was dangerous as hell to try to roll that thing out. It worked pretty good from up in the air. You could see that thing, but short firing was bound to happen especially from the face of that cliff because they'd come in off the water.

"When an air strike wasn't happening, the company commanders would be sending guys like Domenick Tutalo with flame-throwers up there to try to get into that cave and seal it off. Machine guns would be firing right into the opening, trying to keep them down till our guys worked up there, and then, all at once, an air strike would come in. They were bound to get hurt. I think that was the worst I ever saw of something like that. First, second day. Third day I'd say we'd probably taken those guns out of there, and we were past that. Starting to make the swing up the island. We didn't have to go inland too far before we started to swing north.

"The Fourth and Fifth were abreast, and the object was to move right across that short pork chop thing and secure that part and then swing to the right and to the left, that'd be Fifth Division on Suribachi, and then we went to the right, and that's where we spread out and needed some people, and that's when we brought in a few of the Third Marine Division.

"You didn't see too many Japs. Once in a while they'd run from one cave to another. You more or less seen their fire. You could see dust coming. As soon as we'd see that, we'd zone right in, and when we got up there, they'd be layin' there.

"The terrain got rougher and rougher because of the catacombs and stuff where the water had washed in amongst it over the years. Some places you could step over a crack and you'd see a big gap deep down in there. Or you'd go around the corner and they'd be standing right there face-to-face. Whoever shot first was the winner. I saw one marine shoot another marine bone dead right in my squad because he went around this way and the other went around that way and, it was just like I said, you don't have a split second. You just pull the trigger. Shoot first. Whoever does, they're one's going to win. We had to take the guy that shot the other marine, take him clear out because he just went berserk.

"The first day of March I was wounded and evacuated out to a hospital ship. It was shrapnel like I'd got in Saipan. I was taken aboard ship and cleaned up. They picked that stuff out of me. It was mostly like buckshot. One thing about shrapnel: If it hits you the right way and it's a little bit on the spent side, not with full force, it'll burn you, and when it burns you, it cauterizes the wound. That's what it did to me on Saipan because Adrian DeWitt pulled it out of my back and they put some sulfa powder on it and I never had a minute's trouble with it. But the corpsman would bandage it every day for me, check it, and I stayed in action.

"My big problem on Iwo came from a concussion, not that shrapnel. I was in a big hole with ten or twelve other guys, and a shell came right in there. Near as I can remember, I was the only one came out of there alive. We were in reserve. They kept two platoons on the line, and C Company just happened to be in there getting a rest. Give you a little chance to do what you wanted, sit down and cry, or smoke, whatever.

"We were in there grouped up. You didn't group up because it was a bad thing to do, but we did. Otherwise there wouldn't have been as many killed by one shell. One hand grenade'll get you all, if you don't stay spread out. Otis Boxx was my gunner at the time. As people get bumped off, people move up in command. I had moved up to squad leader, and I had to give up the gun for a few weeks. So Otis Boxx from Florida was the gunner. The only thing I really remember is that all that was left of his head was his lower jaw. It was just settin' there. Never moved. Just settin' there.

"I was shocked, no question about it. I come up out of the hole, and somebody grabbed me, and I was just blood everywhere. They thought I was hit worse than I was, but they started getting my dungarees off me and seen that I wasn't really hurt, but my mind was gone.

"I couldn't hear. I remember giving my thirty-eight away to Elmer Neff. They took me back to the beach and took me out to the big boat, and first thing I remember is a corpsman waking me up. Or I came to, apparently. I was talking with him, and I said, 'Where's my clothes?' He said, 'We'll give you clean stuff.' I said, 'Well, get 'em for me. I'd like to get some clothes on.' So I did. Then daylight came, and they were bringing casualties in. They had a stairway up the side of the ship to bring casualties up. They couldn't bring them up the cargo net, but there was a cargo net down there, and I clumb down that cargo net and got in the front of that boat and went ashore. Nobody asked any questions."

Why did he go back?

"I have no idea. I have no idea. They'd dug out shrapnel, give me sulfa, and I had a hell of a headache. My vision and my hearing were bad. When that shell hit, I was out on my feet. A lot of people were killed that way, by concussion. It would just roll them along the ground like a ball. They was dead. Everything confined in that little shell goes out when it explodes, so therefore you go with it.

"I got my thirty-eight back. Elmer Neff had got killed, and somebody picked it up. A day or so later just out of the clear blue sky somebody walked up to me and said, 'Hey, I got that thirty-eight off Elmer when he got hit, so here it is.' I walked right back up there and found out where C Company was, I kept asking, 'Where's C Company?' and I finally found where they were, and I went right back to work.

"I'm not sure who was company commander at that time. It might have been Mike Mervosh. I just don't know who had got killed and evacuated in the line of officers. Mike could very well have been my company commander at that time. We knew each other, hell, yes. We met in New River. He was in First Separate Battalion. We weren't in the same squad, but we were all in C Company. You'd get to know maybe fifty guys. Mike was my section leader at first.

"He became company commander on Iwo Jima. A company commander could have been a major. Mike didn't become a major. You just became the company commander even if you were a buck-ass sergeant because there was nobody else to do it. Then, when you went back to Maui, they'd call you out on the parade deck and have a pretty nice ceremony out of it; they'd call everybody out in formation and either give them their promotion or their Purple Heart or whatever. You didn't know you was getting a Purple Heart because the only thing that gave you a Purple Heart them days was your medical records. The first sergeant wrote in the book you were treated, and you were in line even though your wounds were not serious. They had what they called the walking wounded. And that's the way you were put: WW. And there was

WE, wounded and evacuated. So first I was WE or walking-evacuated, and then I was WW or walking wounded. When I come back off the ship, he put me in as WW.

"Day to day you'd have riflemen go out in front. The number one guy would go so far and keep track of the guy on his left and the guy on his right. There wasn't no talking going on. It seemed like we had to put bait out there to draw their fire. Then we'd find out where it was coming from and focus on that. If their fire was severe enough and determined enough, we had to call for more support. Rockets were a great thing. The Dodge power wagon had these things mounted on them. They'd bring up seven or eight in a bank, and there was probably fifty rockets on each of 'em in a canister and they'd go *chu chu chu*, a hell of a noise, and boy, they just blanketed the target area. They didn't have to be too accurate. And grenades were good. You could damn near throw a grenade ten feet, and it would go down a crevice and you'd hear somebody scream or moan or groan or something. You knew somebody was in there. Grenades were a good thing, and we used a lot of them.

"If your skirmishers found a cave, it would take a considerable amount of time to work your way up to its mouth. The machine gunner would cover the front of it so you could get your flamethrower close enough to shoot flame in. As long as you're firing into that cave, you're keeping their heads down, allowing the flamethrower time to get close, and then the demolition man had to be right there within arm's reach to throw the damn satchel charge. Most of them are still in those caves. We killed more accidentally than we did on purpose, put it that way. Sure we was trying to kill 'em all, but we didn't realize when we sealed a cave how many we killed. We killed thousands.

"Some days we didn't move. One side couldn't move past the other. We had to keep order, especially when the island started getting smaller as we moved up. They'd spell us off, give us a little rest. I can't remember sleeping, but I'm sure I did, and I don't remember ever going to the bathroom. I'm sure I did. There's things you don't remember. I think you're programmed, and you're just like a zombie, but you have to pay attention to your surroundings at the same time. Then you live longer. I think sometimes guys would just forget where they were at, and bingo, they were gone.

"Believe it or not, as a person on the front line you had it better than them in the rear. You were relaxed, you might say, because you knew where the enemy was. They were right in front of us. But if you went into reserve and were trying to crap out like we were in that hole, there's enemies all around you all the time. They can lob a shell at you or get behind you through tunnels going everywhere. You didn't know where the hell they were. That was one small advantage of being on the front line: We knew where they were.

"I was nineteen on Iwo. I came back from wounded and evacuated to walking wounded and finished out the campaign with no more trouble than an infected fingernail."

Glenn married his wife, Needra, in 1949, and they live today in Hubbard, Ohio. They have five children. Glenn farmed most of his life. Did his survival of the battle of Iwo Jima affect the way he lived afterward?

"I don't know. I always tried to do the right thing. I didn't get in too much trouble when I was a kid. I never drank to any extent. Never ran around much. That's why I went to farming. That was a solitary life. I come home from the service, and I broke three vertebrae in my neck falling off a load of hay. That could have killed me right there. I got hurt worse falling off a load of hay than I did in four campaigns in the Pacific. I had to wear a brace eighteen months. I was seventy-nine years old, last year, I'm eighty now, and I fell down eight steps backwards there in the cellar. Could have broke my neck or hit my head on that cement."

Why did he survive the battle?

"When I stop to think about it, I have no idea. I'm a Christian. I believe in God. I believe in the hereafter. But why me? I was no better or no worse than Cooksey or Elmer Neff or Bowman or any of those guys. But yet they took it, you know what I mean? They're gone. Why, I don't know. I can't answer it. I didn't do anything any better than they did. I wasn't a better scholar, I wasn't a better . . . anything. They say every hair of your head is numbered. Well, the fellow who's got that kind of account is in charge, and if he's in charge, then maybe he can answer that question. I don't think God created man to do this to each other, although men have been doing it ever since Christ walked the face of the earth. Otherwise I have no idea. I cannot answer it."

7

PRIVATE FIRST CLASS PETE SANTORO

Boxing Champion; Two Purple Hearts
Twenty-fourth Marines, Fourth Marine Division

In 1938, when I was twenty-one, I won the New England heavyweight amateur championship. I won the Golden Gloves and the Diamond Belt Tournament. I kept that belt in a drawer until I met my wife, Maria Lydia LesCault, and then I took the diamond out and had the jeweler make a ring for her.

Santoro holds a sword he took from a Japanese soldier he killed during the battle of Roi-Namur.

Pete Santoro and his wife, Maria, also known as Bunny, on their wedding day in Norwood, Massachusetts, July 29, 1946. They had five children. Bunny died in 1997.

I was in Pete Santoro's home in Wrentham, Massachusetts, three days before he turned ninety on January 22, 2007. We talked about his life and his military service, and as I got ready to leave, I pulled out my camera and asked if I could take a photo. I saw a sword on the wall. Pete took it down and showed it to me. He said he had seized it from a Japanese soldier he killed one night during the battle of Roi-Namur. Ships offshore were sending up parachute flares. The enemy soldier came up to a foxhole occupied by Pete and two other marines and, speaking in Japanese, brandished the sword over them. "I could see his feet," Santoro recalled. "I just turned and shot him three times. He went down. There was blood on the handle of the sword. I wiped it off. He had no rifle. I was told later I couldn't keep the sword, so when I went aboard ship, I gave it to the chaplain, and he took it home for me, wrapped up with my name on a tag. It was at my sister's when I got home a couple years later. She said a priest had brought it over. It was the chaplain."

Pete Santoro was twenty-seven, old for an enlisted man, when he fought at Iwo Jima in February and March 1945. "I was born January 22, 1917, in Norwood, Massachusetts. By the time I got to tenth grade in 1933 I was sixteen, and my father said, 'OK, get a driver's license. You don't need no more school. You know how to read and write. Drive the truck.' My two brothers Benny and Charlie had the trucks. They worked construction. My brother Benny taught me to drive. My father didn't know how.

"My brother said, 'No, he's going to high school and play football. He can play football in college.' But my father said, 'You can't eat the football. Drive the truck.'

"My father was a bootlegger. He made wine, five or six fifty-gallon barrels a year, both red and white. He also mixed muscatel with California grapes. We'd go to the freight yard with one of the trucks and load up with grapes. My father taught me how to taste them. This one guy had all overripe grapes, and that was what he wanted. They were like raisins, sweet. They made the best wine. Most of the grapes were black.

"We'd drive the truck home, back it into the driveway by the cellar window, and they'd pass the grapes down. My job was to grind them up. The grinder was on a stand. I stood on top. We'd grind seventeen boxes of grapes for each barrel. My father would put a canvas over the cover so it would generate heat, let it all settle, and when the bubbles stopped, he'd drain off the liquid and put it in a separate container and let it ferment for a few months. People would come and buy it by the gallon, three or four dollars a jug. The priest would come down, and we'd give him a gallon, for the altar. Maybe that's how my brother Henry got mixed up in driving a moonshine truck for the Capone gang later on.

"Both my father and mother spoke broken English. His name was Pasquale. He came from the Abruzzi. My mother too. Her name was Carmen; they called her Carmella. Her father and two brothers were fishermen in Pescara, on the Adriatic across from Rome. They had boats. She and my father married and had some kids in Italy, and he came to the States, through Ellis Island."

Pete thought this happened in 1912, but Pasquale actually came in 1909, according to Pete's nephew Patsy Santoro of Branford, Connecticut, the son of Pete's brother Henry and the keeper of the family records, who was born in 1924. Patsy said Pasquale went to Elmira, New York, and worked with the railroad long enough to be able to send for two daughters, who came over and worked with him there, saving money until 1912, when they could afford to send for Carmella and the remaining six children, including Guarino, whom they called Henry once he got to the States.

Through a family connection, Pasquale got a job with Bird and Son, a floor covering and paper products company in Norwood and moved the family there. The Santoros stayed in Norwood, except for a six-month stint in Chicago in the 1920s, according to Patsy. It was here Pasquale had some contact with the Capone gang. "The Italians were everywhere, like horseshit," Patsy observed.

Pasquale found Chicago sooty and unpleasant and so returned to Norwood, where he and Henry got to know associates of Capone's in the Reedville area outside Boston. This was how, both Pete and Patsy maintained, Henry wound up driving a bootlegging truck for gangsters.

"But then one day the truck got shot up by a rival outfit. They didn't kill Henry. They figured they'd be in big trouble if they shot the driver. They just wanted to ruin all the booze. That ended Henry's driving career.

"In 1938 my father and brothers decided to open a bowling alley, with roller skating upstairs, in Norwood. They called it Roll-Land. I worked construction during the day and put my skates on at night. I became a professional skater. I used be able to pick up a partner and skate around, do a deep knee bend with him in my arms. He'd hold a match in his teeth and light it on the floor while I spun him around.

"I started boxing around the age of fifteen. I had a friend I went to school with named Dewey Tronti. He was a welterweight, and he changed his name to Trunny Hogan because you'd get along better if you were Irish. He was pretty good. We trained at night.

"In 1938, when I was twenty-one, I won the New England heavyweight amateur championship. I won the Golden Gloves and the Diamond Belt Tournament. I kept that belt in a drawer until I met my wife, Maria Lydia LesCault, and then I took the diamond out and had the jeweler make a ring for her. We got married July 29, 1946, after the war.

"I had four pro fights after I won the belt, and then I had to quit. I was too small for a heavyweight. I was like Marciano. I wasn't as good as him, but I was pretty good. I fought at one eighty-nine. Marciano was a half a head taller than me. Same build, but he hit harder. He saw me fight when I won the New

England. I beat this guy six foot six, two hundred thirty-five pounds. I saw his belt; it was right at my eyes.

"I won three pro fights, lost one. You know who beat me? Al McCoy. It was a six-round warm-up fight for him. He was going to fight Joe Louis, who was heavyweight champion of the world. McCoy took it a little easy on me because he knew I was just coming in out of the amateurs. I hit him a hard shot, and he come back at me to show who's the boss.

"I joined the Marines in November 1942. What happened was, after I had served three years in the National Guard, I got these papers telling me to report to the Army. I went to the recruiting office in Boston, and I found this Marine major and said, 'Sir, can I speak to you?'

"I told him I didn't want to go in the Army because my mother and father came from Italy, and Italy was fighting against us, and I had relatives in Mussolini's army. I'd said I'd be fighting my own relatives and I'd feel bad shooting at them.

" 'Oh,' he says, 'now I understand. Follow me, son.' He puts his hand on my shoulder, leads me into an office, passes me over to another marine, and says, 'I got a ripe one for you.' I went to Parris Island in November 1942. Boot camp was eight weeks. We trained with the '03 Springfield, but they gave us the M1 before we left. Eight shots, you just kept pulling the trigger. You had to crank each shot with the Springfield. We got on trucks and went to New River for a month and a half of infantry training.

"I was part of a unit they called the Second Separate Battalion, which was to become part of the Fourth Marine Division. We went by train to Camp Pendleton, California, in about March or April of '43. Then it was all ship-to-shore training.

"I was a rifleman. I would have been a squad leader, but I had a little trouble. A guy picked a fight with me, and I had to put him away. I was training boxers, but I couldn't fight because of my pro background. I wouldn't fight those kids; they were too green. I was in G Company, Twenty-fourth Regiment, Second Battalion. Iron Mike Mervosh, who I met back at New River, was in the First Battalion. The First, Second, and Third Battalions made up the Twenty-fourth Regiment. Mike was a good boxer. He used to spar with some of my guys. He was a middleweight. He won the Fourth Division middleweight championship, but then he got wounded and couldn't fight anymore."

Pete saw action at Roi-Namur, where he was slightly injured when a bullet pierced his canteen and grazed his hip.

"They just put a Band-Aid on it, but that kept me from going to Saipan. I was in the rear echelon as backup until we went to Iwo. At that time I was a squad leader, had twelve men. Four of the guys from the boxing team were in my squad.

"We found out aboard ship that we were going to Iwo. It was going to be a piece a cake, they said. It was a piece of cake all right. We got the cake. My outfit, the Twenty-fourth Regiment, Second Battalion, landed side by side with Mike Mervosh's unit. He was in the First Battalion."

Pete had no idea that his nephew Patsy had been at Iwo Jima a week before the invasion began aboard the light cruiser USS *Birmingham*. Patsy, who was a cook, said the ship stayed there and shelled the island throughout the battle before going on to Okinawa, where she was hit by a five-hundred-pound armor-piercing bomb dropped by a kamikaze. "It killed all the doctors and the dentist," Patsy said. "The corpsmen had to take over. They all deserved medals."

"The Japanese let the first wave come in without much firing. I was coming ashore in the second wave around nine-thirty when they opened up. I saw a boatload of marines take a direct hit. Bodies were flying all over. My heart went *boom boom boom*. You're ready to go in, but you see somebody right beside you get blown up and . . .

"Our company captain, Joseph J. McCarthy, who got the Medal of Honor for what he did on Iwo, says, 'Santoro, get your squad. We got to go around this thing here.' It was D plus three, and the Japs were zeroed in on F Company, under Captain Walter Ridlon, and they were tearing hell out of it.

"There were six or seven of us with my captain, McCarthy. I'm behind, trailing a guy, and I said, 'Wait a minute.' There was this big hill they were going around. I thought: I'm going to go over the top; I'm going to see what the fuck's on the other side. So I get up over this bank and look down on the entrance to one of those sulfur mines. Two Japs were lying there, crawling, so I put a shot in each one from up above. Then McCarthy shows up. He doesn't see me up there, and then, bing, bing, he says, 'I got them, I got them.' I was waiting for some more to come out. He spoiled it all. He didn't know they weren't alive. He just saw them and shot.

"We secured that whole area. McCarthy got the medal for killing two dead Japs. [As his Medal of Honor citation makes clear, McCarthy did a whole lot more than shoot two Japanese soldiers dead that day.] I got a Purple Heart.

"I was on Iwo till February 23, the day the flag went up. I was at the second airfield when I saw a hole in the ground, and I was trying to drop a rifle grenade in there when I got a bullet in the back. It hit me like a sledgehammer, tore up the poncho, and shattered an eight-round brass clip on my back. The powder didn't explode, but the brass of the shells shattered, peppering my back. It felt like bee stings. I couldn't move my legs. I thought: What the fuck? Jesus Christ. But if that bullet hadn't hit my clothes and that ammo, I wouldn't be here today. I managed to roll over as some guys came up, and I said, 'Hey, my back, my back.' And they said, 'What the fuck did they shoot you with, a shotgun?' I was all torn up. The X rays at the Quonset hospital in Guam showed a bunch of pieces, and they just left them in there. My wife was pulling that stuff out with tweezers for years afterward."

In 1975 Santoro's commanding officer, Joseph J. McCarthy, who retired a lieutenant colonel, wrote a To Whom It May Concern letter recommending Santoro for disability benefits. Naming Santoro as a private first class with G Company, Second Battalion, Twenty-fourth Marines, Fourth Marine Division, McCarthy described landing on Iwo with 257 men and receiving 90 replacements for a total of 347, only 35 of whom were able to walk off the island when the fighting ended.

Writing about February 21, the day Santoro was shot, McCarthy said his company "was suffering heavy casualties from fortified positions and bunkers." His right assault platoon was pinned down, and he was at his "wit's end, trying to effect an advance of a few yards." He added, "My entire area was also subjected to intermittent large caliber mortar and artillery fire and we were in direct line of fire from one or two high velocity weapons."

As the afternoon wore on, casualties increased until finally McCarthy assigned an assault squad to clean out some pillboxes that were holding back the advance. "Private First Class Santoro was a member of this group," he wrote. The reason he remembered was that the action of the assault team "led to the demolishing of the enemy positions and the advance of my Company to the nearby newly captured ground." Further, he said, the platoon leader was killed in the assault, and several enlisted men were wounded. "I distinctly remember Peter Santoro was one of these men . . . he appeared to be paralyzed from the waist down, from gunshot wounds he received near his spine."

Santoro was evacuated to the USS *Solace*, but despite his injury, he volunteered to return to duty five days later. "I was later wounded myself," McCarthy added. "However, at the time of my evacuation on 6 March 1945, Private Santoro was still serving with the company in spite of his painful wounds."

Santoro remembers: "That slug scraped my vertebrae right at the waist. It was three pieces of lead. They took it out on Guam in a Quonset hut hospital. 'Lay down over here, Santoro. We got to take that piece of shrapnel out of your back.' The surgeon was there. They froze it with a needle. Clunk, clunk, they stitched it up. The surgeon goes, 'You want these?' What I want those for? 'Can I have 'em?' Yeah, you can have the fuckin' things. He had a canful of shrapnel. He had the whole bottom of a hand grenade; he took it out of a guy's jaw.

"They took me off in a stretcher to an LST. They picked up

three stretchers at a time with a crane and a cable. I got on board, and they said, 'Move your toes.' I moved my toes. 'OK, you be good.' If I couldn't move my toes, I'd be paralyzed. Later I transferred from the LST to a hospital ship, the *Solace*. Two days later I started walking, crooked like, you know? They called thirty or forty of us back to the fantail. The colonel wants to talk to you. Then he's telling us how bad guys are needed for backup, with everybody getting slaughtered. He asked for volunteers, walking wounded, to go back to the aid station and wait for the next ship. They had too many critically hurt that had to go to Guam. When I stepped out, three or four more stepped out. That was it. So five days after I was hit I went back to rejoin the company.

"When I came ashore, the ground crew from the P-51 Mustangs were putting up sandbags near the beach. What was that for? Turned out there was a sniper up on the hill, hiding in the rocks lining the edge of the first airfield, Motoyama No. 1, and every night around dusk, about five o'clock, he'd pick off one of the guys between the airfield and the beach. We had people looking for him, but they couldn't find him. They looked all over hell. Had to be up there because if he ran across the field, someone would have seen him. He had to be up there in those rocks.

"I said, 'Gimme a rifle.' I picked one up and walked up there and sat and test fired it. The ocean was here to my right and the runway to the north, and Suribachi was behind me. He wouldn't be there. I sat between two rocks for about two hours. My back just felt numb from the bullet in it. It was just getting dusk when I thought I saw something move. I'm sitting down this way here, I'm looking. The airfield's beside me, I'm watching both sides. Sure enough, I see something move between two rocks. He had half his head out. I shot and blew his face off, killed him. He was camouflaged in a barrel, a big hole, with twigs and stuff. Guys come running up: 'Hey, the marine got him.' I picked up one of his own hand grenades and threw it in there. I hit with my thumb and dropped it in. I didn't want no souvenirs. He was buried right there.

"I got one more Jap after that. We had a couple young marines on ship, replacements just off the ship, and when I caught up with the company, Captain McCarthy told me to take these two guys, keep them separated and make sure they didn't get hurt.

"The three of us were walking down this hill, and I said, 'Stop talking, for Christ's sake, and stay far apart.' Downhill from us, there was a ridge with some rocks sticking out. To me it was a hiding place for a Jap. I told those two kids to stay five feet apart and wait until I circled around. I said, 'I'm going to walk ahead and see what's between those rocks. You two guys stand by.' So I backed up and circled around, and I spotted this Jap watching those two marines. I shot him through the head and then called them up for a look.

"Before he went off with his wound on March 6, McCarthy put me in charge of an ammo and food dump. I had a young fella, baseball player, there with me on March 9, when a big mortar came over, killed him, blew his head off, and I got a concussion out of it. They took me back out to the same ship, the *Solace*. It had come back from Guam for us walking wounded. It took a bunch of us to Guam, and I was there maybe two weeks, before they sent me to a hospital in Honolulu. Then I went on a ship to the States along with a hundred Japanese prisoners under Army guard. We went to Treasure Island at San Francisco, then to San Diego. From there we took a hospital train to Massachusetts. I was discharged at the Boston Navy Yard in November 1945. I had been overseas two years. The doctors listed me with a ten percent disability for the back wound.

"I went back to work at the skating rink, where I met Marie LesCault. Her parents had died, and she was an orphan. She had been brought up by the state. We got married July 29, 1946. We had five kids, four boys and a girl, Diane, Peter, Robert, Bernard, and William Timothy. I stayed with Roll-Land, the roller rink we had bought in 1938 and sold my share a few years ago. My brothers still have it. Now it's called Workout World. It's a gym for physical fitness. Marie died of bone cancer in 1997, two months before our fiftieth anniversary. It was too bad she had to die like that. She would have been with me now."

8

PRIVATE FIRST CLASS DOMENICK TUTALO

Replacement, Flamethrowers and Demolition
Twenty-fourth Marines, Fourth Marine Division

Some guys get it, and some guys don't. That I could never figure out. I'm just thankful it worked out the way it did. There was no way to explain the bullets coming by and other people getting shot and yet they're not hitting you. Why, I don't know. I prayed. I prayed one time, I says, "I'm too young." I says, "I'll never be bad if you let me live."

Domenick and his wife, Maryellen, stand in front of the West Orange, New Jersey, home where they have lived for more than fifty years.

Domenick Tutalo holding a carbine at Camp Linda Vista, California, December 1943. On his left cheek is a bandage covering a boil.

Domenick Tutalo turned eighty-two on February 6, 2007, one day before the fifty-ninth anniversary of his marriage to Maryellen. The three of us were sitting at the dining room table, talking over a glass of wine. He was still working, repairing machines for a screen printing business. Domenick gets to set his own hours, though the owner of the printing business keeps calling him back. He is paid twenty-five dollars an hour. "The money's good; he treats me good," Tutalo said. Besides, he considers the owner's two sons good friends. They accompanied him to the drill instructors' reunion in April 2007. "Yes," said Maryellen, who turned eighty on November 2, 2006, "he's giving it to the grandchildren." Domenick smiled. "I don't mind," he said. "It helps them out."

"I was born February 6, 1925, and I've lived in the same house in West Orange, New Jersey, for fifty-one years. I grew up in Jersey. I quit school in ninth grade and went to work for a butcher, for six dollars a week. It was pretty good money, but I had to put in ninety hours, seven days a week. I was thirteen years old. I used to go to the market with him at four a.m., to buy stuff. That's when they butchered the whole animal. He bought it from Swift, the meatpacking company, hung it, then cut it up.

"My dad worked for the WPA, the Works Progress Administration. He was born in the United States, but my mother came here from Foggia, Italy, at the age of nine.

"When Pearl Harbor came, I was in the Embassy Theater with my uncle. He was in the Army. They stopped the movie and told all the men to report back to base. I don't remember the movie.

"I joined in March of 1943 as soon as I turned eighteen, a year and a half after Pearl Harbor. I was a fairly good meat cutter by then. The whole family was in the Marines: my cousin Phil Petrillo and Jimmy Zarrilla, my father's first cousin, who was killed at Roi-Namur. He was in the same platoon with Lee Marvin, who got shot in the butt on Saipan. Jimmy was supposed to get the Congressional Medal of Honor, but he got the Navy Cross. They said it was better if the colonel got the Medal of Honor instead.

"I was five feet five, and I weighed one hundred twenty-six. To me Parris Island, boot camp, wasn't hard. I was in good shape from being a butcher. We did a lot of running. We trained with sticks, then got the M1. I got out the end of April, and after leave I was put on gate duty at the Philadelphia Navy Yard. I was bored and kept trying to get out. Finally they sent me to New River, which is now Camp Lejeune.

"I joined a replacement outfit, and we trained there, then we took a train to San Diego and the boat to Maui. The Fourth Division went to Roi-Namur, but I went right to Maui. After Saipan they needed machine gunners, so I signed up for that. I was in that about a month; then I volunteered for a demolition outfit being formed by Sergeant Harry Kaff. He was tough. I liked him later, but at that time I thought he was a son of a gun. He was by the book, a Jewish man, but he was religious. You couldn't curse or nothing. When he was there, you watched what you said. We trained for six or eight months, learning how to blow things up with satchel charges and burn with flamethrowers. They used a naphthalike jelly. It shot about twenty feet. You had to be careful, fire in real short bursts. You could run it all out in maybe ten seconds. It weighed about seventy pounds.

"One guy I grew up with was with the Twenty-third Regiment. He thought I was nuts. He said, 'You're cracking up. Don't do it.' He said I had a good thing going, but I wanted to see combat. Why, I don't know. If I had it to do over, would I still do it? Yeah, I think so. I don't know why.... Maybe I wouldn't have went into flamethrowers or something like that, but why I did it, I couldn't tell you. I did believe in serving my country. We were all very patriotic.

"We found out on the transport from Maui that we were going to Iwo, but first we went to Guam, where they put out some smaller boats and let us swim off them. Whoever wanted to swim could just jump in. I did it. I never forgot that because it happened on my birthday, February 6. I was twenty years old.

"We left for Iwo the next day with a company of demolition guys and Harry Kaff. During the landing we were getting shelled as we went in on Higgins boats. There were bodies all over the place.

"What did I feel? Scared. You had the fear, but you didn't have it. I think it's a stupid thing to say it, but whatever they wanted you just did. There was no place to hide, and you have to function if you can control yourself. We got off the boats from the front and charged up the beach. There were cannons, artillery, machine guns, mortars. I'm not that good at relatin' what went on from there. A lot of stuff I forget. I don't know. What I know is we kept doing things on the right flank, we kept moving up by the Quarry. I do remember we spent six days in the same foxhole on Hill 362.

"We were a company of demolition guys, and if they needed somebody, they'd call. If a platoon was pinned down and needed somebody, you'd go in and help. In our first engagement up on the right flank at Iwo everybody got killed but the sergeant and another flamethrower.

"I knew Mike Mervosh, but I didn't know him, you know? You never got that close. We got friendly after the war. I was in C Company, Twenty-fourth Regiment. Up near the Quarry. Our squad leader took us up toward the Quarry, and that's where this sniper just shot nine guys right out in the open dead before a rifleman named Scowie got him. The only reason Jeffries and I survived was we made a run to a cliff where he couldn't shoot us, but we couldn't do nothing either. We were stuck there the whole night. We were in the Quarry most of the battle. We kept moving up the island. I heard about the flag going up, but I didn't see it.

"There was no real strategy on the caves or bunkers. The riflemen gave you cover fire, and your job was to charge as close as you could, then blast it. At a bunker you would try for the slit; if not, the flame would stick wherever it went. You didn't carry a flamethrower all the time. Sometimes you had to carry a rifle. You only got to be a flamethrower when they called for you. They bring you the flamethrower. Then, when you run out of fuel, you just drop it, and they reload it for you. You don't have to run back because somebody else followed you. Once you blasted the opening with flame, somebody would run up and throw a satchel charge. They were mostly caves. I only saw an enemy once. It was hard to stomach. He came running out on fire. I saw a lot of dead bodies. Did I see our guys taking teeth and ears? I'd rather not comment. I picked up a couple souvenirs, like a notepad and money, and I got some wooden dog tags. Tell the truth, I haven't gone through it.

"I was on the island the whole time and was never wounded. I used flamethrowers and threw satchel charges, saw a lot of action, charging tunnels and bunkers. I never went inside.

"They said Iwo was really bad for replacements, who got killed easily because they were green and never had time to get integrated into the units, but I never got hurt. Some guys get it, and some guys don't. That I could never figure out. I'm just thankful it worked out the way it did. There was no way to explain the bullets coming by and other people getting shot and yet they're not hitting you. Why, I don't know. I prayed. I prayed one time, I says, 'I'm too young.' I says, 'I'll never be bad if you let me live.' The worst thing I didn't like was the mopping up. You'd walk the whole island looking for stragglers. That's where a lot of fellows got killed, I think.

"When it was over, we went back to Maui to train for the invasion of Japan. Meantime whoever had enough points were the first ones to go home. It was figured by combat and total time overseas. After Japan surrendered, it didn't matter so much. I was overseas twenty to twenty-two months. I got there January of 1944 and did not get back to the States till November of '45. I was discharged December 10, 1945, in Quantico, Virginia. I still weighed one twenty-five. All my cousins made it through except Jimmy, the one who was killed on Roi-Namur.

"I had three hundred dollars when I got home, and I took a chance and opened a restaurant, a luncheonette, short-order cooking, hamburgers, coffee. I called it Tut's. My mother and sister helped, but I couldn't pay them, couldn't make ends meet. I bought everything on the black market. It closed after about a year.

"Maryellen McDonough lived upstairs with her parents in the same building where we had the restaurant. Her father didn't want her dating Italians, but he and I got to know each other before I started going out with her, and I guess he changed his mind. He was a good man, her father. We got married in February 7, 1948, the day after my birthday. We had two boys and a girl. We bought the West Orange house in 1955. We were married fifty-nine years as of February 7, 2007.

"I started excavating after that, burying four-hundred-fifty-gallon fuel oil tanks for fifty bucks each. I had one helper. We dug the hole and the trench by hand. They supplied all materials; I supplied the truck. I bought a brand-new Ford dump truck for twenty-seven hundred dollars. I don't know why I didn't go into the butcher business. I guess I thought there was more in trucking. From there we went into hauling dirt for contractors, and then we got into landscaping. Tutalo's Contracting, we called it. I had my brother John with me. We got into grading and planting trees for towns. We made a good living.

"I went to my first reunion in 1950, but raising a family, I couldn't afford to go too often. In 1978 I hooked up with Mike [Mervosh] and Glenn Buzzard at the reunion in Philly. We had a little more money and a little more time by then. I didn't meet Pete Santoro yet. I just met all of C Company. Most of them were there, guys I hadn't seen in thirty years.

"I enjoy the reunions. All the years we've been coming we never even mention the service or combat, even with all my friends. Nothing ever came out. Never talked about it, never really realized what it was. We go to reunions, even Parris Island, and there's no talking about the war. Whether the mind went blank or what, I don't know."

[Iron Mike remembers:]
"Tutalo is very modest, and he forgets a lot too. He was a flamethrower and demo man, and that takes a lot of doing. I was in a machine-gun platoon, divided into three sections to support a rifle company. When that became decimated, I became commander of the rifle platoon. The demo men or flamethrowers

were available to whichever platoon needed them. They had their own section within the company.

"Tutalo was a replacement. Replacements usually didn't last long. I had experienced a lot of battle before I went there, and I knew what to expect more than the replacements did. Even if you took care, it was still deadly. Every damn part of the island was covered with something, interlocking fire, artillery, mortars, and rocket fire. You just had to be lucky, damn lucky.

"I seen him in action, applying demolitions and throwing satchel charges in those caves and bunkers. He'd go up to those pillboxes, and we'd give supporting fire, and someone would throw a satchel charge to blow the thing, and then Tutalo comes up and flames it, and anyone left alive comes running out burning from head to toe, you know what I mean? Guys were getting killed left and right, but we considered that routine because hell, that's the job. We didn't think there was anything heroic about it. But we said to Tutalo, 'For what you did, we're going to give you a reward when we get back to rest camp.' But he said, 'I don't need none of that shit.' After that island was secured, he said, 'Hell, I got five medals now: One head, two arms, and two legs. That's the award I got.'

"We got back to Maui to rest camp and he's called front and center with several other marines, and we promoted him to private first class, and that was his reward. He was happier than shit. He says, 'Boy, four dollars more a month.'

"Tutalo was an ordinary marine; that's the way I looked at it. We were all ordinary. I ended up as the company commander, and what was my reward? I got a handshake from the company commander: 'Mervosh, well done.' And that was good enough for me. Hey, we were all ordinary. It was a huge reward just to be alive.

"We built strength among us. We strengthened each other. That's how we survived. The guys would strengthen me, I would strengthen them, and it worked pretty damn good. That's the whole key. You're damn right."

A flamethrowing Sherman "Zippo" tank burns a pillbox near the base of Mount Suribachi.
As they wait to attack, the marines watch for enemy soldiers who
might try to run out and blow up the tank.
U.S. Marine Corps photo by Mark Kaufman

PART THREE

Russell, Tso, Abbatiello, and Waterhouse

The four men in this section had revealing, widely divergent experiences. Gerald Russell commanded a battalion, Samuel Tso sent out in Navajo word that Suribachi had fallen, Al Abbatiello was instrumental in the capture of Suribachi, and Charlie Waterhouse never got to fire a shot. Starting out as an artilleryman, Russell survived Guadalcanal, came back to the States, and transferred to the infantry so he could have more time with his wife. But then, as a brand-new infantry officer, he had to prove himself to the troops right up to the minute he landed on Red Beach One in the third wave at Iwo.

Samuel Tso, nicknamed Chief, had to contend with discrimination everywhere he went. He was denied contact with his family for years because none of them could read or write and there was no telephone on the reservation in northern Arizona.

Al Abbatiello didn't want to become a raider because he thought it would be too dangerous, but then he confronted almost ceaseless combat in his thirty-six days on Iwo.

Charlie Waterhouse, an expert marksman who was to go on to a splendid career as a Marine Corps artist and illustrator, had barely got into the fight when a bullet in the arm stopped him cold, and he was out of it by the third day. After many operations he went home to art school, and eventually made hundreds of paintings of Marine Corps subjects.

9

CAPTAIN GERALD RUSSELL

Battalion Commander
Twenty-seventh Marines, Fifth Marine Division

The most vivid memory I would mention out of all that time was the flies and the smell of the dead. That's something they don't mention in documentaries, but boy, when you have that many bodies all over the place, it's sometimes days and days before they can bring them out.

Gerry Russell, eighty at the time, standing in front of a situation map of the island at the annual Combat Veterans of Iwo Jima Symposium in Alexandria, Virginia, on February 17, 2007.

Major Gerald F. Russell accepts the surrender of the Tsushima Islands in Japan from Lieutenant General Bukei Nagasi in November 1945.

*I first learned it was possible for a civilian to visit Iwo Jima
from Colonel Harvey "Barney" Barnum, USMC (Ret.), who
directed me to Military Historical Tours, founded and operated by another former Marine colonel, Warren Wiedhahn, in
Alexandria, Virginia. I signed up for the Iwo trip and went
down to Virginia to check the place out. Colonel Wiedhahn
managed to have on hand Gerry Russell, one of three battalion commanders from the Iwo campaign who were still alive.
Russell had worked for Penn State in State College, Pennsylvania, for many years, and it turned out he knew Joe Paterno,
the Penn State football coach, very well. Russell and I had a
long, satisfying visit in Colonel Wiedhahn's offices.*

"I grew up outside of Providence, Rhode Island, and went to La
Salle Academy, a Christian Brothers school, and ran track, the
thousand yards, indoors. I won the national championship in a
race in Madison Square Garden, and by virtue of that I got a
scholarship to Boston College. They had me do an extra year, red-
shirting, although they didn't call it that. [Redshirting means
holding an athlete back from intercollegiate competition his or
her first year, so it takes five years to graduate instead of four. This
way the participant has a year to get bigger and stronger before
entering competition.]

"I majored in history, prelegal, and graduated in 1940. Law was
my intention, and I applied for Harvard Law School and Boston
College Law School. I was accepted into both, and my goal was to
get enough funding somehow to go to Harvard. If not, I knew I
could make it at BC.

"Then an interesting thing happened: I had an old Jesuit priest
for an adviser. His name was Father Finnegan. He said, 'You know,
you're a college graduate, and you're single. This guy Roosevelt
wants to get us into a war, and you're going to be the first to go.
They're going to pass a draft law.' And he said, 'What you should

do is try to get into one of these officer reserve programs in the Army or the Navy and then go through and get the commission, and then, if they don't need you, you can just sit and go through school. They'll know they have you.'

"Well, I had some interest in the Marine Corps, so I wrote to the commandant, Major General Thomas Holcomb—this was early summer 1940—and told him what a splendid prospect I was for an officer. I got a response back quite quickly saying, 'We don't want you.' I said, 'Well, I guess that's that.' But then I get another letter from the same outfit saying we're going to start a program. If you're still interested, fill out this form. So I filled it out and was immediately sworn in. I was ordered to Quantico in October of 1940 as part of the very first officer candidate class the Marine Corps ever had.

"Up to that time the Marine Corps would get officers from the Naval Academy or from excess of the various Army Reserve Officers' Training Corps classes around the country. There hadn't been much opportunity for military advancement during the Depression years. The Marines usually got their number one choice because things were so limited.

"The Quantico program was envisioned as nine months, three months as a private first class, three months as a reserve second lieutenant in a classroom environment, then three months of duty with the troops. The fine print said you could go inactive subject to call if the exigencies of the time no longer required your services. I was actually in the first platoon of the first company in the candidates' class. They brought some drill instructors up from Parris Island, and those guys' attitude was: These men are going to be pushing us around one of these days; let's get 'em now. Actually their goal was to make us good Marine officers, and they wanted us to be tough. That three months we were really on the go all the time. It was not unusual for them to break us out late in the evening and have us run five miles in skivvy drawers holding the rifle at high port, you know, all kinds of things. Sometimes we would either march or be trucked over to the Manassas battlegrounds. I think a lot of our tactical problems were based on some of the action that had transpired there during the Civil War, so that was pretty interesting.

"I think we ended up with about two hundred commissioned on 20 February 1941. We were supposed to be commissioned on the first, but the Department of the Navy decided to short-tour the Naval Academy class, so they would be ahead of us on the lineal list, which was very important. They were commissioned on the seventh, and we were delayed until the twentieth.

"We stayed right there for three months after that, until the month of May, and learned tactics in the classroom. Some of my classmates went to troops immediately because the Marine Corps had been so very short of officers. They needed artillery officers. We had base defense units that needed officers. They even had a barrage balloon outfit that needed officers.

"I was selected to go to artillery school. At that point there was no First Marine Division or Second Marine Division. There was no Camp Lejeune, no New River. They hadn't even acquired it yet. I'm sure they were in process. The Fifth Marines was a battalion in Quantico. The Seventh Marines were at the Charleston Navy Yard, and I think the First Marines were at Norfolk. They were not the huge outfits that they later became.

"The Eleventh Marines, the artillery, was situated at Parris Island, so my first duty with troops was at Parris Island, probably August or September. After New River was acquired, we went up there, where the First Division was beginning to form as various units were brought in. The artillery was placed at Courthouse Bay. Of course all the roads were dirt, and the vehicles that were the prime movers for the one fifty-five howitzers had hard rubber tires. In short order those roads were just a muddy mire, and they had to cut trees and corduroy the roads, which was rather primitive but a good way of getting the units together. Not too long after, this battalion of the Eleventh Marines was divided into three. My first assignment was as a supply officer with the Third Battalion.

"Lieutenant Colonel James Keating from Philadelphia was designated battalion commander, and he called me over and said, 'Russell, you're going to be the supply guy. Go down to the quartermaster supply outfit, see where it is. They must have some kind of a list telling you what we rate [qualify for in the way of supplies].' He said, 'Start as soon as you can because we're going to need stuff.'

"Fortuitously we got a supply sergeant who knew the business, so I depended heavily on him. God bless the noncoms, all of them. That's one of the first things I learned, and it helped me through a lot. He was so good we decided to make him a warrant officer, so he became the supply officer. And I wanted to get into a firing battery, so I became the exec of the H Battery of the Third Battalion, Eleventh Marines.

"Things were accelerated once December 7 occurred. I was at Quantico visiting my fiancée, Eileen Herlihy, when Pearl Harbor was attacked. I'll never forget her father. He was old Navy, with the Department of Yards and Docks. He supervised all the barracks building for the Marines. She had spent almost her whole life at Quantico. She told me, 'Well, I'd like it very much if you made a career of the Marine Corps.' As it turned out, we spent the next five or six years involved in it [the Marine Corps] with no flexibility [because of the war]. I liked the Marines. She didn't have to make the decision for me.

"We got married on the twenty-seventh of December, 1941. We were going to get married in April, but we decided it would be good to do it now. Even though she was never officially in the corps, she was a great marine, the greatest asset I could have had. If I have had any success, she was a very significant part of it. We were married fifty-seven years. She died, unfortunately, six years ago from ovarian cancer.

"I was sitting in a hammock on her porch on the base at Quantico when her father came rushing out, saying, 'Those goddamn Japs.' He was a good old Irishman. He kept us posted, listening to the radio. Finally he came out and said all military personnel should report immediately back to their camps. I had ridden up with one of my friends stationed at New River. He had gone on to New York, and he came back shortly after and we went on back to New River. There were four officers in the H Battery. I was of course the junior one. One officer had to stay there for the Christmas holidays. That was me.

"I had the next section beginning on the twenty-seventh, so she came down with her mother and we were married in a church about forty miles from Jacksonville. Her father was sick and couldn't make it. For a honeymoon we got on a bus for a thirty-hour ride to Rhode Island, where I introduced her to my parents. Then we zipped back to North Carolina.

"Our artillery unit had started with French seventy-fives, the seventy-five-millimeter field gun, and then we got seventy-five-millimeter pack howitzers. We got the word to move out in March. It took us a long time to get loaded. I was in charge of my part of the battery. We had the guns and the troops in about eight freight cars and one Pullman. Officers were in the Pullman, and the troops were in the rail cars, where they just nailed bunks together out of two-by-fours. It was miserable. We had our regular field stoves, and they just screwed those into these big old boxcars. We zigzagged back and forth. It took eleven days to get across the country. We had four pieces of artillery, the pack howitzers, all on flatcars. We'd stop at a siding so the cooks could prepare meals. There were no heads or anything like that. They had to use the bushes.

"We finally got to San Francisco, then left there in early May of '42. The First Marine Division's job was to defend New Zealand, so we landed in Wellington. The complexion of things changed drastically after the battle of the Coral Sea and the battle of Midway, and then they discovered the Japanese were building an airstrip on this unknown place, which was a key position to cut off the supply line from the States to Australia and New Zealand. The airstrip came to be known as Henderson Field, and the island was called Guadalcanal. It was in the Solomons. And everybody said, 'Where the hell is that?'

"It had to be taken, so instead of going ashore and into camp in New Zealand, we unloaded. We didn't have all these sophisticated amphibious shiploading techniques. We had one basic approach, and that was: What you want to get off first, put in last. Everything was in these paper cardboard cartons. It was rainy season, so we had to unload on the wharves. They got wet, and we lost an awful lot of stuff, but we got loaded up and took off, probably in July. If you can believe it, when we were leaving the States, we were issued five-gallon aluminum cans of hardtack from World War One.

"Nobody had any idea about Guadalcanal, no charts or anything. And our information was based on a sketch from the manager of a plantation that had been owned by the people who made Palmolive soap. There was no resistance. Carrier aircraft would come in and bomb, and we just sat there and waited, and then we got in the boats and had a successful landing, but it was strictly without opposition. The Japanese were away.

"I went in on the *George Elliott*, which was a transport. The second day the Japanese sent over a big flotilla of twin-engine bombers, and they were after the transports. My battery was attached to the Second Battalion, First Marines, H Battery. The transports had started unloading. Their holds were open, and apparently one of the planes got hit and crashed into the superstructure of the *Elliott,* killed all the people on the bridge. The flaming gasoline spilled into the open hatches, and the ship caught on fire, so I lost everything from the start.

"Fortunately we had the guns off and some of the rations and a good amount of the ammunition. They continued unloading all the other ships. The *Elliott* was the only one that was hit, and the second night was the battle of Savo Island, August 8–9, 1942. I don't think it's possible to describe the thunderous noise and the brightness of the light. It was about midnight, and of course we thought our Navy was really clobbering them. In the morning we had switched positions. We could fire out to the ocean or fire inland, depending on the need. We were watching along the ocean, and we could see sailors swimming or bodies floating, and a couple ships drifted down by there, superstructures all knocked over. This was my first combat.

"We learned fairly soon that we had lost four cruisers, The *Quincy,* the *Historia*, the *Vincennes*, and the *Canberra*, and fortuitously the Japanese didn't follow through. They clobbered them and took off. They could have just wiped everything out. Next day the fleet commander, Admiral Ghormley, decided to husband what units he had, so he pulled everything out. Well, we weren't unloaded completely, so we ended up very short of supplies.

"It was just about this time that I got to know Joe Foss. [Foss received the Medal of Honor for shooting down twenty-six enemy aircraft during the Guadalcanal campaign.] I got to know him because my battery was along this fighter strip, and those guys, aviators, you know, they don't have much sense, and they didn't have any place to protect themselves. So whenever the Japs came in to bomb, they'd come running over to my battery position, and I took care of them. So I knew Joe Foss, I knew him very well. I'm so sorry he passed away; he was a great guy.

"They tried to run supplies in, but they couldn't until finally they did begin to get a few in at night. They had some of these old World War One destroyers they had taken the stacks off. They'd get in about dusk and unload and get out of there before dawn. And even they got hit. We were subject to air bombardment every day, oftentimes several times a day. It was not unusual for a Japanese naval vessel to stand offshore and just lob shells in. One shell landed very close to my position, and a hunk of shrapnel hit me. I saved one piece. It got me in the arm and the side. By that time we all had malaria too, you know. Malaria was endemic. The shrapnel didn't stop me. It wasn't that serious, and you couldn't evacuate casualties anyway. I got a Purple Heart out of it. I got one on Iwo Jima too. I was promoted to captain a year and half after being commissioned and served as battery commander for quite a while on Guadalcanal.

"Finally the First Marine Division units were being relieved by Second Marine Division units, and then some Army elements came in. I think the Army took over responsibility probably in March or April of '43. We went to Brisbane, then Sydney and finally Melbourne. We didn't suffer the high rate of casualties we were to have at Iwo. I'd say about eighty percent of the battery was intact. From Melbourne we moved out to an old Australian army camp, and I got sent back to the States because of my malaria.

"They were just starting the First Marine Corps Command and

Staff School at Quantico, and of course my wife was there. I was assigned, and about that time I got promoted to major. I was there six or eight weeks and then got ordered to an advanced officers' course at Fort Sill, Oklahoma, for ten weeks. My wife was able to accompany me; this was still '43. When I got back to Camp Lejeune, they were just beginning to form the Fifth Marine Division. The artillery for the division was the Thirteenth Marines, and I was ordered to the Third Battalion. The rest of the Fifth Division was being formed at Camp Pendleton in California, so we got the Third Battalion fairly well formed and then moved to Pendleton in the late summer of '44."

Russell was the battalion executive officer, but there was a great deal of rotation going on as more senior officers came back from the field. He was pushed out of the exec job to operations officer, somebody else came in, and he was pushed out of that.

"They were talking about sending me back out. I hated like heck to have to leave my wife when we were finally getting acquainted after three or four years of marriage" [so he transferred to an infantry battalion and became the exec there]. So I became an oh-eight/oh-three, artillery-infantry.

"It wasn't easy because the Marine Corps had these raider and paratroop outfits, and I think, wisely, they decided to disband them. A marine is a marine. They didn't need all this fancy raider stuff. But all those people, these prima donnas, were thrown into this regiment, and they were horrified to have an artilleryman in the outfit. I had to really work and work and work to gain their respect. Any time there was a hike I was always leading it. They had a lot of swimming pools, for amphibious training. They had a platform twenty or thirty feet high. You'd have to climb up that with your full pack on and either be pushed off or jump off into this pool. And of course the pool was crystal clear, and it looked like you were up about four hundred feet.

"When it came time, I was the one designated to take the battalion up. And you know, all the troops are looking and wondering what the heck's going on, so who has to go up the damn ladder? First one was me. Oh, I tell you when I looked down there, I thought there were a lot of places I'd rather have been. But I said, 'I gotta go, and I'll show these so-and-sos.' So I went. Full pack, combat boots, everything. It gradually got to the point where I had the confidence of the troops and the company commanders, so everyone was comfortable with me by the time we got the word for Iwo Jima.

"We made the landing on Red Beach One. I landed in the third wave, which was the first of the LCVPs [landing craft, vehicle, personnel] fourteen to twenty minutes after the first waves landed at eight-twenty. The first two waves were amtracs. Our mission was to cut across and go up the other side.

"When I got out, I had my jeep in this boat, and when we got out, I kept yelling to the troops, 'Get off the beach! Get off the beach! Get up on the high ground!' And of course they were trying to climb up that soft volcanic sand. It was extremely difficult. You'd go up, and you'd go sliding back, and already there were a lot of casualties. There was firing on the beach, not the heavy volume that came later, but there was firing.

"I got the troops out, and the driver of the jeep got it across the ramp, and as soon as the front wheels hit the soil, it started to spin. He couldn't get it any farther than that. We were trying to get up the hill, and when I looked back he had got out of the jeep. One of the kids had been hit, and I was seeing how bad he was hurt. When I looked around, the driver had gotten out, and he must have got hit; there was this enfilade fire coming up the beach, and it looked as though he was just broken in half. He must have got it in the midriff. One of the sailors on the ramp just reached over and dragged him in. The coxswain then took the LCVP and jiggled it back and forth back and forth to get rid of the jeep and I just remember seeing my jeep just gradually slipping down into the sand. It became part of that pileup of debris all along the beach.

"We were under fire from all directions, heavy fire from just all over. I don't remember being appalled. I was kind of dismayed, I guess you could say, but I was more interested in getting the troops up and on the higher ground where they wouldn't be so vulnerable. I did not know Fred Haynes then [see Chapter 4]. I may have known him as officer in the Twenty-eighth Regiment. My regiment was the Twenty-seventh. My job as executive officer was to get the troops in and coordinate the command post.

"Iwo Jima was an action of constant, constant fire all the way through, twenty-four hours a day even to the thirty-sixth day. It was just constant. Guadalcanal was spasmodic; there were times you could just take it easy. Korea you were in trenches. But at Iwo there was artillery, mortars, machine guns, rifles, everything, and they would pop up from places you least expected. Of course they don't mention it much, but we thought this was gonna be a piece of cake. We were going in there for ninety-six hours just to kind of, you know, wipe up what was left, and go on and support the Okinawa operation.

"The fact that they had all these troops in tunnels came as a big surprise. When I went back the first time, I was almost confused. There was something different. All of a sudden I realized that when we landed, there wasn't a blade of grass on that thing. They had pulverized it. I mean everything. It was just bare soil, and it was hard to imagine that anybody could survive in that, but they were so far down. Last time I went out I was amazed that the caves held up so well even after all these years, because of the consistency of the rock. They just chipped away and chipped away. They didn't need anything to support it.

"I recall having two code talkers with my unit. My experience with them went back to our training base in the Hawaiian Islands. We worked for quite a while with them when they first joined us. I had one, and the battalion CO had one. He might send a message to me saying, 'I got a call from the Baker Company or Easy. They need some ammunition. Get it for them.' He'd write it out in longhand, and the code talker would go off and transpose it. Then he'd get on the radio and send it and nod to the battalion CO that it was on the way. Then I'd see that Navajo on my end pick up his phone and start writing. Then he'd go off to the side, transpose it into English, and hand me the thing. They were very well organized. They went through the routine and knew exactly what to do.

"But the first five days on Iwo were so heavy I really don't recall using them too much. That action was so concentrated. It was just day and night. You hear people say, 'Well, when did you sleep?' You didn't sleep; you just got by. It rained the first couple days. You'd stick the poncho over your head, and after a while you'd get soaking wet, but you just took it. That's the way it was.

"For meals, you grabbed something when you could. We did have some canned C rations. It was interesting, you could dig down six or eight inches, put the can in, and in a half hour it would be cooked. If you dug a foxhole, you had to wait for it to cool off before you could get in it. It was an amazing phenomenon.

"I was taking care of all the details that came up, making sure there was ammunition or rations or that casualties were taken care off, radios, runners, telephones. Hell, the ground looked like spaghetti, with telephone wire going everywhere. My battalion CO was a major named John Antonelli. He got through OK. About the sixth or seventh day we had been pulled off the line. Of our original twelve hundred, we were down to around four hundred men. By this time Suribachi had been taken, so they could bring in replacements. So we were pulled off the line and brought down, and we got our replacements, and we were trying to filter them in where we needed them. We got a good meal for the first time, had a chance to bathe a little bit.

"Next morning the regimental CO called the battalion commanding officer so he could show him where the battalion would be moved back up to the front. The battalion CO went up in his jeep, and I led the troops up. I was out in front of them, and I had them spread out with a good interval between each one, two rows going up this full road. I came up on the top of the hill, and there was a cut in the road, not quite as wide as this room, and when I got to the top, I could see all the way to the end of the island, and just as I got there, a shell hit the side of the hill.

"It threw shrapnel all over, and I got hit in the face. It barely missed my eye. I landed in the ditch on the side of the road. I was groggy, but I told the headquarters company commander to take the troops down around the back of the hill and then notify the battalion CO. Next thing you know I was being driven down to the beach by the regimental CO. I was sitting in the front seat with blood all over me, and the battalion CO was holding me so I wouldn't fall over.

"We used to get these two-ounce bottles of Lejeune medicinal brandy, and they were giving that to me, plus I think the regimental CO had a bottle, so by the time I got to the beach I didn't know much of anything. Anyway, they claim I insisted that I not be evacuated. I remember vaguely going through the next few days with a big patch on my face. Three or four days after that, halfway through the operation, well into March, Antonelli, the battalion CO, got hit, and he was evacuated. That's when they talk about me being one of the last remaining battalion commanders because Antonelli died four or five years ago. At any rate, I took over the battalion and brought it all the way through for the rest of the campaign, right to the end.

"We always tried to dig in for the command post. We tried to be as close to the front as we could, and usually we were one hill behind the front lines. Take the case of First Lieutenant Jack Lummus, who was to receive the Medal of Honor for all the stuff he did on March 8. His action was up front of us, on sort of a mound, you might say, and the CP was behind it. I remember when they brought him back. He had stepped on a mine, and both of his legs were blown off. They weren't bleeding.

"He was on a stretcher, and I lit a cigarette and held it for him. Jack had been an All-American at Baylor and was an end for the New York Giants. He talked reasonably cogent, and of course I was shocked that he wasn't bleeding. I learned later that shock just clamps things off. Anyway, he said, 'Well, I guess the Giants have lost a good end.' And I said, 'Jack, the Marine Corps has lost one hell of a good officer.' They took him in the jeep down to the clearance station. I talked to a doctor down there afterward, and he said he didn't have a chance. He said what you didn't see was the fact that his stomach was all ripped open. He said he could reach in and pull a handful of dirt out of it.

"We went through the whole thing on the front lines all the time. On the morning of the fifth day we had swung up to the north, and we were having a hell of a time. Our two code talkers got clobbered that fifth day, and one of them was in a shell hole for two days before we could get to him, the action was so intense.

"We were facing away in a kind of crevice, and one of the kids yelled, 'Look!' He pointed up, and there on the top of Mount Suribachi we could see this small group of men and Old Glory. It was very emotional. You can't imagine how I felt. There was an old gunnery sergeant standing near me. He was about six feet two and had been in the Marines for I don't know how many years, the Old Corps, you know?

"This guy had the most colorfully profane vocabulary I've ever heard. How he could conjure up some of these things was just amazing. He never showed any emotion or anything else, and on the fifth day we were coated with that black grime. We barely had enough water to drink, let alone to wash. When the flag went up, I couldn't say anything. I had a lump in my throat, and I don't know if I had any tears, but I looked at this guy who I never thought had an ounce of emotion in his body, and he looked at me and you could see tears coming down through this grime on his face, and he said—and I'll never forget it—he said, 'God, that's the most beautiful sight I have ever seen.'

"I've said this in Flag Day speeches and stuff that up to that point, we weren't sure whether we were going to succeed or not. But from that moment on, when the flag went up, we knew we were. It didn't get any easier, but we knew we were going to win. We were reminded of what we were there for. I don't know which flag it was, but it was in the morning. We just kept going. We were just relieved that they had taken it.

"Iwo was a place where you had to go in and dig the enemy out, where you had to use flamethrowers and satchel charges. It wasn't just huge barrages of fire. For example, we were in an area where the rocky formations were such that every time our troops would try to maneuver, the Japs could come out of these caves and fire on them. We needed some kind of heavy fire, and there was no way we could get a tank in there.

"Being an old artilleryman, I suggested we get a pack howitzer, because it breaks down into seven or eight pieces. It was originally designed to be carried by donkeys or mules. It was easily portable. This weapon was designed primarily as mountain artillery that could be broken down and taken ashore in six loads from a boat. It became an important support weapon of the Marine Corps at every major landing in the Pacific. It was crewed by five men and could throw a sixteen-pound shell almost ten thousand yards. So I recommended we get one up there at night, set it up, and start using it during the daytime.

"But the regimental executive officer of the artillery said, 'That's damn foolishness; it'd never work.' But apparently General Rockey, the division commander, said in no uncertain words, 'If they want it, get it and give it to them.' So they brought it up, just this little group with one gun. They put up the gun at night, camouflaged and put rocks around to protect it. We used it, and we moved right through after that. But again it was that individual action, individual initiative.

"We kept losing men after I took over the battalion, and we got a few more replacements. But by the end of the operation there were so few left in the whole regiment that they consolidated the First, Second, and Third into a sort of temporary battalion. There was just one lieutenant colonel left, a guy named Don Robertson. He took over.

"The most vivid memory I would mention out of all that time was the flies and the smell of the dead. That's something they don't mention in documentaries, but boy, when you have that many bodies all over the place, it's sometimes days and days before they can bring them out. The flies and the stench were pretty bad.

"I carried a forty-five, but I never fired it. Three or four days before the end of the operation I had the remnants of my companies together, and we were dug in. I was in a foxhole myself, and I had a phone from each one of the companies. They were having trouble, and we needed some heavy fire. I had requested a tank. When it came up, I went around to the side away from where the Japanese were, so I had some shelter. I got the phone from the side of the tank, and I told them inside exactly what fire we needed and where. I vividly remember that when the sixty-millimeter small-caliber mortar shells would explode, they gave off that yellow picric acid kind of smell. When they acknowledged my message, I ran like heck back and jumped into my hole. Well, while I was gone, a shell had landed in there and chewed up all three phones and everything else. We always have an expression: If your name is on it, no matter what happens, you're going to get it. I guess mine wasn't on it. To this day I kinda sweat a little bit when I think about that one, right up almost to the end. They didn't give up. They fought all the way. Talk about a hunk of hell, it really was.

"I think the battle of Iwo Jima is one of the truly great landmarks in the overall history of the Marine Corps. It was an achievement tremendous in its significance because of the way we were able to handle it, win it.

"The performance of the troops became a defining statement for what marines can accomplish because at times it seemed hopeless. We were still able to keep going, day after day, with an unbelievable number of casualties. It was unsurpassed. We never had anything like it before. The troops, those marines proved that no matter what, we would succeed.

"After Iwo, and as soon as we got back to the base camp at Hilo in the Hawaiian Islands, we immediately started getting ready for Operation Olympic, to land on Kyushu. We trained, got replacements, then the two atomic bombs were dropped, and the Japanese sued for the armistice.

"They took the First Battalion, Twenty-seventh Marines, and the First Battalion, Twenty-sixth Marines, to make a preliminary landing during the occupation. We didn't know what to expect from the Japanese. They had been treacherous, mistreated our prisoners of war, and so we went in ready to fight. But they were the most docile, cooperative people you could ask for. Honor is so important to them, and the emperor said, 'Do what you're told, and cooperate.' I never had one bit of trouble with them.

"So I spent almost a year in the occupation, and I got a couple key assignments. One was to accept the surrender of the Tsushima

Islands under Lieutenant General Bukei Nagasi. The Tsushimas were the pair of islands in the Sea of Japan with Korea on one side and Kyushu on the other. I got some pictures of the guns we had to blow up, fourteen-inch naval guns.

"I went in with my battalion on LSTs. I had a group of twelve interpreters from the Home Ministry. General Nagasi was from the old warrior class, very distinguished, a very proud, very pleasant guy. He had eight thousand troops, and I had a little over a thousand, and his were crack troops, and I wanted to get them the hell out of there. I commandeered every damn fishing boat, everything I could find, and put them aboard and sent them back to the mainland.

"I'm still just a major in my mid-twenties, and this lieutenant general kept saying, 'Well, when can we make arrangements to have a surrender?' He kept saying, 'Well, when is your general coming?' And I had to tell this poor old—you know honor would dictate somebody of the same rank would accept the surrender, and here he has to surrender to this punky major. By virtue of that, I got to know the Japanese people and everything, so I could see their side. There were some things I had come to understand about them where they felt justified in a way.

"Japan was a small country, very short of minerals, and all the metals of the world were right there in their backyard, all controlled by countries half a world away. They got it through colonial efforts; why can't we do the same thing? I think they felt we'd back down if they showed any force. They thought the United States was a bunch of pussycats, wouldn't be willing to fight. Of course Kuribayashi and I think Yamamoto knew better, but nobody listened to them."

Gerry Russell retired from the Marines in 1968 as a full colonel following service in World War II and Korea, then as a regimental commander after that. He commanded the ground transport in Guantánamo during the Cuban missile crisis in 1962. He and his wife had two daughters, Eileen and Maureen. He spent his post-military years at Penn State University in State College, Pennsylvania. He has been the chief finish judge of the Millrose Games for many years. He never made it to Harvard.

10

PRIVATE FIRST CLASS SAMUEL TSO
Code Talker
Reconnaissance Company, Fifth Marine Division

They called me Chief, and I resented that for a long time. I don't know what they mean by that at the time, but later on I decided, oh, they give me a promotion from PFC, and from then on I don't bother with it.

Samuel Tso in Albuquerque, New Mexico, in October 2006. The Navajo code talkers were honored by President George W. Bush in 2001 with the Congressional Gold Medal, the highest civilian honor Congress can bestow.

Private First Class Samuel Tso, displaying one battle star for service on Iwo Jima, is photographed in Camp Pendleton, California, in 1946.

There were twenty-nine original code talkers, four of whom were still living in the spring of 2007. Sam Tso was recruited for a later group. He and I were at Iwo Jima in March 2006, but I didn't really get acquainted with him until we met again in Albuquerque in October of that year. He was there with several other code talkers to sign copies of three different books to help raise funds for their association. I bought all the books. They signed them. You couldn't help liking these guys.

"I'm from Arizona, above Window Rock. It's way up by a place called Black Mountain, about eighty miles from Gallup, New Mexico. We didn't live on top but down below, on the east side of the mountain. The nearest town or store was twenty-five miles away. My father and mother raised sheep. They'd sell wool and sometimes sell the lambs. I had brothers and sisters; there were ten of us.

"I don't know what year I was born. The only thing my mother remembered was it was sometime close to the midsummer, probably around 1926. When I finish eighth grade, I'm ready for high school, so they send me to Fort Wingate, New Mexico. In that four years I never came back home. I learned to read and write. It was a boarding school paid for by the federal government. We lived in dormitories. We were mostly Navajo, but other Indians were sent there too. During the summer everybody goes home except me. I had to go look for a job. I found out the government was running an experimental sheep station close by there. So I went and herded sheep for them. They were experimenting with wool. Old Navajo sheep wool had a hole through every strand, and to get rid of that, they brought in Rambouillet rams to crossbreed and change the wool so it was solid.

"After high school I didn't get a chance to go home at all. The federal government just told me, 'There's a road down that way.

Somewhere you'll find a job.' So I picked up my suitcase and started walking.

"You know what? I sure hate to tell anybody, but I really resented it. I really resented it. I just kept it inside me all those years. In fact, when I started school, they told me not to speak my language, Navajo, at Indian school. We used to get punished for it.

"It took me approximately nine years before I got back home. I did not get home until after the war. When I got home, I found out my father, my mother, and one of my sisters, that I used to herd sheep with all the time, they were all dead. There were no phones, and no one ever wrote; they couldn't write. They were uneducated.

"When I come out of high school, the only job available was with the railroad company in Gallup, so I went there and asked for a job. They asked how old I was. I said nineteen. Then I found out they didn't employ nineteen-year-olds, so in the morning I was nineteen, but by the afternoon, when I got hired, I became twenty-one years old and signed a contract saying I was born June 22, 1922. This was 1943. It was an easy birthday to remember. But that's how I came to be drafted.

"When I got the job from Gallup, they transported me all the way to Barstow, California. We were replacing old ties underneath the tracks. While we were out there, the draft board came around and told me to report to the San Bernardino board. I went over there and signed in. About a month later they called me. I was drafted and sent back to Arizona. Instead of going home, I hitchhiked from Gallup over to the draft board at St. Johns, Arizona, to report. I didn't know a bus had been set aside for the draftees, so I hitchhiked all day, a long ways. It was in 1943, March.

"The guys I worked with on the railroad had bought me a charcoal-colored civilian suit, and they told me to wear that coming back. I was hitchhiking with that suit on when I got to St. John. I found the guys there resented it. Right after lunch they ganged up on me and tore some of my suit, took my hat away from me and stomped on it. They were all Navajos. Jealous. The guy in charge, I guess he was the sergeant, came out and broke it up. Next morning they put us on the bus to Phoenix, for our physical exams. Only three of us were selected out of those two busloads of guys. We found out the rest of them don't know how to speak English very good. I found out that to go in the service, you had to speak good English, read and write. Those others did not know how to read or write.

"After we were drafted, they found out we were Navajos, so they put us into the Marines because the Marines had the [code talker] program. Two of us went through boot camp in San Diego together. The third one came later, in the next platoon. It was 1943, March 13, when we started. We finished in April, then went to Camp Elliott, east of San Diego. We trained as infantrymen. We were ready to be shipped out when all of a sudden they pulled my seabag to the side. The rest of the guys I trained with, all white guys, were hauled off and sent to the Pacific.

"They took me to Camp Pendleton and put me in the code talker school. I said, 'Hey, you didn't want me to speak my language. How come? Now you want it.' At least this time they said please. Before that they never said please.

"The way I heard it there were thirty original code talkers. Something happened to one, so there were only twenty-nine. A guy by the name of Johnston ran the school. Later on I found out he was the son of a missionary that was on our Navajo reservation. The first day I reported to Pendleton I met Mr. Johnston, and all of a sudden he talked to me in Navajo. I was really surprised that he could speak Navajo. His terms and tenses were all mixed up, but I could understand him.

"I believe I was there about a month, maybe more. We were at least one class, close to twenty. As soon as they got trained there, they got sent out. We were all from Arizona, New Mexico, and Utah. I did not know any one of them. I learned all the code signals, and they gave me a partner and took us out in the field to set up the radio and practice sending messages back and forth. We noticed that some of the Anglo kids that taught us how to set up the radios were listening to us and memorizing all the coded words. Right there me and my partner said, 'Hey, if these kids can memorize that in such a short time, the Japanese will do the same thing.'

[The original code, invented in 1942, contained 236 terms. By 1945 it had grown to more than 400, all memorized. The expanded code uses alternate words for common letters of the alphabet. The letter *A* could be "ant," "apple," or "ax." The word for *America* was *Ne-he-mah*, meaning "our mother." The word for *battleship* was *lo-tso*, meaning "whale."]

"We started making another set of twenty-six symbols for the letters in the alphabet, and then we started on a third set, and somewhere along the third set we were ready to be sent out for further training. So that's where we started the other sets. And when we started it, we started jumping around between those sets, and the kids that memorized the first set got confused. We mixed it all up, so the Japanese could not memorize it.

"We were sent out as soon as we were trained. Six of us went to a recon company. We trained up in mountains, down on the beach, out on an island, even in submarines. The sub would come in offshore; we would paddle over there and go into the sub. It dives, takes us out somewhere, comes in, and surfaces, and then we get out and use rubber boats to go along the shore. They told us to look for military installations, ammo dumps, or fuel dumps. When we got back to the submarine, we would dive again, then get together and report what we saw. After about half a year they sent us to Hilo, Hawaii, in early 1944.

"We left Hilo on Christmas night of '44 and went to Honolulu. They told us to go to town and do what we liked. I didn't know anybody, at the time, to go into bars and drink beers and stuff. As I remember, we Navajos were told not to do that because the federal government put restrictions on us. So I didn't bother to go to any bars. I went to one show and then another one. It was real close to sundown, so I went by myself to the ship, I got aboard, and in about two hours there was all this commotion. All those guys were coming in, some so drunk they couldn't walk up the gangplank. So they let the cargo nets down, put 'em in there and hoisted them up and dumped them on the deck. This was the Fifth Marine Division. There were six of us code talkers in that company. All the rest got drunk, and I was the only one sober. Some got so sick they just puked all over the place.

"The boat left for Guam that same night, sneaked out, zigzagging all the way. Some guys said later the reason was to avoid Japanese submarines. From Guam we went to Saipan and practiced landing there. A recon company was practicing landing there, and I found out that some of these guys who could really swim good belonged to an underwater demolition team, UDT. I got to be real good friends with a guy named Al Mertz, one of the UDT experts. We sort of stayed together. He was from the Ozarks in Arkansas, Pine Bluff. I remember because he used to get letters. Me, I never got no letters. My father, my mother, my brothers and sisters were uneducated. They couldn't write anything. I never got a letter from anyone all that time. I didn't even have a girlfriend. Mostly I kept by myself.

"We didn't know we were going to Iwo until we were out there at Saipan. I can't remember what wave I went in with, but when we landed, there was no fire from the Japanese. But after we went on top and started spreading out, they opened fire. Some of the guys jumped in an artillery crater. We jumped in on the south side of it, and the guys who jumped in on the north side got shot because they were exposed. My personal sergeant was a guy named Barnes; when we started moving forward, he got blown up. He told me to go around to the other side and stay behind. He went straight ahead and stepped on a mine. If I'd followed him, I'd have been killed.

"Let me tell you, I was scared stiff. The only thing that helped me go on was the fact that I was committed to the fellows that I trained with. We were told that you go in as a team, that you must watch out for each other. That's what kept me going, even though I was scared.

"When we went ashore, our mission was to cut the island in half, but they held some of us behind. They put us by the airfield and said, 'You hold this for a certain day and then follow.' My job was to receive and send messages from the ships or the command post or whatever it is. You receive it and send it on. All in Navajo. All the radio guys were Navajos doing code. I don't know how many there were altogether. I know my recon company had six. Sam Billison was supposed to be with us, but they selected him to be with headquarters command. All messages went in code. Major Howard Connor said he had six Navajo networks going twenty-four hours, and they sent and received eight hundred messages without an error.

"On February 23, 1945, just somewhere close to noontime, all of sudden the radio signaled, 'Message for Arizona.' So I just grabbed my papers and my pencil and just sent it. They sent this message: *DIBE BINAR NAAZII*: 'Sheep's eyes is cured: Mount Suribachi is secure.' *Sheep Uncle Ram Ice Bear Ant Cat Horse Itch* spelled *Suribachi*. And it was encoded too. It was sent out, and I caught it there by the airfield. And the marines that were there saw me writing it down, and they all said, "What's up, Chief?" All I did was just point up to the flag, and they saw it. Oh, gosh, those guys just jumped up and started celebrating there. They forgot the Japanese were still shooting. As I remember Sergeant Thomas screamed at us, said, 'Damn you knotheads! Get back in your foxholes there!' And then the guys stopped celebrating, and they jumped back into their foxholes.

"They called me Chief, and I resented that for a long time. I don't know what they mean by that at the time, but later on I decided, oh, they give me a promotion from PFC, and from then on I don't bother with it.

"One night, sometime early in the morning, my buddy Paul Blatchfield kicked me, and he said, 'Hey, Sam! Are you having a nightmare?'

"And I woke up, stood up, then sat down. I was dreaming about a young Indian maiden who came to me, and gave me something.

She says, 'Here, you wear this, and you'll come back to us.' It was so real that I got up and just set there thinking about it. And all of sudden they called the rest of the marines to go eat. Everybody went to go eat, but I just set there and thought about it.

"They came back and said, 'Hey, Chief, are you still here?' I said, 'Yeah, I'm just thinking.' Then, mail call. They all went over there. I know I don't get no mail, so I don't go. All of sudden, here this Mertz came running back, and he said, 'Hey, Chief, you got a letter! You got a letter!' He brought it over, and he said, 'There's something in it.' We opened it and here is the necklace that Indian maiden tried to give me in my dream, it's in that letter. That letter, I was so stunned I didn't know what to do about it . . . oh, yeah . . . I was supposed to wear it. I put it on; as soon as I put it on, all that fear disappeared.

"The necklace was made out of what we call cedar tree berries. The berry has seeds in it, and it's formed into something like one of those Catholic Church rosaries, and at the end it has a cross made out of cedarwood. I wore it and wore it and wore it. I don't know when that thing broke. It just fell apart.

"Who sent it? I never knew. My name is on the envelope, but there's no return address or nothing. No note. Just plain the necklace. And the dream. After that I wasn't afraid anymore. That's the reason why. We were sent to run across a place called Death Valley. This Death Valley is on the north side; there's a valley there the marines tried to cross and on the other side a Japanese machine gun. When the marines tried to cross, they'd just mow them down. We were sent to cross that valley and locate the Japanese machine gun . . . the recon guys. I was selected to take the farthest point. Me and another guy were both assigned over there.

"They told us, 'At noontime we will give you the signal to cross the valley and get to the machine-gun nest.' So we strung out all the way. I believe a platoon, don't know which one it was. Sergeant Thomas told us, 'If you get hit, we're going to come and get you; we won't leave you out there.' Gave us that pep talk. At noontime they gave us the signal, and we took off. Just beyond the boulders, oh, man, there were bodies laying on top of each other, some still alive, some reaching out for help. We tried to stop and help, but the sergeant screamed at us to keep going. You complete your mission first. I took off again. We ran smack into a Japanese submachine gun. They told us those Japanese soldiers would get their food ration at noontime. When they go out there, that's when they sent us out, and we ran into that submachine gun. I think my buddy just threw a hand grenade over there, and we beat it back to report.

"The sergeant called me over and just chewed me up and down: 'Don't you know how to take orders?' and all that stuff. He was mad because we had tried to help the wounded. That was not our mission; our mission was to locate the machine gun. The other two code talkers sent the coordinates and ordered mortar fire, rocket fire, and artillery fire, all three at the same time, at one machine-gun nest. Within five minutes you could hear all the explosions coming in, you could see rockets coming over, mortars coughing and going over. That place was just completely . . . Rocks were flying all over the place. Within maybe twenty or thirty minutes they stopped. Before the dust and all that settled they ordered the marines to cross. The marines they just walked right across without any Japanese fire. We found out stretcher bearers were all kneeling down waiting to go get our wounded out.

"Anyway, that's where that dream helped. It kept all my fear away, and I said, 'I'm going home, I'm going home.' And sure enough, I came back.

"I was on Iwo for the whole battle. We carried M1s. Guys don't believe me, but one time we were out on a ledge at the front and they told us to hold that point at all costs. Sometime late in the afternoon the sun was almost down, and the guys become real spooky, and one said, 'You hear that?' 'Hear what?' 'That popping sound?' As soon as we heard that popping sound, we could see that Japanese hand grenade coming. And we just grabbed the M1, used it like a bat and whammed the grenade back instead of trying to pick it up. Then we found out the M1 was a good bat too.

"I was never wounded. [Gestures left.] A guy got shot here [gestures right], another guy got shot there. Why I wasn't hit is beyond me. The maiden in the dream? I believe that's what it is. I believe I know for sure of three code talkers that got killed on Iwo Jima.

"They found out that carrying the radio on Iwo Jima was all right for a wide-open area but too risky in real close fighting. They used the telephone, a regular telephone receiver, mostly. Most of the code talkers had to string the wire. If it broke, you had go back and repair it or string another one. Some guys set up radios for relays in certain areas; that's where I intercepted that message coming in about Suribachi.

"The radiomen, they always said, 'Message for Arizona!' And that meant a code talker needed to receive it, even on the radio. Message for Arizona. Can you hear it? A lot of people don't understand that this Navajo code language was not written. It's only a spoken language. You can't read it, and you can't write it. You have to decode it in your head and change it to English. It's only in the head here. A rich language.

"Now they're trying to pass a law that all Indian languages should be taught in public schools. It is being taught on the reservation and on the university level, at New Mexico State, University of Arizona, Northern Arizona, and at Arizona State. But back then they wouldn't let us speak it; they wanted everybody to be Anglo. I went to speak in Washington, D.C., last April 12 [2006]. I talked to some congressmen, Senators Daniel Inouye and Daniel Akaka and some others. We talked about the Native American language. I told them it was very valuable. This was about legislation saying that Native American languages will be taught in states where they have reservations. The other was to recognize code talkers from other tribes, like the Sioux, the Choctaw, Comanches, Sac and Fox, and some others. They were used as translators in their own languages, but ours was coded.

"During the war there were guards assigned to protect us. Some code talkers had bodyguards. I wasn't told I had one, but there was a guy who stayed with me all the time: 'Hey, Chief, where you going?' 'Oh, I got go to the restroom.' And he comes along. He followed me all over that place. The guard was supposed to protect you.

"That *Windtalker* movie? One of the guys who saw it, one of the original twenty-nine, said that's eighty percent correct and twenty percent Hollywood. But another guy says it's fifty percent OK and fifty percent bull hit the snake. That's Navajo code for *bullshit*. When Tokyo Rose used to come on the radio, this guy by the name of Chester Soul always used to say, 'Oh, that's bull hit the snake.' That means 'bullshit.'

"Chester trained with us. Groups came in later. Some joined and learned the code, but they never saw action. Altogether there's about four hundred twenty code talkers, all marines, in the First, Second, Third, Fourth, Fifth, and Sixth Divisions. They were at Okinawa too. Every theater. Last March, when we were back over there, we stopped at Okinawa, and man, oh, man, there were people out there who really appreciated the Navajo code talkers.

"I didn't go to Okinawa during the war. Iwo was my last action. When we got back to Hawaii, they were getting ready to invade the mainland. Japan. I came back to the States sometime in February of 1946. If my family had said, 'Write to me,' I would have seen my mother again. But nobody could write, no telephone. That's the one that really hurts.

"I got out March 29, 1946. They tried to keep me in the Marines. They said, 'We'll give you a corporal rating if you stay in.' I said, 'No, thank you. You don't give me no promotion or nothing all this time, and I'm supposed to be a specialist. I'll take my chances on the outside.'

"I was released in San Diego, and from there they took us to Camp Pendleton, and we waited a whole month to get discharged. The bus depot, the train station, everything was all jammed. I had to stand in line almost two nights just to get on a bus. Some would get so disgusted they'd take their seabag and try to hitchhike. I got on a bus as far as Winslow, Arizona. It turned south there, so I took my seabag and hitchhiked to Gallup. A guy from New York picked me up. He wanted to stop at Petrified National Forest before we got to Gallup, so I went along with him. We saw it, came back, and he decided to eat. We went and sat at a restaurant, and to my surprise he ordered beer for us. Then the guy that owned the place said, 'No beer for this Indian!'

"And the guy from New York got into an argument with the owner. He was mad at that guy. He said this man just risked his hind end for you guys, and you won't even give him a beer. So they argued. I was beginning to think they might get into a fight, and I said, 'Forget it, forget it, let it go. I'm used to it now.' But he finally talked the owner into it. He says, 'OK, then you be responsible for him.' 'Responsible for what? It's just one beer.' So we had a beer, and then we went on to Gallup.

"From Gallup there was no transportation to the reservation, and it was more than ninety miles to Black Mountain. I had to wait for the mail truck to Chinle early next morning. There was no transportation from Chinle to Black Mountain. Nobody knew anything about where I was.

"So I had to walk again, had to walk all day. Just before sundown I got to a place where they have rocks piled up on the south side. There was a mirror hidden underneath, so I took that mirror out and started flashing out toward the Black Mountain, where my home was. All of sudden I saw a horse coming. I put the mirror back in there and walked a little ways. The horse came bearing my brother. I hadn't seen him in nine years. I left my seabag there till they could come for it with a wagon. We rode back home, and I found my father had died.

"Then just before dawn I got up and walked out of there because there was nothing for me to stay for. A big cedar tree is still standing just a little ways from where we lived. Underneath that tree is where I was born. When you stay with the sheep, you have to move here and there every month so they don't overgraze. You don't move the hogan, which is your home. At that time we didn't have any tent. All we had was sheepskins spread over a lean-to. I was born in a lean-to under that tree.

"I looked over there at that tree and saw there's a family living there. I asked, 'Who's that?' They said, 'They own that place now.' And here that was supposed to be mine. And I talked with the guy who lived there, and he told me, 'This is mine because you been away all these years. To own this land, you're supposed to live on it, and tend to it but you've been gone all these years.'

"I said, 'Hey. I been fighting for that land. The government took me away.' But that's tribal law. He still lives on it.

"I just walked out of there. My brother found out I just left. He brought a horse over to me and asked where I'm going. I said, 'I don't know where I'm going. I'm just going. The first thing I need to do, I need to get to Chinle and that mail truck.' So he gave me the horse and gave me instruction. 'You ride this over there and leave the saddle and the bridle at the church and put my name on it and turn the horse loose. He'll come back,' he said.

"I rode the horse to Chinle, got on the mail truck, and went back to Gallup. From Gallup I bought a bus ticket all the way to San Francisco. I had found out one of my sisters got married and she and her husband lived there. She didn't know our mother, our father, and my other sister had died. She couldn't communicate with them either."

Sam worked in San Francisco and then back on the railroad, and then he went to Lawrence, Kansas, where he spent two years at the Haskell Institute vocational school, a trade school for Indians. He learned electrical work and refrigeration. Here he met his wife, Anne, also a student. He went on to Oregon while Anne found a job at a new school for Navajo children in Brigham City, Utah. Eventually Sam joined her there and obtained a degree in elementary education. They were married in June 1952 and had a son and a daughter. For thirty years he taught Navajo children at the Intermountain Schools and up in Lukachukai, "a little bitty settlement," about twenty miles from where he was born.

So how does Sam Tso feel today about the treatment he received at the hands of the government and about his service on the Island of Iwo Jima?

"Let me tell you. We are still part of the United States, whether it's called a reservation or not. We are still part of the United States. When I thought about it, I felt that, if were not for the United States, some other country would have come in and taken over, and what would we be? I doubt we would be a democracy. I found out in high school that a democratic form of government is best for people. And that's what made me decide to go and help in the war.

"People aren't stupid. Sooner or later they are going to learn to respect everybody. Not only one group, but everybody. It's best that we be patient. Coming back from the war, I found out that the people of America were really thankful. The reason I say this is because one time President Clinton invited us to go with him to Hawaii to celebrate V-J Day. We followed him over there, and we were at the Punch Bowl, where all those dead soldiers were buried. It was a lot of people. He made a speech, and then he introduced a lot of the top brasses from different parts of the services.

"At the end he introduced us Navajo code talkers. Man, oh, man, I just couldn't believe it. All the people in that bowl just stood up, yelling and clapping. Some even started running up here to shake our hands, and then one right after another had to have us sign autographs. People wanted to take our pictures. I just couldn't know how to take that.

"That same year, 1995, the *National Geographic* paid my transportation back to Iwo Jima. They made a documentary film over there, *War Code Navajo*. They sent me a copy. I later found out it won an Emmy award."

11

CORPORAL AL ABBATIELLO

Combat Engineer
Twenty-eighth Marines, Fifth Marine Division

If they took Truman out of his grave, I'd kiss his ass right now for dropping that bomb because he saved our hide.

Al Abbatiello, eighty-one, displays the Purple Heart he never wanted and he never wore. He came home from Iwo Jima with two samurai swords, one of which he took off a dead officer near the end of the battle and the second from a supply cave for noncommissioned officers; three Japanese rifles; and a couple of Nambu pistols. He hid them in a trailer that held demolition supplies and had them shipped to Hawaii, then sent home from there.

Corporal Al Abbatiello sports a goatee along with a very large grin shortly after reaching Hawaii on the return from Iwo Jima. "The big reason I'm smiling," he said, "is because I'm still alive." The whiskers came off shortly afterward.

I met with Al Abbatiello early in 2007 in his Lighthouse Point, Florida, condominium, not far from Fort Lauderdale. He was eighty-one at the time. I was inspired to contact him by the former Marine Corps historian John Ripley, who said, "Al is one of my favorite Iwo veterans from all the trips I have taken there. He is the real deal, authentic and accurate in all his recounted stories. He was also the stereotypical marine in his day, big, tough, hard, and a real professional. I also like his entire family, all of whom admire him, which says a lot about any family."

"I was born in New York June 26, 1925. For some reason my mother didn't want to put me in kindergarten when the time came, so she lied about my age and put me in first grade, and as a result, I graduated from Christopher Columbus [High School] in the Bronx in January, before I turned seventeen. I wanted to go into the Marine Corps after my birthday in June, but my dad would not sign the papers. He was the straightest guy. If a nickel ever came out of a phone booth, he'd put it back in again. 'Don't screw around,' he said. 'That's the way you gotta be.' So later the following year, when the draft was coming up, he finally agreed to sign for me. I was one month short of eighteen. It was 1943.

"I went down the Marine Corps recruiting station and they said enlistments were closed because you couldn't be more than seventeen and ten months, but then they arranged it finally, and I left August 1. I took a train to Yemassee (we used to sing 'Beautiful Beaufort, by the sea, just twenty-eight miles from Yemassee'). We took a truck to Beaufort. Then I actually went by barge out to Parris Island, even though they had the causeway from the mainland. I think they wanted us to feel isolated.

"Boot camp was tough. I was a six-footer from the Bronx, one hundred eighty-five pounds, and I was in good shape. I did an awful lot of swimming. I was supposed to be a tough guy, so I got picked on all the time by the drill instructor. He'd come over and say, 'You think you could handle this or that guy?' He was always on my butt. I had done a little boxing with one of the guys in a neighborhood youth organization, and somebody mentioned it, so all of sudden the DI said, 'You are the boxer.' You'd compete between platoons. It worked that way.

"After boot camp we went to New River, part of Camp Lejeune, and that was where they'd give you what they now call your MOS, military occupational specialty, and with a name like Abbatiello, I'm the first one in line. ABBA, you know? The only guy who ever beat me was Aaron, AA. They called my name and said I was going for raider training. That's when they had Carlson's Raiders. I said, 'Oh, my God, I joined the Marine Corps, but I don't want to be a raider,' you know? I had a ten-day furlough, and when we reported back, some guy was reading the roster off, and he looked at me and said, 'What's your background?' I said I'd worked with my dad as a carpenter's helper. He said, 'OK, we're going to put you in engineers. You got a good strong back.' I said to myself, 'Thank God, I don't have to be a raider.'

"At first we did pontoon bridges, building stuff like that, and then we got into demolition. The majority of demo guys were engineers, and as an engineer, what are you going to do in combat? Build something? No. You blow things up. I took a course and did a lot of demolition work along with everything else. We worked with blocks of TNT. Later on we trained with C2, which was a plastic explosive we used on Iwo Jima most of the time.

"I was in the Fifth Division, Fifth Engineer Battalion, attached to G Company of the Twenty-eighth Marines as assault demolition. We did flamethrowing, we blasted pillboxes, blockhouses, caves and mines and took care of minefields, anything to do with demolition. Mainly we worked with the frontline troops. We did lay out mats to keep vehicles from getting stuck in the sand. We had armored dozers. One platoon had all the heavy equipment.

"We used C2 when we could get it. When you couldn't, you

used blocks of TNT, which was not as stable. The satchel charges contained six sticks of C2, two inches square. You'd put a fifteen-second delayed detonator in there and then throw it. One stick would blow the others, so the whole sack would go. It was heavy, I'd say ten or fifteen pounds.

"I landed with two of them when we hit the beach. I had the demolition kit, with all the stuff in it, different fuses, and it was on my chest, and I had two sacks of C2 and the regular half a pack they gave you and a gas mask. I was so covered with stuff when I hit the beach the first thing that went was the gas mask. Everybody threw that away.

"We were supposed to be reserve, but they called us in early. We must have landed an hour or two after H hour. We got into Higgins boats, and the coxswain was going around in circles, waiting to hit the line of departure, and he said, 'They're walking up the beach in formation; the place is secured.' The first few waves didn't get no resistance. Then, when they called us in, it got hot. I was on the last boat on the left on Green Beach. There was nothing between me and Suribachi, and we were getting all the fire from Suribachi. They were really giving us hell.

"I had a hole a shell had made, a big crater, so I dove into that. I hit about four guys on the side. Then another guy comes flying in. When he turns around, you can see he's got his helmet on backwards. This was my first combat, but he's a veteran. He says, 'Man, this is a hot fucking place. This is going to be great!' Holy Christ. I said, 'You got your helmet on backwards.' He said, 'Yeah, it gets my face deeper in the sand.'

"We were right on the base of Suribachi. We went up to the right a little bit. We had a rendezvous area where we were supposed to meet some people. You couldn't just walk there. You were doing flopovers behind dead guys and in and out of holes till you got to where you were supposed to be. We spent the first night right above the beach, then moved across the island the second day. We found the G Company commander by word of mouth. They set up the battalion CP, we dug in, and that was it. I was the assistant squad leader. We moved out to work with G Company on the right side of Suribachi the following morning, blowing up tunnels and cave openings.

"I got wounded on the twenty-third, the same day the flag went up. Actually I was in battalion aid at that point. We had been working on a cave with a big coastal gun emplacement. One of the guys set a couple of charges up on top because it was surrounded by concrete, and our stuff wouldn't do anything but make a big loud noise. We figured if we could get something up high, we could drop half the mountain on it.

"The guy with the charge climbed up the side and got it set. We were covering him, and the infantry was covering us. They even brought up a couple tanks to give us cover. Anyway, he got up there and came back down, but the charge didn't go off. Something was wrong with the detonator. So I took a charge myself and climbed up and put it on top of the other charge. I waited a decent amount of time and put it on the charge, and I wanted to get away from there in a hurry. Coming down, I tripped. I slipped, fell, and rolled all the way down. There were huge explosions going all over the place. When I hit the hole, somebody said, 'Oh, my God, your face is gone.' I said, 'What are you talking about?' Turned out I was full of blood. Since I fell, I figured all the pain was from the fall, but actually it was a piece of shrapnel, probably from a Japanese grenade that was rolled down there.

"They dug something out of my nose and out of the side of my cheek . . . over here. Something ripped out the side of my nose and gum, and my cheek was cut wide open. I thought it came from the fall. The lieutenant checking in on us said, 'Get yourself to the aid station,' so I went over to battalion aid midway across the neck. You know what a million-dollar wound is, where you get hurt, but not bad, but bad enough so you have to pull out? This young kid corpsman was treating me. He had been on the ship with us. He patched me up, a couple Band-Aids, this and that and the other thing. 'You didn't sew it, though,' I said to him. 'A million-dollar wound, huh?' He looked at me and said, 'Get the hell out of here.' I was there the whole thirty-six days and was not hit again.

"As he was patching me up, somebody said, 'There goes the flag,' so I broke away, and I looked outside. I was still bloody. There were these big field binoculars you could look into, and I saw where first flag had gone up. Nobody paid any attention to the second flag. Later somebody said they put a bigger flag up. Nobody cared.

"Near the end of the operation, we had secured the island pretty close, and we were mopping up. I had the squad just going around, blasting anything that could be bad. We went out on patrol, and they put a corpsman to go with six of us. It was that same kid who treated my face injury. He was running around all over the place with a forty-five, and my BAR guy said, 'Get him off my back; he's going to shoot me.' Anyway, a charge goes off, and I hear this screaming. There's a big rock right over the corpsman. He's lucky, having just enough space under it so it broke his leg but didn't crush him. We drug him out and sent him to battalion aid, and when we got back that evening, somebody said, 'Hey, a guy wants to see you over in sick bay.' So I go to the battalion aid station, and he's laying on the floor. He's got a cast on him, and he looks at me and goes like this [waves his hand]. I figure he can't talk loud, so I lean over, and he kisses me. He says, 'Million-dollar wound!' I say, 'You son of a bitch!'

"We worked with C2 till we ran out, and then they dropped us in some dynamite from Guam. Sixty dynamite, it was called, and it's bad stuff because I think it's sixty percent nitro, which is not very stable. Forty is what everybody uses for construction. But they dropped us some sixty, and we were using that to blow up caves, blockhouses, pillboxes until we got some more C2.

"Here's how we operated: The engineer battalion broke down into companies, then platoons, then squads. My unit, C Company, was attached to the Twenty-eighth Marine Regiment. They had four battalions. I was in the third platoon, so we were attached to the Third Battalion. The first platoon was attached to the First

Battalion, the next to the Second, and the fourth to the Fourth. Each platoon works out of a battalion command post. The fourth platoon goes to the Headquarters Battalion. Within the Third Battalion, the first squad goes with G Company, the second squad with H Company, the third with I Company, and the fourth squad goes with the Headquarters Company. That's one platoon.

"Nobody wore bars or any kind of rank insignia. It was all just numbers. Number 414 was our outfit; it meant engineers. So Number 1414 meant a private in engineers. Mine was 2414 because I was a corporal. It was stenciled, with your name, on the chest of your jacket. Everybody wore the same cover [hat, or helmet].

"When we got to other end, when there were not so many people around anymore—I'm talking a lot of casualties—we used to bleed over. If another company needed a little more demo, then we'd work with them, although at night we always went back to the battalion CP and stay there as protection for them, plus we'd blast caves around them at night. It wouldn't be dark yet when we'd pull back and dig around the CP, blast caves and stuff, find out what could be the worst thing on the perimeter and lay charges in there. But not after dark. That was the given rule: Nobody got out of that hole after dark. If there was anybody walking around, and it was dark, you shot him. That's the way it went. Then, when morning came, you'd go to your designated area and meet with the head guy of whatever company you were assigned to and he'd tell you where to go.

"After a while we hit an area where they had sunk these antiboat mines, which were like ones you float, with ears sticking out. Only they were half of a complete mine, and they would bury them in the beach. There was a minefield inland with all these things on it, so they called us in to clear it. When you go for mines, you dig all around with a bayonet to make sure there's no connections that are going to explode when you pull the mine up.

"The artillery was giving us cover as we were doing that, but then we had a short round, which happened to be a dud, hit behind us. It went flying through this minefield, and luckily it didn't hit any of the mines, but from that moment on we didn't fool around with the bayonet. We just reached out and picked them up. They had handles. There's acid inside, and when you break it, a battery is activated, and that sets off the charge. But you could grab them by the handle and set them to the side, so everybody could go around them. They were semicircular, heavy, and had handles on both sides. Did I ever wish I had gone into the raiders instead? At times, yes.

"The thing I remember most vividly was the steam and stuff coming out of the ground on the upper part of the island. You couldn't sleep in a foxhole—you got burned. It was that hot. We used to take a canteen and bury it, and it would come up boiling. And, like I said, you never got out of your foxhole at night, but you're sitting there and you're seeing all these things, people moving, but actually it's steam coming out of the ground but you're picturing people. I shot more steam than I did anything else, you know? You very seldom saw the enemy. You never saw them. You could hear them; you could hear them digging. You'd close up the cave, and you could hear them digging at night, trying to get out.

"I didn't recognize the place when I went back in 2005. The whole island was completely green, and I didn't see one little bit of green in that place when we were there the first time. I did find the cave where we had buried two of my guys. It was just something that bugged us. We had just a few men left in the squad; they had put a sergeant from headquarters in charge, a guy named Joquist. I had the other half of the squad.

"This was near the end, almost mop-up, you know? They said on March 15 the island was secure, but it wasn't. We had a lot more fighting after that. Anyway, it was near Kitano Point on the north end, and we were coming down around a rock wall, and up there a little bit was a cave, and above it was another cave, a small hole.

"Joquist turned around, motioned to me, and pointed up. A Jap was trying to get into the other cave. I signaled my BAR guy, and he took a shot at him with the BAR, but the gun jammed on him.

The Jap blew himself up with a grenade. We threw smoke in there, and smoke came out around the bend. So a couple of the guys went over there to take care of it. I guess they assumed there was enough rock and debris on top so that if they blasted, it would drop down on the cave. For some reason, two of them went in, and they both got shot. One was killed, and the other crawled out. Why did they go in? I don't know. Maybe to set a charge. To this day we don't know. That would have been a no-no and a half.

"The guy who got killed was my foxhole buddy John Babich. He looked like a kid. They called him Young Babich. The other guy was Sam Queen, the Mississippi gambler who had come in as a replacement. He was in a different squad, but they had shoved him from headquarters as a replacement into my squad because we had lost three or four guys. This Joquist put a call out to the lieutenant, and he came down with a runner, Madsen, who was originally from my squad. They tried to get Babich out. They pulled Sam Queen out. He had a bullet through his belly, and he said, 'Don't go in; he's dead. Babich is dead. Don't go in there.' But you could see him laying there. The lieutenant came, and they got a piece of pipe, put a rope on it, and tried to get to him.

"Anyway, Madsen was trying to get a rope on the feet to drag Babich out, and the Japs reached around and shot him in the head. He fell in there, and so now the lieutenant orders the cave shut with a bulldozer. He didn't want to blast it. So we got Kingsbury to come down, and he scraped dirt off the top of it and buried it, closed the cave.

"When you leave somebody, you got to give the location to Graves and Registration so they can reclaim it. So when I was planning on going back, I always had the—I wanted to go to that cave. I wanted to go see if the thing had been opened and if they got the bodies out. I talked to the lieutenant, he's over in Oregon, and I got his letter here somewhere showing where he had marked the coordinates. He had a letter from Graves and Registration saying they could not locate him. I always wondered did they ever get him out. You hate to leave anybody; you know how the marines are. There was somebody who said they went and saw Babich's grave up in upstate New York, but I never could verify it.

"When we got to Iwo, my son, Don, and daughter Lisa and I went looking for it. We were part of a Discovery Channel film. I'm ninety-eight percent sure I located the cave, but it didn't look the same because the whole roof had been caved in. The lieutenant had given me the coordinates. It looked like somebody had dug it out, and then the roof had collapsed, probably because they used a backhoe. There were tracks all over the place. There was no sign of Babich or Madsen. I mailed that Discovery tape to my lieutenant. I wanted to verify the site. I haven't heard from him yet.

"Why didn't we throw smoke to rescue Babich? You don't know why you don't do nothing. First of all, the lieutenant's in charge. This sergeant, Joquist, was the one who summoned the lieutenant, and he made the decision on what we were going to do. After it's all over, you think, why the heck didn't we reach down and flip in a couple smoke grenades or get a flamethrower and turn it around the corner? There were ways of getting them out; it just didn't happen.

"We blew some of Kuribayashi's cave. There was a small entrance, but inside were a series of rooms that were all connected. My son went in one, and he said it was enormous. He went in that small entrance, passed cutouts for munitions, for a radio room, and it all opened up into an enormous cave. We blasted all those caves hard. There was a blockhouse too we assumed was his headquarters. We had a hell of a time trying to blow that up.

"My Purple Heart? That's another story. We all refused the Purple Heart. Most of the guys in the outfit had some sort of damage, but they never put in for it. But when I got out, my discharge papers were one year shy in showing the time I had spent overseas. In New York they had a bonus so that the more time you had overseas, the more money you got. So I sent to Washington to have my discharge corrected, and when they fixed the time and wrote me back, they also sent me the Purple Heart. It reads the twenty-second of February but it was actually the twenty-third."

The citation reads: "Dear Mr. Abbatiello, I am directed by the Commandant of the Marine Corps to inform you that you are entitled to a Purple Heart, awarded in the name of the President and by order of the Secretary of the Navy."

"I never wore it. I don't even mention it when I go to the convention because every one of those guys rates one. They interviewed my lieutenant, and he said if it was the Army, the whole platoon would have Purple Hearts. The company I was attached to came out with about one hundred ninety men. They supposedly had one hundred eight percent casualties, meaning the entire company was replaced, with a few more thrown in. And my name was first on the wounded list.

"When we first went in on D-day, I was scared shitless, but then after that I don't know if I was scared or not. I don't remember being frightened. You just hoped it worked out the right way. I did what I was told to do, and I did it when I was told to do it. I'm not saying I was gung ho and not scared, but I don't remember it being so bad that it affected my ability to do what I was supposed to.

"One instance that happened came when my friend Red Brown got killed. I had half the squad, and we were backup, waiting to rejoin the action, and here came a couple guys dragging Red Brown. So I jumped in and grabbed a hold of him. He was still alive, but he had a bullet in the head. Part of his head was . . . anyway, I got in and helped carry him down to the battalion aid station. The lieutenant, Herb Hammond, was there.

"And what bugged me so badly was I'm up at the battalion aid station and I had left four guys down there, and here I was the assistant squad leader, when I all at once thought: Oh, my God, the lieutenant's going to think that I'm scared, that I'm yellow. It hit me hard that I had left my post because Red Brown was my best buddy and he's lying there with half his head blown away. He's still alive, still breathing, but he died when we got him up there.

"Anyway, I took off down the road and went back to them, but that bugged me for years. It always bugged me that maybe they thought I ran out of that area because it was hot, that I had come back to the battalion aid station and left my men down below. I mentioned it to the lieutenant not too long ago, and he said, 'What? Are you kidding me, Abbatiello?' But that always bugged me.

"They said it was going to cost one million lives to conquer Japan. If they took Truman out of his grave, I'd kiss his ass right now for dropping that bomb, because he saved our hide. I got sent to China, sort of shanghaied, to fix roads for a spell after the war and then got discharged on Mother's Day, May 12, 1946. When I got sent home, they said I would automatically be raised to sergeant if I came back within ninety days.

"But then I met this gal, Mary Ganguzza, a Sicilian, and that was it. I was a Neapolitan. I loved swimming. We lived right off Pelham Bay. I was down swimming, and she happened to be there with a couple friends. She was a good-looking gal, tough. We got friendly, and it escalated from there. We got married in 1947.

"We had two daughters, Lisa and Angela, and a son, Don. All live locally. Moved to Florida in 1974 from Puerto Rico. I worked forty years for a contractor as a superintendent in charge of concrete construction. I worked in New York, New Jersey, and then in Puerto Rico for ten or eleven years. We did all the bank buildings. I had the whole family with me. We moved to Florida in 1974. But they kept calling me back to Puerto Rico as a consultant. I was there four years ago; we did an addition to the Hilton.

"I'm eighty-one now. I retired more or less when I was sixty-six or sixty-seven, but it didn't last long. I'd stay home a couple months, and they would call me for a job, and I would go back. I worked up until just before my wife passed away three and half years ago. She died very peacefully. I went to call her, and she didn't wake up. We were married close to fifty-nine years. I sure miss her."

[A newspaper article written in February 1945 by a combat correspondent credited Al's Company C, Fifth Engineer Battalion with a "a major assist in the seizure of Mount Suribachi." He wrote that the company killed six hundred Japanese, "three times their own number," and that they moved in front of the infantry, "smashing pillboxes, blockhouses, minefields, tank traps and emplacements." He added: 'With explosives lashed to their backs and dangling from their belts, the engineers knocked out more than 165 concrete pillboxes and blockhouses; they blasted 15 strong bunkers, naval gun positions and dug up or exploded 1000 mines and booby traps, filled in 200 caves with bulldozers, trapping more than 100 Japs in one cave alone. Some of the caves were three stories high and blocked by heavy reinforced steel doors. In addition, they evacuated hundreds of wounded Marines, buried more than 200 Japs, built more than 1500 yards of roads and tank paths around the crater, saved six trapped tanks in one day, built retreat roads for the tanks with broken ammunition cases, strung barbed wire at night and kept illuminating flares soaring over the enemy."

[Asked if this account was accurate, Abbatiello replied, "I don't know. Like I said, I was only a little part of the company. We did our part, which would be a portion of that. I was just a run-of-the-mill guy doing a job. No big heroics. You did what you had to do."]

12

PRIVATE FIRST CLASS
CHARLES WATERHOUSE

Wounded at Iwo Jima
Twenty-eighth Marines, Fifth Marine Division

Al Abbatiello was in my squad, the engineers. He was very tough, a tough, tough guy. There used to be an ad in the magazines in the forties, something about shaving cream, how it was "tough but ever so gentle." That was Al. He was big, and he could break you in half, but he was a tender guy. Very nice guy. We keep in touch.

Colonel Charles Waterhouse, USMC (Ret.), eighty-two, stands beside his painting of a young marine facing a cemetery and Mount Suribachi, one of several works Waterhouse has done on the Iwo Jima campaign.

Charlie Waterhouse shot expert on the rifle range, and it was a great disappointment to him that he never got a chance to shoot back at the enemy on Iwo Jima. This photo was taken in January 1944 at a May Company department store in Los Angeles.
Photo courtesy of Waterhouse Museum

I spent an afternoon with Colonel Waterhouse in his museum in Toms River, New Jersey. He was extremely gracious and cordial, granting me all the time I wished even though his wife was home and not feeling well. We talked at length, and he gave me a tour. I saw action illustrations of the Medal of Honor recipients Hector Cafferata at Fox Hill in Korea and Mitchell Paige at Guadalcanal, among others. He also had a compelling work of Colonel John Ripley hanging off the bridge at Dong Ha. I said I couldn't understand why Ripley had not received the Medal of Honor for his feat that day. He said he couldn't either. I asked how he liked being described as the Norman Rockwell of the Marine Corps. "That's the ultimate compliment," he replied.

"The first wave shoved off at Iwo at nine o'clock. The waves came in about five minutes apart, and we were in the seventh or eighth. I came in at 0937. We didn't expect to go in that fast, but the first couple waves got in so quickly, zip, they sent us in. Kuribayashi opened up while we were in the water: machine guns, mortars, artillery, everything. We were in the left-flank landing craft, Abbatiello too, and the coxswains got mixed up. They saw this marker they thought was in the center, but it was the left end of the beach.

"We were fortunate to be on the left flank because the machine-gun fire and stuff were going over us at boats to our right. We landed much closer to it than we were supposed to. When the ramp went down, there were no footprints, but there were lots of people shooting at us from Suribachi. It seemed like we were getting fire from three directions, from Suribachi, from the neck of Iwo, and from up north, by the Quarry. We were immediately in a firefight, all this shooting, and you could not see where any of it came from.

"We faced a series of at least three terraces. Our orders were to go two hundred fifty yards inland, turn left and dig a hole, and sit there until we had orders what to do. As we went in, we kept edging to the right. We found a nice-sized ridge thirty feet high or so, and that's where we dug in.

"We saw a few people getting hurt, but luckily nobody from my platoon did. We had a guy named Danaluk from Brooklyn, New York, whose draft number had come up. He wanted to get in the Coast Guard because he lived in Brooklyn and figured he could get a job on a ship patrolling New York Harbor, see? So he said to them, 'I want the Coast Guard.' They said, 'You're in the Marines.' 'No, no, no, I want the Coast Guard.' They finally convinced him he had no say in the matter and that he was going to be a marine. So every morning, as he threw the blankets off, his first words, the first thing he'd say was, 'Oh, that effing [fucking] draft board!' Every day. So, in his honor, when the ramp let down on Green Beach, the whole boatload of us hollered, "Oh, that effing draft board!" That was for Danny. The Japs must have thought: Here comes a bunch of nuts. Guys I haven't heard from for thirty years, I'll suddenly get a Christmas card, and it'll say, 'I'll never forget, Oh, that effing draft board!'

"The first day we made our two hundred fifty yards up the beach; the second day we didn't make fifty yards. The third day we got to the base of Suribachi. Each one of our engineer squads was assigned to a different company in the Twenty-eighth. Harold Pierce was a buck sergeant in my company. The lieutenant said to him, 'There's Easy Company. You're going to support them. Crap out here with your people until I get back and tell you what to do.'

"So the lieutenant's gone, and somebody walks up behind Pierce and gives him a kick and says, 'Hey, why don't you go down there and blow up some pillboxes or something?'

"And Pierce says, 'Well, sir, I can't order my squad to do that. My lieutenant told me to stay here with my men until he came back and told us what to do.'

"Well, the guy who gave Pierce the kick was none other than

Colonel Chandler Johnson, they called him Jellybelly, and he sent Pierce and some of the squad up to where Easy Company was going to jump off. Pierce caught up to the rear elements of the assault and said, 'What do you want me to do? I'm a demo man.' And they said, 'Well, there's a big cave over there.' He'd picked up a BAR from a dead marine, and he started for the cave with that.

"Pierce spent the whole day taking out caves. He wasn't supporting an attack. He was making attacks. Three or four times he came back to get more explosives, and he finally got hit by fragments from a knee mortar. Then a machine gun stitched him up one arm. He wasn't going to have somebody take him back to the aid station. Instead he helped another wounded guy get back. Chandler Johnson has been watching this all day, and at the end he said, 'I sent that guy down there to do something, and he did it. Put him down for a Navy Cross.' A week later Johnson was dead. I think Pierce was from Braintree, Massachusetts.

"Why did I want to join the Marine Corps? When I was twelve years old, they took us to the library for the first time, a real library. Naturally you want an exciting book, and I'm looking and looking, and finally I see something. It says, '*Fix Bayonets!*' I figured that would be exciting. It was by John Thomason. His writings influenced many, many young men between World War One and World War Two to join the Marine Corps. He treated his characters like they could walk on water. I took it out so often they wouldn't let me take it out anymore. He drew pictures too, and I'd try and copy his pictures. I wanted to be one of those good guys.

"I was born September 22, 1924, and I grew up in Perth Amboy, New Jersey. I was seventeen when I graduated from high school in 1942. When I got to be eighteen, a group of kids I hung out with, five of us, were going to join the Marines. So we went up to North Jersey to sign up, and we all got separated, and when we came outside, they said, 'Are you in?' 'Yeah, I'm in.' But they're all different. One's in the Air Force, one's in the Army, one's in the Navy, one's in the Seabees. It's fate.

"It took thirty-three hours to get to Parris Island. They put us on a Higgins boat even though the causeway was built. They wanted to make you unhappy. And while you were going, you'd hear the chant 'You'll be sorreee!' I couldn't imagine what they meant. But then I thought I was in jail; I thought I signed the wrong papers. Boot camp was twelve weeks. I shot expert with the M1, got an extra five bucks a month.

"After boot camp we got a ten-day leave, then showed up at Camp Lejeune. My application form asked what did I do when I graduated high school. Well, I wrote I'd worked four or five months in the engineering room of a copperworks factory, copying these big old drawings on transparencies to be put in a mountain in Pennsylvania for protection in case the Germans bombed us. So they put me down as a draftsman and said, 'OK, you're an engineer.'

"I met Abbatiello right away. We moved to a tent camp out in the woods and did all kinds of things. I remember it snowed like crazy. They had us riding around in trucks shoveling out the officers' quarters. They issued us long winter underwear, and everybody's running around singing 'The Man on the Flying Trapeze.' A week after New Year's 1943 we got on a train and went to Camp Pendleton in California. That was where our training really started.

"The Fourth Marine Division was loading its ships to go as we were unloading our trains. They went right into combat while we trained at Pendleton for a year and a half or more and didn't ship out until September of 1944. We finished training cycles a couple of times, and they still didn't ship us out. We were going to be reserve for the battle of Saipan, but they never called for us.

"We went to the Second Division's Camp Tarawa on the big island of Hawaii that September, and here's something you never read about: We ended our training cycle that September, and we were supposed to hit Iwo in November, but MacArthur had tied up all the shipping in the Philippines and they couldn't get adequate space aboard ship. This was going be a big deal, eight hundred ships, equipment for three divisions, and we didn't get it.

Now you read about how Kuribayashi in that time doubled the number of tunnels, doubled the number of pillboxes. If we had invaded in November, it might have been a different story. It might not have been the greatest battle in the world.

"It was always the same drill: The Twenty-seventh and Twenty-sixth would be on the right, and we would land in a column of battalions, in a line. We'd train, go so far inland, turn left, and here's this big hill. We would assault it over and over again. It was Suribachi. It got to be like walking in your sleep. You knew exactly what you were supposed to do: Go two hundred fifty yards and turn left.

"They closed the Green Beaches the afternoon of D-day. A destroyer came damn near into shore, and he kept pumping five-inch shells. There was one huge vertical cave slit in the mountain, and you could see the shells go right inside. The beaches were closed the second day also.

"I was wounded at one o'clock in the afternoon of the third day. They finally decided to go inland another two hundred fifty yards and make a left turn to support the attack on Suribachi. The two forward holes facing Suribachi were occupied by Barney Barnstein, with the radio, and me. I was thanking God just the other day because if Kuribayashi had said, 'Hey, banzai banzai banzai,' mine was the first hole they would have hit.

"Anyway, Barney had a radio aerial sticking up, and the machine guns were really working over us two and the foxholes in back. All this lead was flying right above your nose, and when it stopped, the platoon sergeant come running over. He stood right where the beating zone was, where the bullets were flying. He says, 'Waterhouse, you follow the lieutenant. Don't let anything happen to him. We're moving inland.' So I got my stuff together, and by the time I got up there I could see the sergeant and the lieutenant. The sergeant got hit in the legs. They ran with blood pumping out of him, and then he fell down. The lieutenant was on top of him, trying to put first aid on his legs, and the sergeant reaches up and yells to the lieutenant to get down. They were very close. The sergeant had been on Guadalcanal and Cape Gloucester. He was real tough.

"Meanwhile I get up almost to them, and the lieutenant hollers to everyone to leave their packs in the holes and to come with weapons and shovels. I took my pack off and ran back with it. I'm waving the shovel and the rifle, and I go to jump in the hole, and something hits me in the left shoulder. The corpsman offers to come over, and I say no, but then I figured maybe he'd better because they say if you don't feel it, it's bad. And I didn't feel any pain. I was completely numb in the hand, from the shoulder down. So he ran over and put a dressing on it, and then they had to go. The last guy that went by said, 'Charlie, give me your carbine,' and he hands me his rifle, and they were gone into the smoke.

"I got out of there in a quiet time and edged sideways and went down beside a pillbox, and I took this rifle and I'm trying to work it. It's all coated with ashes, and it won't work. I wanted to just shoot a clip, just to whom it may concern, you know? At Suribachi. I swore at that guy who took my carbine. If I ever saw him again, I'd kill him.

"So I never fired a shot. At what? I was the best shot in the platoon, expert, and you couldn't see a thing. It was starting to rain again, so I went down past a thirty-seven-millimeter gun armed with canister, persuaded them not to shoot me, and then made my way down to the beach. It got messier and messier; it looked like a junkyard.

"There was a hole not quite as big as this table, and it had two shelter halves over it. I figured that must be the aid station. I tried to get in, but these two doctors said it wasn't big enough for any more people. Told me to find myself a spot to crap out. I figured office hours are over, and the doctor's not in, so I looked around for a spot that wasn't littered and lay there. I laid there in the rain thinking if they had a barrage or started sending mortars, it wouldn't look too good. Finally a Higgins boat came in, and they hollered, 'Casualties! Casualties!' People started getting up from different piles of stuff with litters and bringing them, so I shuffled down. I think I was the only ambulatory guy. The rest were all on litters. They closed the ramp and started backing off. I'm in the boat water, and it's red as can be: All the guys are bleeding. I found out what it was like to get seasick immediately.

"Gradually the sound of the motors were louder than what was going on ashore, but then they couldn't find the ship. They started getting rejection slips from ships that were loaded with casualties, and it was raining. The LCVP [landing craft, vehicle, personnel] crewmen were getting worried. It's getting dark; it's raining. They could float out to the sea, you know? We went the whole range of the beachhead, from Green all the way near the end to Blue. The Fourth Division command ship was there with generals on it, and they took us aboard.

"And I'm thinking: How the hell am I going to climb the nets? I'm dead from the shoulder down. They sent down a hoist with five or six wooden things on it and started loading stretchers. I climbed on and held on to a greasy cable. When we got to the top, a corpsman lifted me over the rail, and that was it. I was the first man down because I could walk, and they checked me over, then sent me down a hatch. I went down, found a bottom bunk, and I figured this is it, I'm off that [out of the battle].

"I was in the dark, like, and I felt like an animal licking his wounds in the cave. I went to sleep, and after a while I came to. There's only one little red light on, and here from the sack above me is an arm with a knife. He's swinging this thing, and I'm huddled against the bulkhead and the corpsmen are scattered all over. He's having nightmares: 'You effing Japs!'

"That scared the heck out of me, but they finally quieted him down and then, about two hours later, I wake up, and here's a guy six feet away, directly across from me, and he's got a submachine gun. The corpsmen are trying to take it from him, and he says, 'The goddamn Japs can't do it. You can't do it.' And he's cocking it, and I'm thinking, holy mackerel. He finally went to sleep with it.

"Two days later two officers came down and said, 'Guys, we

need people on the beach. This is the worst one yet, the very worst, and we need people who think they can go back.' And everybody started, 'Oh, my head's bleeding, oh, my guts, oh, my legs, oh.' But an hour later this bunk's empty, that one's empty, hey, I'm going back. I didn't want to. It's only supposed to take five days, you know. They said it would take three days of fighting, like Tarawa, two days to mop up, and off we go to Guam.

"I had to see a doctor for real first. It turned out I had a bullet through the shoulder, under the arm, at an angle that cut these nerves. The first thing the doctor said was, 'Make up a cast.' I said, 'Sir, my arm's not broken.' He said, 'Make up a cast.' They put me in a cast with my hand up in the air, fingers curled over. I'm still complaining. What the hell do I need that for?

"The bullet had cut the nerves, and he knew it. He punched me with needles. I couldn't feel a thing. He knew. Anyway, I get two cartons of cigarettes, a fountain pen, and whatnot in a little bag, and I'm going back to the beach. A half dozen guys had got up on deck early, waiting for the boats to come alongside, and I'm there, and then it hit me: How do I get down the nets? They're not going to lower something just for me.

"And I cried.

"It was the only time I ever felt like crying. I prayed: Help me! I never cried again after that. It was a big tragedy for me. I didn't want to go, but I had it all figured out: I know they're going to land on the Fourth Division beaches and I'm going to have to make my way down to Green Beach because those people are still filling in the holes around Suribachi. I know you can pick up helmets and guns and all kind of things [so he can get all the gear he needs].

"It didn't happen. [Charlie did not go ashore.]

"I was aboard ship when the flag went up on the fifth day. They announced it on the loudspeaker. The ship had been hit that morning, and I went up to get some fresh air and saw splinters on the bulkhead. Looking ashore, I could see demo teams working in the north. We were on the extreme north, right off the Quarry. I could see teams blowing caves, and I'm thinking: Gee, if I can see them, they can see me, but they were busy. I walked up to the front of ship and looked to the south, and I could see a speck of a flag, and I'm thinking: Hey, that's my people.

"Later, on March 1, the day the Twenty-eighth came north to attack Hill 362, they sent all the wounded topside, and there was a Higgins boat . . . on deck . . . and they just walked us onto it, lifted it up, set it down in the water, and took us out to a Coast Guard boat loaded with wounded, going to Guam. They transferred us same way, just picked up the boat and set it on deck. That ship didn't have room for anything. It was packed with wounded.

"We left that night, and next day, during a rainstorm, they buried a number of marines at sea. I went out on the deck, getting soaking wet to watch.

"On Guam the first thing you know they got me in a cast with my arm raised up with a brace wrapped around the chest to keep it up in the air. I looked like a secret weapon. You know Bob Dole? He's got a hand like that. Once they leave it that way, it stays. With the cast I couldn't get in the sack by myself. I was dangerous. Walking like this, I could knock your brains out. Sleep wasn't easy.

"I had two operations, one on an artery immediately. This doctor says, 'I haven't checked you.' So he looks me over and says, 'How long have you been walking around?' Since it happened. He said, 'Lie down.' Twenty minutes later I was in the operating room. Turned out that bullet had nicked an artery, and it could have gone, just like that, any minute. He picked it up with the stethoscope.

"I ended up in a series of hospitals. I flew back to the States, took a medical train to the East Coast, and ended up in St. Albans Hospital on Long Island that July, where they operated on the nerves. I was released from the Marine Corps in May of 1946.

"I had met my wife-to-be, Barbara Andersen, on a blind date in 1945. When I got out of the car to let her out that night, there was no running board, I still had that cast on, and I fell into the gutter. My future mother-in-law said to her daughter, 'You'll never go out with that drunken marine again.' And I wasn't drunk. We got married June 6, 1948. We had two daughters, Amy and Jane.

"How did I get into drawing? They had the GI Bill, and you couldn't beat it. If you served three years' time, you qualified for three whole years of study, three hundred and sixty-five days. You could go to college, and they gave ninety dollars a month if you were married, eighty if not. That was a big deal. I had been drawing a cartoon strip of the battle of Iwo Jima, and I went to King Features with it, and they said, 'Christopher Columbus! We just got rid of four years of war, and you're drawing a war thing? Why don't you go to art school?' So I did. I started school the following January 1947. I found out there was an art school in Newark, New Jersey. I figured, that's close to home. I studied for three years, didn't get a degree. I was hired immediately by the Prudential Insurance Company. They had eighteen artists doing everything from cartoons to paintings. It was a marvelous chance for experience. I worked there over five years. Then I figured: Someday I'm going to be an old man, I'll be in my sixties, I'll be smoking a cigar, and I'll have the eighteen people running around, but I won't be making any pictures, and I'll say I always thought I wanted to make pictures for magazines. So I talked it over with my wife, and she said, 'Do it.'

"It was the day my second daughter, Amy, was born. I went to work, and I said, 'Mr. Gasser'—he was a famous watercolor painter, head of the art department—I said, 'Sir, I quit.' His cigar fell right out of his mouth, just like in the movies. Because they had it all figured out: Hey, he's got another mouth to feed. He's gotta come in for a raise, and we'll say, 'In a little while we'll see that you get a raise.' Instead I quit.

"I had an arrangement with the director of the school I had gone to. I taught one day a week, a class in illustration, something to base an income on.

"I had gone out and got some freelance jobs by showing pictures I had done at Prudential. I was working on illustration jobs for three different magazines while Amy was in the hospital with her mother—a story from a detective magazine, a story from a children's grade school publication, and one for an adventure magazine—and they all were due on the same day. One paid on delivery, one on publication, which was four months later, and one had a different deadline, so you were never sure when you were going to get paid. I did that for twenty-odd years. I didn't work the slick women's things, but *Saga, Argosy, Man's True Whatever, True Man's Whatever*. They were always starting magazines. If they caught on in four months, that was OK, but if they didn't, they dropped them. You always hoped you got paid before they dropped them.

"I belonged to the Society of Illustrators and the Salmagundi Club, and both had connections with the military, and you could get jobs to go paint weather balloons or ships, so when you did something for a magazine about ships, you had some idea of what to do. It was cashless, but you got experience.

"Then one day this friend of mine said, 'Hey, Charlie, why don't you go to Vietnam?' He worked for the Air Force. The war was on then, and he had just come back. He was in the Society of Illustrators. I said, 'I don't paint airplanes; I paint marines.' He said, 'Well, go down to the Salmagundi Club.' I sent down a portfolio and got a call from the man who ran the program, and he asked if would go to Vietnam.

"I said, 'I will if my wife will let me.' This was in January of 1967, and I went for a month and a half, February and March. I did a book of sketches and things. I figured I could use some of the ideas. Vietnam was just becoming a dirty word, and I had people saying, 'I shouldn't look at this,' or what was I doing? Was I trying to sell the war? I said, 'No, I'm trying to show that I can draw pictures on the spot.'

"I went a second time for the Air Force, flew on a B-52 mission over Laos, hitting some Ho Chi Minh trails, a thirteen-hour roundtrip from Guam. We refueled over the Philippines. I went a third time for Navy medicine, and the first person I met was a Navy corpsman. He said, 'Come on down to my village. I've got five marine advisers.' So off I went. There was a patrol boat a hundred yards across a very muddy beach. He said, 'OK, follow me.'

I'm going in mud sucking up to my knees, slothering in it with my paint stuff.

"Three years later he calls, says he wants to come visit me with his Vietnamese wife. He says, 'You know, Mr. Waterhouse, I hated you. I thought you were one of those damn media people.' He says, 'There was a dock out there we could have walked out on, but I made you walk through the mud.' I said, 'You had to walk through the damn stuff too.'

"Eventually I went all over. I ended up on missile cruisers, carriers, destroyers. They lowered me in a monsoon from a helicopter to the fantail of a destroyer, and when my feet hit the deck, a wave hit me this high. I thought: I'm not going to like this. I was seasick from that moment until the next morning, when a helicopter came, dropped a life preserver, and took me off.

"The pay was terrible, fifteen dollars per diem in the States, and when I got to Vietnam it was nine dollars and fifty cents, and then, when I got back, the Navy Department docked me four dollars fifty cents for chow and a buck a night for quarters, even though I slept in foxholes at times, five hundred yards from the demilitarized zone. I didn't go with the idea of making money, but I always thought at least Barbara would get a check while I was gone, to buy some groceries. It didn't happen.

"Finally I get a call from a Major Dyer at the Marine Corps Museum in Washington, asking me to paint something for the bicentennial. I said sure. Then he said, 'Write us a letter saying you can't. We want to convince the powers that be that this has to be funded.' So I wrote a letter to General Simmons, said I was thoroughly professional, had worked at all the magazines and I had a wife, two daughters, two cats, and a dog, and we all ate, and while I would love to do this, I could not accept the job unless it was funded.

"I had a double-page book jacket for the Rutgers Press showing Washington and his men slogging through the snow, going to fight the battle of Princeton. This thing arrived while I was writing the letter, so when I finished, I folded up one of the proofs and put it in there. The general was impressed, thank God. If it had been Chesty Puller, he would have said, 'What the hell do we need pictures for?'

"A week later Major Dyer calls and asked me to make seven paintings. I said, 'Last week it was paint one, then don't do any, and now it's seven. I'm confused.' He said, 'So are we.'

"Then he says, 'Could you come on active duty?' I said, 'Well, if my wife doesn't mind.' So now I'm forty-seven years old, and I'm going to the draft board in Newark to get drafted and all these eighteen-year-old bushy-headed kids are standing in line. It was just like a TV show. 'What the hell do you want?' I says I come for my physical. You know how Jack Benny used to do double takes? Everybody's head turned. They thought it was *Candid Camera*. It took four months, paperwork, FBI checks, all kinds of junk.

"And then it was, 'Oh, by the way, sir, we can only make you a major.' At the end of the war, I had been a corporal, just like Hitler and Napoleon had started, and I thought if they can do it, I can do it. They weren't marines, though.

"I didn't have to do any training. I'd have been dead. First day I came down, they drove me to lunch and there's thirty marines running in their red skivvies, and they say, 'Here's what we do at lunchtime, Major.' I said, 'You do that to me, and I'll be in Arlington, not running through it.'

"I became the only artist in residence the Marines ever had. I always loved historical things, and I did over five hundred paintings for the Corps. When I came on duty, they asked me what I liked to paint, and how big. I said I paint historical pictures, and I like 'em big. The first picture had fifty-three people in it. All my work went to the museum from that point on. It is not on exhibit, however. It's in Washington, D.C., in the archives.

"The new museum at Quantico? They're exhibiting one picture, probably. I had a wonderful relationship with the Marine Corps. I did dozens of covers for the *Marine Corps Gazette*, for officers, for *Leatherneck*, which was for enlisted, and for the *Marine Corps League* magazine.

"Everything is acrylic. Sometimes it's thin, like watercolor;

sometimes it's black and white, it's just black acrylic instead of ink. It's the magic medium for me. All art students and artists look for the one that works; well, this works. Acrylic won't turn black; it won't crack and eat the canvas.

"I retired for the second time 19 February 1991. I had seven guys from my platoon at retirement at the museum in Washington, D.C. The commandant, Al Gray, made a surprise visit, gave a speech. He knew more about me than I did. He was very nice to us.

"My museum in Toms River opened six years ago. I needed a place to hang stuff. It's all supported by contributions. I'm working now on a series featuring Marine Corps recipients of the Medal of Honor.

"I've been back to Iwo Jima three or four times. I spent at least a week there on two occasions. I painted a number of little pictures on the spot, including the admiral's cave. I got friendly with some Japanese who were there, including one who had been wounded twenty-seven times. He had an artificial nose. He said it was 'made in the USA.'"

The day the flags went up: Little Joe Rosenthal of the Associated Press stands near
the summit of Mount Suribachi overlooking the invasion beaches. He holds
the Speed Graphic camera he used to photograph the flag raising.
U.S. Marine Corps photo, National Archive, by Private Robert R. Campbell

PART FOUR

The Flag Raisings

Inseparable from the campaign to conquer Iwo Jima is the photograph by Joe Rosenthal of the flag being raised on Mount Suribachi. Five marines and a Navy corpsman put it up on February 23, 1945, five days after D-day. Back in the states, the photograph was an instant sensation. It appeared on the front page of dozens of newspapers across the country on Sunday, February 25. The success of Rosenthal's image obscured the fact that it merely recorded the second flag raising on the mountain. Six other marines had erected the first flag a few hours earlier. The planting of the second flag was a routine incident, not even mentioned in the daily logs.

That first flag, fifty-four inches long and twenty-eight inches deep, was put up by Lieutenant Harold Schrier, Platoon Sergeant Ernest T. Thomas, Sergeant Henry O. Hansen, Corporal Charles W. Lindberg, and Privates First Class Louis C. Charlo and James Michels. Three of the marines who raised the first flag were to die in combat, just as three from the second flag raising were also killed. Staff Sergeant Lou Lowery, a staff photographer for the Marine Corps magazine *Leatherneck*, took a picture of three marines tying the first flag to a pipe and another after it was in place, with some marines standing around. The second photo is static and uninspired.

Lindberg, the last living member of the twelve flag raisers, told me shortly before he died in June 2007 that it went up at 10:30 a.m. Much was made in the press at the time about the ferocious fighting the patrol endured in order to get the flag to the summit, but it was all grossly exaggerated. Both the first and the second group of flag raisers scaled the 556-foot elevation with minimal interference from the enemy.

No one is quite sure why they had such an easy time. There were still plenty of Japanese in various caves and tunnels all the way to the summit. For whatever reason, however, none emerged until after the first flag had gone up. Lindberg thought the Japanese troops stayed inside because Suribachi had taken such a terrible pounding from the ships before the patrols ascended its slopes. In any case, most of the fight for Suribachi occurred around its base in the four days preceding the flag raisings.

The second flag, which was eight feet long and four feet eight inches deep, almost twice the size of the first, was raised early in the afternoon. Present besides Rosenthal were Sergeant Bill Genaust, a Marine motion-picture photographer, and Private Bob Campbell, a still photographer. Rosenthal took several pictures, including what he called a posed "gung ho" group shot. The story of this posed photograph later helped foster confusion over the assertion that the famous flag raising shot had been staged. Genaust shot a sequence of the flag going up that later confirmed the validity of Rosenthal's photo. Rosenthal took his picture with a 4 x 5 Speed Graphic at 1/400th of a second, lens aperture between f8 and f11 on sheet No. 10 of a twelve-sheet film pack, according to Hal Buell. Campbell got a nice shot showing the new flag in place while the first one was being gathered in.

Hal Buell, who spent forty years as a photo editor with the Associated Press, including twenty-five as the head man, reports in his authoritative book *Uncommon Valor, Common Virtue: Iwo Jima and the Photograph that Captured America* that three other photographers were present before the second flag went up.

Of course it was Rosenthal's photo that got the attention. Three of the flag raisers—the Navy corpsman Pharmacist's Mate Second Class John H. Bradley, Private First Class Ira H. Hayes, and Private First Class Rene A. Gagnon—were later brought home and feted as heroes as they led a nationwide bond drive to help raise money for the war effort. The other three—Private First Class Franklin R. Sousley, Sergeant Mike Strank, and Corporal Harlon H. Block—were all killed in the weeks following the flag raising.

Lowery initially resented the attention Rosenthal received and thought his shot had to be a fake because he wasn't even there when the first flag went up. Chuck Lindberg too maintained that Rosenthal was a self-promoter who helped set it all up, but this was not the case. Rosenthal was just a news photographer, trying to get a good shot, and things went his way. His material got back to Guam quickly, got sorted out and sent to the States right away, where it became an immediate hit.

I interviewed Joe Rosenthal in 1995, when *Parade* magazine ran his photo on its cover to accompany a fiftieth anniversary piece on the battle of Iwo Jima, written by James Brady. You always hear about famous photos being staged, so we ran a sidebar with Joe explaining how he had come to get the shot, emphasizing that it had not been posed. "I backed off thirty-five feet and stood on a couple of old Japanese sandbags and some rocks," he told me. It was around noon, he said. "The light from above tends to sculpt your subject. The tension in the picture comes from the weight of the pole, which was about one hundred fifty pounds. Other guys jumped in to help when they saw it was heavy. I never would have used that many in the shot."

Since he worked for the AP when he took the photo, the agency owned the rights. He got a raise, though, and won a Pulitzer Prize. Ten years later, on February 18, 1955, he told the full story with W. C. Heinz in an article for *Collier's* magazine. Rosenthal down-played his part in the story, and his last line was the best. Yes, he said, he took the picture, but the marines took the island. Rosen-thal went on to a full career with the *San Francisco Chronicle*.

Though the Associated Press owns the copyright to the photo-graph, the Marine Corps has the right to distribute it. According to Hal Buell, proceeds from commercial use go to the Navy Relief Fund. Though it is one of the most memorable images of the twentieth century, the AP doesn't make any money off it. "Every-body knew the picture was going to be around forever," says Buell.

Rosenthal was "a delightful human being, witty, insightful, easy to talk to, very friendly, and unassuming to a point of distraction," Buell recalls. He was a small man, five feet five, 130 pounds. He wore horn-rimmed glasses. He had volunteered for all the serv-ices, and they all had turned him down because his eyesight was so bad. Buell adds, "As I say in the book, he was painfully modest. There was a story I heard after I did the book: He'd been out on assignment with some young reporter at the *Chronicle*, and she introduced Joe this way: 'You know he's the man who made that famous picture.' And Joe took her aside and said, 'Don't ever do that again. Don't introduce me that way. I'm Joe Rosenthal, a photographer for the *San Francisco Chronicle.*' He was very modest about it; I used to give him a hard time because he always said the picture was a lucky shot.

"Serendipity is part of every picture ever made, but there's a lot more to it than that. He wanted at first to make a picture of one flag going up, the other one coming down, and then he thought: No, that wouldn't, might not work. It was too much like a football play. Go this way or that way, and you could miss it. So he went around to the front, then had to step back so he could get the whole swing of the flag. If you notice in the [Genaust] film, the flag goes up and out of the frame, and he didn't want that to happen, so he stepped down.

"Then he built a little platform that cut down the foreground, and then Genaust walks in front of him and they get involved in a 'Am I in your way?' 'No, you're not—whoops, there it goes,' and he raised the camera and—bang—right at the perfect peak of the action. So there's a lot of skillful photography involved. It wasn't lucky. There was some luck, but it was mostly Joe making a good picture, taking the time to make it right.

"Some photographers go to war because it's a way to make a career; a great war picture can make a career. Some photographers go because it's a way to make a buck; there's a story to be covered, and you can sell your pictures and make some money. And some photographers go because they sincerely feel that the story should be told because they can help change the world. A lot of photographers are motivated by that. Photographers are basically emotional journalists. The nature of the work is emotional, instinctive, and intuitive, and so the mind works that way all the time. There's a swashbuckling element involved as well, something that takes you to the place where the action occurs.

"Joe's flag, the second flag, flew till March 15. There's a lot of irony in that too. They said the island was now secure. So they declared a headquarters company and put a flag up, and that became the flag on Iwo Jima, and the flag on the mountain was taken down. But there were a lot of people died after March 15." Both flags now hang in the Marine Corps Museum in Quantico.

"You know Rosenthal's favorite picture from the invasion days is not that good, but Joe was crazy about it. [The photo shows two slain marines in the foreground, with another marine advancing over the sand from right to left.] The reason he liked it was, he said, he was so impressed by the fact that no matter how many marines fell, they just kept coming. They just kept coming. They just kept coming. And I think that's why they weren't annihilated, because the Japanese couldn't kill them all. There were too many of them. Once they got up off the beach, it was a little tougher to get them."

Joe Rosenthal died in California on Sunday, August 20, 2006. He was ninety-four.

13

WARRANT OFFICER NORMAN HATCH
Photo Officer, Fifth Marine Division

[T]he brave ones were shooting the enemy; the crazy ones were shooting film.

Norman Hatch, eighty-seven, in the study of his Alexandria, Virginia, home in March 2007, in front of a poster for the movie *Sands of Iwo Jima* with John Wayne. Behind and to his right is a colored chalk portrait of the twenty-three-year-old Hatch, then a tech sergeant, in 1942, after he returned to Boston from Tarawa. It was commissioned by an uncle.

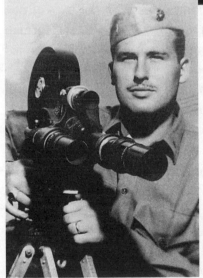

Warrant Officer Norman T. Hatch, photo officer of the Fifth Marine Division, at Camp Kamuela on the Big Island of Hawaii in January 1945 just before departing for the Iwo Jima campaign. He holds a thirty-five-millimeter Bell & Howell Eyemo Model Q motion picture camera. "In those days we were shooting black-and-white film only for newsreel use. All other Marine cinematographers were filming with sixteen-millimeter cameras and color film." The Eyemo had a four-hundred-foot magazine that could not be used in combat because it required a motor drive and heavy battery instead of being hand-cranked. The camera would be handheld without the tripod. The Eyemo, without the magazine and the motor, held a roll of one hundred feet that ran through the camera at ninety feet a minute.   Photo from Norman Hatch collection

A cassette tape of "Pennsylvania 6-5000," a tune made popular during the war by Glenn Miller, began playing in Norman Hatch's car as he started it up. He was driving me to the Metro station in Alexandria, Virginia, so I could catch the subway to my train at Union Station in Washington, D.C., in mid-March 2007. We had just spent nearly three hours in his basement office, a long railroad car of a room filled with memorabilia and files. His backyard contained several very large boxwood shrubs, which he said had been very small when he planted them after he and his wife, Lois, moved into the house in 1951. On the way to the Metro, he said something about how you just have to take chances in life and make things come to you, even if you do fail now and then.

Perhaps not many people know the Marine Corps won an Oscar, but in 1944 it was awarded an Academy Award for the best short documentary of 1944, *With the Marines at Tarawa*. One of ten men assigned to film the bloody invasion, which took the lives of one thousand marines and forty-seven hundred Japanese, was Norman Hatch, who is credited as the cinematographer. Hatch also landed on Iwo Jima on D-day, February 19, two years later and stayed there eighteen days until he left for Washington to play a crucial role in sorting out for the commandant of the Marine Corps charges that Joe Rosenthal's photograph on Suribachi was faked.

The invasion of Tarawa took place November 20, 1943.

"I went in practically with the first wave. I was the only cameraman to get on the beach for the first day and half. It was not the fault of the other cameramen. After the first three waves of amphibious tractors hit the beach, all hell broke loose. It wasn't just Kuribayashi on Iwo who did this. The Japanese always waited for you to get on the beach. That was their philosophy: Let 'em get on the beach, and then annihilate them.

"I was sitting on the engine hatch of a Higgins boat with Major

Jim Crowe, the commander of the Second Battalion, Eighth Marines, and he saw he was losing his beachhead there at Tarawa. He was not due to come in until later. His exec was on the beach with the first waves, but they were losing the beachfront because a Japanese guy in a tank turret buried in the sand was firing a machine gun at the amtracs. They were like tin; they didn't have any armor, and those thirty-caliber and fifty-caliber rounds would go right through them. The drivers were getting scared and pinching in away from the gun, and Major Crowe said, 'Jesus Christ, I'm losing my beachhead. Coxswain, put this goddamn boat in right now!'

"So we were the only boat to hit the beach at that particular time. We got in and walked ashore with no problem. A couple guys got hit and dropped in the water. My assistant, Obie Newcomb, and I are lugging black-and-white camera gear on our shoulders, and we get onto the beach, and then the fire opens up. We could lie there dug in and watch a landing craft come in, drop the ramp, and then a shell would land right on the ramp.

"The Japanese knew where the reef was, and they knew where the boats would have to stop, and they had it all zeroed in. After they blasted a half a dozen boats, the guys on the beach radioed out to the ship and said, 'Jesus, don't send any more until we figure this thing out.' I doubt we had six hundred or seven hundred men on the beach at that stage of the game.

"Anyway, all the rest of the Higgins boats, which had been loaded up at nine o'clock in the morning, were held off overnight, so everybody had to spend the night in those things getting seasick and dashed with spray. And there I am on the beach. I don't know that these guys are all afloat, and I'm shooting the war as it's happening pretty much in front of me.

"It winds up that I've got the only real combat footage of the fight because, when they come in about ten o'clock the next morning, there's some fighting to be done but it's mostly wrap-up stuff. The first nine hundred guys who got ashore did most of the action, and I filmed it in black and white. Why is the movie in sixteen-millimeter color? The kids that we trained shot color, a lot of the boat stuff, island shots, and planes dropping bombs, but when you get to the combat, it's my thirty-five-millimeter black and white that you see. We tinted it so there wouldn't be such a sharp contrast.

"I was able to catch the only shot, not just in the Pacific but the European war, that had both the enemy and our guys in the same frame of footage. I'd attended a briefing on Tarawa with Major Crowe and with the battalion exec, Major Bill Chamberlain, who said to me, 'We're going to take that big blockhouse up there. Do you want to come and cover it?' Well, you know, a staff sergeant doesn't argue with a superior, so I said sure. We had been sitting there in his CP, his command post, which was a big shell hole, and he's got his senior NCOs and a couple of officers, and they plan the attack. What they're going to do is go over the top of the blockhouse and do some damage to the air vents, drop grenades down the smoke pipes, and it's going to happen at nine o'clock. It was just like a World War One movie, with everybody synchronizing their watches.

"All the people went back to their command units, and Chamberlain looks at me and says, 'Are you ready?' I says, 'Yup.' He gets up and yells, 'Follow me!' He waves his hand, and the two of us run up, climb onto the top of this thing and get all the way across and look down the other side, and there's a dozen Japanese looking up at us, wondering what the hell we're doing on top of their blockhouse.

"We turn around, and there's nobody in sight. We're the only two people on top of the world entirely. And I looked at the major. He didn't have a weapon. I said, 'Where the hell is your rifle?' He said, 'I gave it to somebody that lost his coming in.' Where was his pistol? He lost it. I had one, but it was in back of me behind all the camera gear. And I said, 'I think we better get the hell out of here.' He agreed. We ran back and down off the side. He held another meeting, with a little ass chewing, and then we started to take the place. I was standing at the foot of it at that point in time, filming some stuff, and somebody yells. 'Here come the Japs!' So I just stood in position, moved over, and that's when I got the shot. I was within thirty or forty feet of the enemy.

"I had a marine in the foreground, pretty much in the middle, with a machine gun, while the Japanese can be seen running across from right to left in the background. When I got back to Pearl Harbor, I sent a telegram to my wife saying I think I got a shot of both of our forces fighting and, if I did, it's a lucky shot. It turned out that way. Andy Warhol said everybody should have his fifteen minutes of fame. Well, I got fifteen seconds of fame. That's about the length of time it took, sixteen seconds, to go through the camera. Later people asked me how I could walk through a battle like that, taking pictures as I went, and that was when I said the brave ones were shooting the enemy; the crazy ones were shooting film. You have to remember the island of Tarawa is only about one-third the size of Central Park in midtown Manhattan. Within seventy-six hours, over forty-seven hundred Japanese and one thousand marines were killed. We only took seventeen Japanese prisoners."

The color film went to Washington, where it was put together by Warner Brothers' Office of War Information. Hatch's black-and-white went to San Francisco and eventually wound up in newsreels that were shown in movie theaters, which is how Hatch's name ended up on marquees. "Of course, being a dumb photographer, I never took a picture of it," he recalled. Hatch eventually worked with the director Frank Capra to combine Hatch's three thousand feet of black-and-white with the color footage to make a training film, *Army-Navy Screen Magazine No. 21*, to be shown to troops all over the world.

"Tarawa had hit the press in a heavy way with all those casualties occurring in such a short space of time. It was also the first time in the history of the world that anybody had assaulted a heavily fortified beachhead from the sea and succeeded. There's a rumor—I can't validate it, but it's a hell of a good story—that Churchill was having trouble with Eisenhower and his own staff about the landings they were planning on the French coast. He couldn't get them to agree that it should be done. He was watching what happened at Tarawa, and after he saw we had done it, he came to both commands, Eisenhower and the Brits, and said if they can do it, we can do it. Did that happen? I don't know, but it's a hell of a good story.

"I was born March 2, 1921, in Gloucester, Massachusetts. I enlisted July 7, 1939. My father had told me I should join the Navy because it could teach me a vocation, and I signed up, but they kept putting me off. They were only accepting twelve or fifteen a month from all of New England. In June of '39 I walked in again and said, 'When are you going to take me?' I'd been doing odd jobs to earn a little money. I bought a Ford dump truck for seventy-five bucks with another guy, and we were hauling loam all over the city of Boston. The Navy rep told me it would be another three to five months, so on the way out I went by the Marine Corps office, walked in on a whim, and said to the sergeant, 'If I wanted to join the Marine Corps, how long would it be before you took me?' He said, 'Do you want to leave Friday or two weeks from Friday?'

"I left on the seventh of July 1939. I was eighteen. When we got off the train at Yemassee, we were met by a sergeant who picked us up and took us by gig, by boat, from Beaufort to Parris Island. My senior drill instructor was a sergeant named Johnny Watkins. He wasn't cruel, but he had his own ways. He carried the steel shaft of a golf club, which he would use to whap you on the back if you didn't do things just right. In the early stages of training, if you didn't do a facing maneuver properly, while marching, he would likely run at you and jump and hit you in the middle of the back with his elbows and his knees. You'd have a rifle, you'd go flying, and you might take three guys with you. And he'd say, 'Now will you do it correctly?' He was nimble. He was a little guy too. There was a kid, a little Jewish boy, who couldn't get anything right. Drilling to him was just anathema, and so Watkins had him pushing a peanut with his nose on the sidewalk all the way around the barracks.

"One time Watkins didn't like the way we were drilling, so he had us go behind the barracks, stack our rifles, then march out into the bay. It was all mud, just icky, gooey mud, and you'd get it up to about waist high, and you'd begin to founder. You couldn't stand up straight. Some of the kids were getting scared because they really couldn't swim that well. Finally we turned around and walked in and took showers with all our clothes on.

"Another day I was corporal of the barracks guard for the

evening, and Watkins came in and said, 'Will you mail this letter for me tomorrow?' I saw it was addressed to Mrs. Johnny Watkins, such and such, Shanghai, China. But Johnny also had a wife over in Beaufort. That's Old Corps for you. They could get away with things like that. There would be girls coming on the base to clean various offices, and when they passed you, they would say very quietly, so the DI couldn't hear them, 'Ah'm available for twenty-five cents; Ah'm available for twenty-five cents.' They knew all these guys would be horny anyway, and they were just trying to get some guys to slip out, which was damn near impossible. Parris Island was something else in those days.

"Boot camp ended in September, and I was scheduled to go to sea school in Norfolk, which meant I'd be trained in how to react aboard a ship and wear blues and look pretty all day long. But coming from Gloucester, I'd spent a lot of time aboard ship, and I knew what shipboard life was like, and I thought: Hell, I don't want to get sent into that. I didn't think I could plan my future very well that way.

"While I was in boot camp, they told us to religiously read the bulletin board every day because it would tell you what your commander was doing and what the Marine Corps was doing. I followed this advice and saw an opening for an English instructor at the Marine Corps Institute at Eighth and I in Washington, D.C. I applied and forgot about it, and two days before I was supposed to ship out for Norfolk, Johnny Watkins comes up to me with a piece of paper and says, 'God damn it, Hatch, what have you been doing? This says you're going to teach English. What the hell kind of job is that for a marine?'"

Norman Hatch then found himself in a succession of jobs in the Marine Corps, from English teacher to an assistant editor at *Leatherneck* to public affairs, at which time he got to know the radio personality Arthur Godfrey, and finally, on October 1, 1941, to a class in photojournalism in New York City, with an emphasis on motion pictures and still photography. His film career began with another trip to the bulletin board, but it took three tries. Nothing came of these three trips. "Everything sort of happened because I either slept next to somebody or knew somebody," he said. He was lucky enough to meet an important person. In this case it was the director Louis de Rochemont, who got him into the class. The idea was to learn how to tell a story with a camera and not just settle for the "grip and grin."

"Even back in high school I'd liked photography. To get our so-called degree, in New York, we had to take one roll of film out into the city and come back with a complete story done in one roll, which ran through the camera at ninety feet a minute and there was only one hundred feet in there. I went out to one of these concrete chess boards in Manhattan where a lot of old men sat and played. That was my story. You had to learn to think out ahead what you were going to do.

"From there I went to Quantico, where we were doing training films, and all of a sudden two of us were ordered to the Second Marine Division. I was promoted to corporal, and we were supposed to be on the train to California Saturday night. I came up to Washington and told my girlfriend, Lois, I was getting ready to go, so we decided to get married that Saturday morning, September 19, 1942. Some cousins drove us down so she could say good-bye to me at the train. I called Johnny Ercole and said, 'Pack everything. I'm not coming back to the barracks.'

"We were at Camp Elliott while the Second Division completed its forming, and then we sailed for New Zealand in late September. We were there eleven months and then landed at Tarawa November 20, 1943. The director John Ford had won an Academy Award in 1942 and again in 1943, for his filming of the battle of Midway, and we used to say that when we got to the front, we were going to make a film and get an Academy Award, just like Ford.

"After the filming at Tarawa and my return to the States and the war loan drive, I wound up as a photo officer with the Fifth Division on the big island of Hawaii the summer of 1944. I had insisted that we forget the thirty-five-millimeter black-and-white camera and go to the sixteen-millimeter color. It was a lot easier to carry, and the success of the Tarawa film proved its worth. So we were the first ones in the services to go completely all color. We were on the Parker ranch, one of the largest in the world, training for Iwo even though we didn't know it. I made frequent trips back and forth to Oahu for staff meetings and got to know Herb Schlosberg, the photo officer for the Fourth Division, and he and I became very good friends. I had been promoted to warrant officer by then, the highest rank you can reach as an enlisted man."

Bill Genaust, who shot the motion-picture film of the second flag raising, joined Hatch's group in Hawaii.

"Genaust was one of the supernumeraries I got in the pool from Cincpac. We knew action was coming, and I had sent a request to the Marine Pacific headquarters at Pearl for more photographers and motion-picture cameramen for the next action. We ended up with probably ninety cameramen on the beach at Iwo, thirty for each division. Genaust had been wounded on Saipan and had come back on active duty. He didn't want to return to the States, so he was assigned to me when I requested more people. I wrote up the order of photographers prior to taking off from Hilo. We sent him up Suribachi even though nobody knew for sure if there was even going to be a second flag raising.

"I went ashore on Iwo Jima right after the first wave. Once I knew the philosophy of the Japanese, I promised myself I'd always go in the first wave, I wanted to get on the beach and dig in before things hit the fan, and sure enough, that's what happened. They let 'em get on the beach and gave them hell after that.

"I was near Suribachi when we hit the beach. I had been briefed by the colonel as to where they were going to set up once they got ashore, and it was right near the tail end of Motoyama No. 1. I had Obadiah Newcomb, the still man who had been with me on Tarawa, as my assistant photo officer now. I said, 'Obie, we got to get up there by Motoyama No. 1. I don't know how we're going to make it.' We had the broad expanse of Iwo in front of us. We'd gotten up over the hump, and I said to Obie, 'I want you to look out behind us, and I'll look in front of us. We don't want some goddamn Nip coming out of a hole in the ground and shooting us in the back. We'll take pictures as we move.' We didn't have any trouble. We walked right up to Motoyama No. 1, probably twenty minutes after we landed. I found a fifty-caliber gun mount circled by fifty-gallon drums loaded with sand. The mount was sticking up, but the gun wasn't there. It made a perfect tent pole, and I covered the whole thing with a big tarp I found nearby. That was my command post.

"I was all dug in and Obie was out shooting stills when finally the guys began to infiltrate in. They'd also been told we'd be somewhere near the end of Motoyama No. 1. We had ten guys shooting motion-picture film. The rest were still men except for a camera repair guy.

"The Navy had noticed in looking at all the film from previous actions that everybody's footage was the same in every battle: Guys running here, guys running there. So we determined to select and assign various topics to various men. I had a tank battalion, a medical battalion, and a signal battalion I would cover. I had one still man and one movie man assigned to them and nothing else. Out of that came several good training films. One film has a very distinctive name, *Glamour Gal*, which was painted on the barrel of a howitzer. We also had free roamers, guys attached to a unit, a battalion or a regiment, to document whatever was going on. This way we avoided duplication.

"The whole thing was planned out to the extent that three times a day an LCVP came in from the command ship. It had great big letters across both sides: PRESS. Anybody, meaning civilian press or our public affairs writers or combat correspondents, would go down to that boat and turn their stuff in. It would go to the command ship and then be packaged individually and flown to Guam, where the Navy had a big photo lab set up. They processed all the film. There was total censorship all through the Pacific war, and all military and civilian stuff had to be looked at before it was released.

"That's how Joe Rosenthal's shot of the second flag raising and his other stuff was sent in. He went back to the ship in the press boat that night. He went back and forth for four days. There wasn't any sense in him sleeping on the beach at nighttime, so he'd go back, write his captions, turn his stuff in, and it'd be flown to Guam. So he never saw it until he arrived there around D plus eight. Herb Schlosberg, the photo officer for the Fourth, was on that boat with him. Schlosberg had orders to take all the Marine motion-picture film from D plus one to D plus eight to Washington and to Hollywood, where Warner Brothers could edit the film. We figured it would be smart to have the film edited and ready by the time the battle was over. I took the film between D plus eight and eighteen to Washington.

"For the second flag raising, my boss, Colonel George Roll, the division intelligence officer, came to me and said General Rockey wanted a bigger flag up there because nobody could see the first one, it was so small. I said, 'Where the hell are they gonna get a bigger flag? Nobody's carrying any holiday or Sunday flags.' He said there were LSTs on the beach, and maybe they would find one there. The official Marine Corps position is quite simple: Lieutenant Tuttle, who was an aide to the battalion commander, was sent out to get some supplies from some of those ships and to look at the same time for a larger flag. He was lucky because LST 799, I think it is, had one, and the lieutenant JG gave it to him. It was eight feet long, and if he'd tried to fly it on the stern of the LST, it probably would have dragged in the water."

Hatch, aware that the marines were going to try to raise a second flag, knew he ought to have someone there to film it.

"I didn't have anybody to send out, but then in walked Bill Genaust and Bob Campbell to turn in film and get new stuff. I had assigned them to the Twenty-eighth Marines.

"I said, 'You guys have to turn around and go right back. There's a possibility that a second flag is going to be put up. Just go up there and sit on top of the mountain and shoot whatever you see, and if a flag goes up, shoot that too.'

"They headed back down. It was kind of dangerous, getting from my CP at the foot of Motoyama No. 1 airstrip over to the mountain. It was a good quarter mile, and there was nothing but firefights going on. But they got over there and ran into Rosenthal going up. He and Bob Campbell had worked on the same newspaper in San Francisco, and they were friends. They joked about going up, and

Because it showed the second, larger flag flying while the smaller one was coming down,
this photo by Marine Private Robert R. "Bob" Campbell helped dispel
later assertions that there was no second flag raising.
U.S. Marine Corps photo, National Archive

Rosenthal apparently said, 'Oh, you guys are carrying guns. You can protect me.' But it was pretty secure on the mountain at that point. They get up there, and it was only seconds later that the second flag went up. They were already putting it on a new pole, and Bob Campbell shot the perfect picture of the one flag coming down, the other going up, crossing each other. This disproved a lot of arguments people have brought up that there weren't two flags.

"For his part on the summit, Joe had built a little rock cairn to stand on, and Genaust was over to the left of him. But Genaust figured that was not a good shot, so he started to move across, and that's when Joe said, 'Hurry up, it's going up.' Genaust got on Joe's right, and that's the way the shot worked out. Campbell didn't want to stand next to Rosenthal and get the same picture, so he moved over to the side and down at a lower angle, and that's how he got that beautiful shot of the two flags.

"When Rosenthal's stuff came through processing at the Cincpac lab in Guam, somebody, and I don't know who—nobody's been able to put a finger on it—whether it was the lab man or the Associated Press photo editor on the island, but somebody made a decision. I always say in a talk, 'There's another man involved in the Rosenthal picture.' He is the person who changed that picture from a horizontal to a vertical, and that made the photo. Because if you look at the horizontal, it shows the top of the mountain, it shows the debris around the place, it shows part of the beach over here, you can even see very faint lines of ships out to sea. It's got too much crap in it. I've said often that if that picture as taken were sent out and printed that way, I don't know if very many people would have done anything with it. But in turning it into a vertical, he did something that artists, true artists, really like: It's got a triangle in it; it's got action in a still photo. You get the feeling of the movement up there, and it tells the story without the caption.

"Of course the picture was a sensation. It was put out the Sunday after Rosenthal took it, and it was on the front page of damn near every major newspaper across the country. Then word got out that it was phony, that it had been staged.

"What happened was Lou Lowery, who shot the first flag raising, got together with a Time-Life correspondent, Bob Sherrod, on the island after we'd heard about this wonderful picture via radio. We hadn't seen it. This was part of that thing we'd determined at Pearl beforehand: We'd get lots of info back on what the press was saying. Everybody was extolling the wonderful picture. Now Lowery had been up there and was part of that little attack that went on up there and jumped off the side of the mountain and busted both his cameras. He couldn't understand why this guy who had gone up and just shot a replacement flag was getting all this credit. No combat, no nothing, you know?

Sergeant Louis R. Lowery's photograph of the first flag raising did not compare with the impact of the picture Joe Rosenthal was to take a few hours later.
Louis R. Lowery

"He was pissed off enough that he sat down with Sherrod and he told him the story. He said, 'There's something phony about this. It's just not right.' Plus a lot of professional photographers thought it was a staged picture from the start.

"What Bob Sherrod told me later was that when he sent it in, he put a note on the piece he had written as a result of talking with Lou. He said, 'Don't run this until you check with AP.' Now that's good reporting. And they didn't publish it per se. But there's always a glitch somewheres. Time-Life in New York at Thirty Rock [Rockefeller Center in midtown Manhattan] was as big as the Pentagon. It was on a great number of floors, and there was also a radio station in there that received copies of all the correspondences going through Time-Life from around the world. So Sherrod's story comes through all the various stations, goes through this radio desk, and there's no hold on it; the hold had dropped off somewhere along the line. So they ran with it, U.S. wide, a phony story, phony flag. And then, when Joe hit Guam, he was met by a press conference of his pals saying, 'What a wonderful picture.' Well, he hadn't seen it yet. Someone in the course of asking questions said, 'Did you pose any pictures?' He said, 'Oh, yes, sure.' Well, he didn't pose the flag raising, but he did get one of everybody standing around the flagpole. We called that the banzai (or gung ho) shot. It was taken all over the goddamn Pacific. That's how the misunderstanding arose.

"And that's what I was up against. The reason I went to Washington was I was taking the film in, from D plus eight to D eighteen, following Herb Schlosberg. I was met at National Airport on March 17 by a lieutenant colonel who was deputy director of public affairs for the Marine Corps. I knew him. His name was Ed Hagenah. I said, 'Jesus, this is really nice, for a colonel to come over in a car to pick up a warrant officer. I'm really proud.' He laughed and said, 'No, I've got to take you into headquarters.' I said, 'I can't go like this.' I hadn't shaved for a day and a half, I was partly in uniform, still had combat gear on. I had been five days getting from Iwo to Washington.

"He said, 'Get in the car, and I'll explain.' I did so and he told me we were going to the commandant's office. I said, 'Oh, for chrissake, Ed. Let me go home and shower and shave, put on a uniform. I only live five minutes away.' He said no, because in the office waiting for us was the bureau chief of Time-Life in Washington, the executive vice-president of the Associated Press, a bunch of horse holders, and the commandant of the Marine Corps, General A. A. Vandegrift. He said they all wanted to know

The "gung ho" or banzai shot that led to the confusion over Joe Rosenthal's flag raising photo.
Asked in Guam whether he had posed the picture, Rosenthal said yes,
but he meant this image, not the flag raising shot.
AP Wide World Photo by Joe Rosenthal

about the two flag raisings. There was contention about the fact that Time-Life had said Rosenthal's shot was a phony picture. Now AP wants to sue Time-Life, and it wants to sue Sherrod, and I'm supposed to settle the goddamn argument.

" 'That's all I need,' I said, 'to be in the middle of two warring major news organizations.' So I get there, and the commandant looks at me and kind of grins. He said, 'Gunner [in those days warrant officers wore the bursting bomb on their covers, or hats, and they were called gunners even though they had nothing to do with guns], he said, 'Gunner, we don't know the real story about the two flags. You're the first one to come back here who might be able fill us in on it. Tell us what the story is.'

"I told them the first flag was put up by the patrol that went up there, and it was considered too small. There was a desire to put up a larger flag, but nobody knew where the hell they'd find one, but they finally did find one on the LST. They took it up and put it up. I said that was all there was to it. It was a replacement flag. I said I thought one of the problems was simply that the AP was calling it *the* flag raising, and it's not. *The* flag raising referred to the one that went up at ten-twenty, the first flag. This one, Genaust and Rosenthal's, was a replacement flag. Lowery shot the first one. In fact, there is nothing reported in the records about that second flag going up. If you didn't have a picture of it, you wouldn't know it was there. The battalion log has nothing; the D-2 log, intelligence, has nothing, the D-3 log, operations, has nothing. It was just a replacement flag, a routine action.

"There was a definite second flag raising, I explained, that had been photographed by Joe Rosenthal, and he hadn't planned it, he hadn't promoted it, he hadn't staged it. So that cleared things up. I hadn't seen Genaust's film at all. He was killed March 4, and his film was on the West Coast. The crux came when the commandant said to Alan J. Gould, the senior vice-president who pretty much ran AP, 'This is a wonderful photo, and I think we could use it a lot in the future. Would you give us permission to use it?'

"The guy said something typical, normal and natural for anybody in that business, with a stock photo library, to say. He told the commandant, 'Well, yes, I'll give you a couple duplicate negatives, but it will cost you a dollar apiece for every eight-by-ten that you make.'

"Well, there was dead silence in the room. It felt like icicles. You could feel the horse holders sitting around thinking: If it hadn't been for the Marine Corps, Rosenthal wouldn't have been up there taking the picture in the first place, and now they want to charge us for it? So the commandant turned to me, and said, 'Gunner, what do you think about that?'

"And I thought: Well, here goes nothin'. I said, 'That is a normal position, for them to come back with a normal response to a request for a stock photo, but if we don't decide to go with that, we have the sixteen-millimeter color film of the flag raising taken by Bill Genaust and,' I said, 'you can always find one frame that's fairly sharp. We can blow that up to eight-by-ten, make color or black-and-white prints of the exact same shot.'

"Now I didn't know whether Genaust's film was underexposed, overexposed, or whether there was dirt or scratches in the film or what the hell might have happened. His motor might have been running slow. I could see the wheels turning over in Gould's eyes as I was saying this. I could see him thinking there was going to be two pictures out there, one a little fuzzy and the other good and sharp, but the public wouldn't know the difference. He very quickly came back and said to the commandant, 'Well, as an after-thought, I'll give you the two dupe negatives and you can use them in perpetuity at no cost.' That ended the whole conversation.

"The first thing I did when I got home was call Schlosberg. I got him in the cutting room, and I said, 'Have you seen Bill Genaust's film yet?' He said yes. I said, 'How is it?' He said, 'It's beautiful.' I said, 'Thank God,' because all I could picture was that if by any chance, the decision had gone the way I suggested and the film was bad, I'd have been shipped to Iceland or someplace.

"At first Lou Lowery was embittered that Joe got all the atten-tion, but once he saw the photo, he didn't have any doubt that it was a good one, so the animosity sort of drained out of him. But he was pretty bitter there on the beach. He came to me and said, 'God damn it, what the hell is this?' I said, 'Lou, don't get excited until we find out what it is. We haven't seen it.' Later on he and I were very friendly. We worked together on several Marine Corps photo contests as judges. He and Rosenthal became good friends. In fact, Rosenthal came all the way east for Lou's funeral.

"I never got to know Rosenthal real well, but we talked on the phone over the years. It'd be like, have you heard about this? One of the funniest stories we traded was about some Air Force captain or lieutenant who was having trouble with his P-51 fighter. He put down on the Iwo airstrip, and while he was waiting for the mechanics to fix it, he said, 'Well, as long as I'm here, I might as well go get a good look at the island.' So, he said, he walked over and climbed Suribachi just in time to help put the flag up.

"Besides Genaust, we lost one other film guy, Fox, on Iwo after

I left. I never did a lot of filming there myself although I went out a couple times. I stayed pretty close to the CP, the command post, in case the colonel needed me.

"I had left the island by the time Genaust was killed March 4. A funny thing happened about ten years ago, 1997 or thereabouts, here at my home in Arlington. I heard a knock on the door one Saturday morning, and a tall gentleman introduced himself as former Lieutenant John K. McLean. He lived right up the street. He said he was an interpreter who was on the patrol when Genaust was killed. A report had come back to division intelligence that a Japanese was sitting at a table in a cave with lots of papers, working on something, but nobody could talk to him. It was thought the papers might be valuable; it was thought it might be a trap, so McLean was sent out with a patrol to find out what this guy was doing. Bill tagged along, looking for a story. It was a rainy, misty day. They got there, and here was this guy sitting at a table down inside this cave, which was quite large. The lieutenant tries to talk to him: 'Why are you there? What are you doing?' No answer.

"So the patrol leader says, 'We'll go down there and find out what's happening.' but he didn't have a flashlight, and nobody else had one, except Bill. He said, 'Oh, hell, I got the flashlight. I'll go down there.' He was that type. I mean, he'd been in combat. He knew his way around. He knew what to do. But why he did this one, I'll never know.

"To get into the cave, you had to climb over a large berm formed by dirt taken out of there. There was just enough room to squeeze through. Bill went down into the cave while McLean and two or three other members of the patrol squeezed through behind him. But they didn't descend. Genaust got two-thirds of the way down there, and a Nambu machine gun opened up from a tunnel off to the right, which they could not see from the entrance. It killed him.

"The Japanese guy starts to pick up his papers, and McLean immediately ordered his men to kill him. But the Nambu scared the living shit out of them, and they turned around and had a hell of a time climbing back out through all that volcanic ash, plus it was so narrow. They were scared to death, and they just piled ass out of there. They got out, but nobody fired at them. Genaust was too far down for anybody to reach without getting shot. So they called for a dozer to close up the cave. McLean, who has since died himself, said he went back a couple days later, but he couldn't find the cave, and I guess it has been lost ever since.

"Just last week [March 2007] I was at a meeting with a group of Japanese who had come from an organization that looks for bodies, and they were going to make their fifty-fourth or fifty-fifth trip to Iwo and wanted to talk to some marines who had been there during the fighting. The question of Genaust came up, and I gave them a copy of McLean's story. Of course our own guys have looked for Genaust for years. [At the time this book was going to press, there had been no word from the Japanese contingent.]

"Was the Marine Corps thrilled when the Tarawa film won the Academy Award in '44? I guess they were. I haven't the slightest idea. I wasn't there. General Julian C. Smith, who was the division commander on Tarawa as a major general, was a lieutenant general by then and director of the Department of the Pacific, in San Francisco. He and his wife were invited down to the awards to sit at the table of Twentieth Century Fox, even though they didn't have anything to do with the film, which was produced by Warner Brothers.

"He accepted the award. I don't know if you know it or not, but this was not *the* award. It was a little wooden plaque. Because of the metal shortage, they weren't making any Oscars during the whole war period. After the war they went back and made Oscars for those who didn't get any. The Marine Corps Museum's got it in Quantico. I often used to ask Happy Smith, the general's wife, whose real name was Harriet, 'Would you let me take that so I can keep it on my mantel? Whenever the general passes on, I'll turn it in, to the Marine Corps historical people.' But she never would agree to that. It was kind of a joke between us. Still, I thought it would be kind of nice to have that plaque sitting there on my mantelpiece."

After a hitch in Japan during the occupation, Norman Hatch wound up back in Washington as an operations officer for photographic services for the Marine Corps, first as a military man, then in 1946 as a civilian. He and his wife, Lois, had a son, Skip, and later a daughter, Colby. Following that, he worked in procurement, then joined Bell & Howell in Chicago for a stretch, did some freelancing back east, and finally, in July 1956, became the chief of the Defense Department's newsreel setup, where he spent the next twenty-three years. As newsreels phased out, he created a radio-TV-newsfilm branch and then became operations officer for the audiovisual division. There he came to work with folks like John Wayne, who wanted Marine Corps authenticity in his film *The Green Berets.*

"John Wayne was fine to work with. He was emotionally involved with his project, and he thought it was wonderful and great, and it was pretty good in the sense that it didn't hurt the service any, but there were little things that aggravated us, relationships he portrayed that were farfetched. But then he built a whole Vietnamese village at Fort Benning and gave it to the Army to train guys.

"I retired as a major in January 1979, after forty-one years' service. There were several retirements in there: the Marine Corps, the Defense Department. It's like I've been on the crest of a wave ever since I got out of the Marine Corps. I went from one good job to another. Now I am doing something like this interview for this book, I just did a similar thing for somebody writing an article, and they're asking me now to write for the Second Marine Division newsletter. Everybody's asking me to write a book, a fellow in New Zealand is writing a book, and I got to dictate something for him, so I'm busier now than I was before."

14

CORPORAL CHARLES "CHUCK" LINDBERG

Last of the Flag Raisers; Silver Star, Purple Heart
Twenty-eighth Marines, Fifth Marine Division

*It still bugs me that we never got recognition for
being the first to raise the flag on Iwo Jima.*

Chuck Lindberg in his Richfield, Minnesota, home on May 8, 2007, when he
granted an interview to the author, who
took this photograph. Lindberg's Silver
Star and his Purple Heart rest beside
him on the arm of his easy chair.

Corporal Charles W. Lindberg,
grenades hanging off his jacket,
flamethrower in hand, looks for
cave entrances along the summit
of Mount Suribachi shortly after
the first flag was raised on the
morning of February 23, 1945.

I was sitting talking with Chuck Lindberg and his wife, Vi (for Violette), in the living room of the modest Minneapolis home they had shared for more than fifty years when I noticed after some time that half the forefinger on his left hand was missing. Thinking it got shot off in the war, I asked about it. But no, he had lost it as a twelve-year-old reaching into some rocks at a dam, trying to catch a bullhead, when the rocks loosened, came down, and crushed the front part of the finger. "Them days," Chuck said, "they didn't have what they have today or they could have saved it. But when I got to the Marine Corps recruiter in Seattle in 1942, he took a look at it and said, 'Is that your trigger finger?' I said, 'Nope.' And he said, 'You're accepted.' I couldn't get in now, if I wanted to, with a finger like that."

"I'm from Grand Forks, North Dakota. I was born June 26, 1920. I quit high school in tenth grade, in 1937, and joined the Civilian Conservation Corps, the CCCs, planting trees, down around Fargo, mostly, for about six months or a year. When that ended, I went to work on a farm outside Grand Forks, getting a whole ten dollars a month in the winter and twenty-five dollars in the summer. One winter day this big Lincoln Zephyr pulled up in the yard. As soon as the driver got, out I recognized him as Archie Simonson, a man I used to take care of horses for back in my school days. He owned three or four gas stations in Fargo, Grand Forks, and St. Cloud. He kept some big workhorses up there and sent them down to the woods for the winter. I took care of them for him. He remembered me and where I was. He said he was starting a gas station in Fargo and he'd give me ninety dollars a month and a room. Oh, boy! I jumped this high.

"I worked for him about a year and then got acquainted with the road boss of some truckers hauling cars. I asked him one day,

'Hey, I'd like to get another job and get out of here.' He says, 'I'll give you a job. You can make yourself two hundred forty bucks a month.' Pretty soon I was driving a big truck hauling cars from Detroit to Spokane.

"That was my big move. I drove truck till war was declared, and then, when I found out two months later there was no more cars to be delivered, I went up to the Marine Corps. It was January of '42, and I was stranded in Spokane. I always had great respect for the Marine Corps, from books, posters, and movies. I joined in January 8,1942. I knew the draft would get me eventually anyway. I was single; I was twenty-one. I had six brothers and three sisters. My folks didn't know I was in the Marines until I wrote home. By the time they got it I was on my way overseas.

"I had to go to Seattle to get sworn in. They sent me to boot camp in San Diego. When you're driving trucks all the time, you get weak, and boot camp was tough even though it only lasted five weeks. Them marines don't monkey around. The day we finished boot camp they marched us down to the parade grounds, and here was a big platform and Carlson (Lieutenant Colonel E. F. Carlson) and Jimmy Roosevelt was there. But Carlson was talking, recruiting men for his raider outfit. He says, 'I want men who ain't afraid to die, I want men who ain't afraid to kill. I want men who'll walk fifty miles in a day.' I raised my hand. I put my like in him right away. I liked his way of talking. They sent us up to Jacques Farm for training; they put us in pup tents on the crick. There was a house sitting there, and I thought, first thing, I thought there's where the officers are going to sleep. But about ten o'clock that night here come the officers, all of 'em, and they get in the pup tents. That's the way he run it. He'd eat, sleep, and go with the men all the time. The officers didn't get fed any better. We liked that.

"I stayed with them until they were disbanded, after Guadalcanal and Bougainville. We come into Guadalcanal November 2 at Aola Bay and went on what they called the Long Patrol, thirty-two days behind enemy lines, from November 4 to December 4, 1942. It was said to be the longest patrol of World War Two. I was a rifleman. [Lieutenant Colonel Carlson led the guerrilla raid, for which he received a Navy Cross. His men were credited with killing 488 Japanese while 16 raiders were killed and 18 wounded.]

"After that we went to Hebrides, and then they called us back north again. I was a private first class. Later we made the invasion of Bougainville in 1943. We were there three months, and then they brought us back to the States, disbanded the raiders, like they did the paratroopers, and put us all in the Fifth Marine Division. After I returned from leave to Camp Pendleton, I saw the flamethrower unit and volunteered for it. Everybody said I was nuts, but I made corporal, and they gave me an assault squad. I was five feet ten and weighed a hundred seventy pounds. The flamethrower weighed seventy-two pounds. It carried five gallons of jellied gasoline, and you could empty it in six seconds.

"After several months at Pendleton, we went to the Big Island at Hawaii and trained more there, at Camp Tarawa. From there it was on to Iwo. We didn't have too good info on that island. From Hawaii we stopped at Guam and switched from big ships to LSTs. Was it bumpy? Oh, Jesus, you can say that again. It went plop plop plop through the sea.

"I was in the Third Platoon of E Company, Second Battalion, Twenty-eighth Marines, under John Keith Wells until he got injured. Then Lieutenant Harold Schrier took over. We came in next to Suribachi in the eighth or ninth wave. Kuribayashi opened up when we come ashore. It was really bloody, with guys lying all over the place. They mortared us up and down the beach. They had it all bracketed. I found out later their plan was to let us get on the beach and annihilate us. But we got off the beach and up behind the sand ridges. There were tunnels and mines and booby traps all around Suribachi. I was used to combat, so that never worried me too much. We got to the base of the mountain February 21. We got across the island and cut Suribachi off that first day. We thought we were really doing something.

"We spent the next few days attacking the mountain, taking out caves, pillboxes. I never seen so many caves and bunkers. Ever bunker was attached to another one, and they'd go by one connector on down fifteen feet, and then someone would come up behind and shoot you in the back. Our casualties was high on that Third Platoon.

"With the flamethrower you had to sneak up on them, and once you got within thirty or forty feet you could use it. It would reach sixty feet under good conditions. Once you sent that load of gas in there, you didn't have to worry too much, as long as they didn't have another way out. I can't say how many I hit, maybe ten or fifteen. The biggest one I got was on top of the mountain when we went up at eight a.m. on February 23, forty of us. I was on that first combat patrol with Schrier. They came the night before and said we were going to start climbing in the morning. We had a kind of jittery night. The next morning we reported to Colonel Chandler Johnson, who handed Schrier a flag and said, 'If you get to the top, raise it.' We thought it was going to be a slaughterhouse, but it turned out we went up that mountain with no resistance.

"I was back a bit. The scouts and riflemen go first. We didn't hit the cave right away. The first thing they told us was to get the flag up. When we got there, I took the flamethrower off and laid it beside me. We found a water pipe to tie the flag to laying on the ground. It was about four inches thick and twenty feet long. It was heavy. I helped tie the flag on with Thomas and Schrier and Hansen. Then we went to the highest spot we could find and stood it up. It hit my helmet going up and knocked it off. There were horns honking, guys cheering; it was just wild. All the ships out there tooting their horns. We felt very good about it.

In his excellent account of all aspects of both flag raisings, *Uncommon Valor, Common Virtue: Iwo Jima and the Photograph that Captured America*, Hal Buell quotes Chuck Lindberg from an oral history collection, *Never in Doubt*: "It was a great patriotic feeling, this chill that runs through you. . . . My proudest moment of my time in the Marines was raising the American flag on Iwo Jima. My feeling of being a Marine is I served with the finest, and I feel proud every day that I can tell somebody that."

"Once we put up the flag, the Japs started coming out of the caves. I know the first one we got wasn't more than one hundred or two hundred feet from where we put up the flag. And we were right near the edge where you go over to go down where that cave went in. I went around the back of it and found another entrance. Somebody had dropped something big and knocked a hole in the cave. I sent a good blast in there. The other guys were standing on top, trying to get something to shoot at, but nobody came out. We thought that was kind of funny, so we blew both ends of that cave shut. Then two days later we dug it open, went in there, and found seventy-two dead Japs. My theory has always been that before we started up that mountain, they ordered barrages and Colonel Johnson just pulverized it, with planes, battlewagons, the whole thing. I think they were afraid to come out. Then, after we got up there, they started shooting at us from this one cave, and that's the one we went after first. It sat right on the rim of the volcano, a big rocky opening.

"You know about Donald Ruhl, who got the Medal of Honor? Before we went up the mountain, he and Hansen were down on edge of a big hole, looking for targets for me, and all of a sudden a grenade came over, right between them. I was right directly back. Ruhl he just gave Hansen a shove, and he fell on it. He was a good man; there was no doubt. The trouble is, you know, then Hansen was killed March 1, the same day I was shot. [In addition to falling on the grenade on February 21, Ruhl was cited for his bravery over the previous three days in attacking the enemy and rescuing under heavy fire a wounded fellow marine.]

"Sergeant Lou Lowery, the *Leatherneck* magazine photographer who took the pictures of our flag raising, was trying to get away from a grenade when he fell down the side of the mountain and busted his camera. I knew him very well. Lowery was with us off and on. He was unhappy, he told me after, when Rosenthal's photo got all the attention. He was unhappy over that. I was very good friends with him after the war too. I even went to his funeral at Quantico, after he died in 1973. The thing that got me was here come Joe Rosenthal too. He took the second flag raising picture. 'Oh,' he says, 'you were on the real one, wasn't ya?' He wasn't told to do that, in my opinion. He wanted a picture, and he was going to get a picture. Oh, you bet. It's a good picture. I even told Rosenthal it was a good picture. But me and him got into a few arguments.

"How did I feel about it? It still bugs me that we never got recognition for being the first to raise the flag on Iwo Jima. Why, here you were doing the dirty work, and they get the credit for it. They were called heroes. The mountain was secured. All they did was come up, put the flag up, and go back down again. And when I got home and started talking about this, I was called a liar and everything else. It was terrible.

"We spent from the twenty-third to the twenty-eighth on the summit. I reloaded and went back up several times because there were a lot of places we wanted to burn up there. You didn't know if they were in there or not and you couldn't blast them out, so you used the flamethrower. I and Robert Goode were flamethrowers for the company. I had a whole squad, and where we were needed, we went.

"We moved on the twenty-eighth, went up to Hill 362 Able. We stayed there the first night, and then the next night Hansen was shot. We were all settin', kind of got to talking, when all of a sudden a sniper nailed him right there, at noon. And that's where I was shot, March 1, that same afternoon. I was trying to get to a mortar position, kind of running across the side of a ridge there, and all of sudden—*boom!*—a bullet went right straight through my right forearm and on through my jacket. I was bent over like this, and if I'd been standing straight, another inch or two, it would have got me. But because I was bent over, it missed my stomach. It shattered my forearm bone. You bet I went down. I hollered, 'Corpsman,' and here come John Bradley, from the second flag raising. I knew him very good. He was our platoon corpsman, a wonderful corpsman, I'll tell you that. He was from Wisconsin [Bradley's son James, with Ron Powers, wrote *Flags of Our Fathers*, the best-selling story of those who raised the second flag and the basis for the Clint Eastwood film]. We saw each other after the war, and I saw them in Chicago when they were on that bond drive. I was back in Great Lakes Hospital by then.

"Anyways, I'm on the ground lying there, not feeling too bad.

He got some splints on it and gave me a shot of some kind. He was going to take me back, but I said, 'No, I'll go by myself,' which I did. I left the flamethrower behind. I walked from Hill 362 to the beach; I didn't know if I could make it or not. It was a long way too. When I got to the Higgins boat, they stripped me of all my equipment, my rifle, pistol, the works, and away I go. They set my arm on the hospital ship, but I got the best deal when I got back to Pearl Harbor. They really worked on it.

"I went from the hospital ship at Iwo to Saipan. After about a week a guy says to me, 'You want to see a picture of the flag raising?' I said sure. He hands me a picture, I look at it, and that's not the one we put up. I didn't know a thing about it. Nobody said anything about it. I was astounded. After they sent me on to Pearl Harbor, *Yank* magazine came out with pictures of the first flag and the second flag, and then I saw what happened.

"But we hadn't known the flag was being replaced. Nobody said anything about it. We were busy hitting caves when the second patrol came up with big flag. We had the mountain secure by one o'clock, and I went down to the bottom because my tanks were empty. I was being assisted by Robert Goode. We left the mountain at one-thirty, went straight down, and Rosenthal came up over to the other side. I didn't see him go up. I don't think anybody knew the flag was being replaced. Nobody cheered. Everybody knew the flag was up. They weren't paying attention to that anymore. If it were not for the photo, nobody would have noticed. The mountain was secure when he came up there. He didn't go under fire. We didn't even go up under fire. Nobody fired at us.

"Rosenthal pulled a rotten trick there, I thought. He was behind that second flag; he was going to get a picture. They weren't going to use ours. Give us our share of credit for what we did. People today don't know the difference. They called him a hero, called the six men who raised the second flag heroes when they sat at the bottom while we went up. To their credit, they didn't consider themselves heroes.

"I talked to them guys on the bond drive when I was at the Great Lakes Naval Hospital in Chicago, where I spent several months after being treated in Guam, Hawaii, and Camp Pendleton; that's where they cured me. We found out they were going to be at Wrigley Field, so I and another guy went down there. Huge crowd. They were really eating that up. That Gagnon, he got me. He introduced me around as a guy that killed a lot of men. I didn't like him as well. He wanted to be in the movies. Bradley introduced me to other people too. We didn't talk too long. My arm was still in a cast. I never talked to Gagnon.

"I kind of felt sorry for Ira Hayes, the Indian. He did it wrong [lost control of his life], but he was a good marine. He was a paratrooper. I talked to him quite a bit. We came back on the same ship together, seventeen days from Guadalcanal to San Diego. He'd drink, but it wasn't that way [not to excess]. I imagine everybody had some. I took a drink myself.

"After that they sent me down to Charleston, South Carolina, and made me a guard in the naval brig for two or three months. That was an easy racket. I was discharged down there January 16, 1946. When they pay you, they pay you from where you enlisted at. I had enlisted in Seattle and was discharged in Charleston, so that was a nice check, including travel pay for all that distance.

"I met my wife, Vi, in November of 1946 at the Legion Hall in East Grand Forks, Minnesota. I belonged to it. I was a past commander of the post. I was the bouncer, and I let them in free, four good-looking girls. She's from Minnesota. We got married in October 1947. We had two sons and two daughters.

"I was an electrician by then, wiring farms up there. I had run into an old friend in Grand Forks that I used to work for long ago, and he says, 'Can you wire a house?' I said, 'I don't know.' I tried it, and I guess I got it wired all right, with a few mistakes. That was my start in the electrical trade, and I did that for thirty-nine years, IBEW Local 292 Minneapolis. I retired in 1985. Two years ago they put up a new building in St. Michael's for training apprentices, and they told me they were going to name it after me, the Charles Chuck Lindberg Training Center.

"We had some attention for raising the flag but just not what you'd think, not like those other guys got. I was invited to Washington quite a few times. I was there for the dedication of the flag raising monument in 1964. Harold Schrier was there, and Lou Lowery. Nobody recognized us at all. Eisenhower was there. Nixon was vice president. I shook hands with him. He was shaking hands with me and looking over at somebody else. I met President Clinton and went to the dedication of the new Marine Corps Museum in Quantico November of 2006. I got sent a lot of stuff, and you ought to see the statue they got of me in Bemidji. It's beautiful, six feet tall, over in the center of the state. Vi and I went to Washington on a private plane, just the two of us for the Veterans Day dedication of the new museum last November. Seven of us were there from the Third Platoon. That's all that were left.

"It's taken half a century, but I think I've finally helped set the record straight."

On February 24, 2001, then eighty-year-old Charles Lindberg was presented with a letter from the commandant of the Marine Corps honoring him for his role in the raising of the U.S. flag at Iwo Jima. Lindberg also holds a Purple Heart, of course, and the Silver Star, awarded for his performance at Suribachi and on Hill 362. Part of the citation reads:

> *Repeatedly exposing himself to hostile grenades and machine-gun fire in order that he might reach and neutralize enemy pillboxes at the base of Mount Suribachi, Corporal Lindberg courageously approached within ten or fifteen yards of the emplacements before discharging his weapon, thereby assuring the annihilation of the enemy and the successful completion of his platoon's mission. While engaged in an attack on hostile cave positions on March 1, he fearlessly exposed himself to accurate enemy fire and was subsequently wounded and evacuated.*

Chuck Lindberg died on Sunday, June 26, only weeks after I visited with him and his wife at their Richfield, Minnesota, home on May 8. He and Vi had been married fifty-nine years.

LSTs, called the workhorses of the invasion, are fixed against the beach while marines form a bucket brigade to unload supplies on Red Beach Two. Supplies had to be hand carried because the trucks and tractors were bogged down in Iwo's volcanic black sands.
U.S. Coast Guard photo

PART FIVE

The LST, Workhorse of the Invasion

The LST, or landing ship, tank, was 327 feet long and 50 feet wide and was manned by a crew of seventy plus seven officers.

About a thousand were built during the entire war, at Evansville, Indiana, and floated down the Ohio to the Mississippi and New Orleans.

Seventy-five to one hundred were used for the invasion of Iwo Jima, according to William E. Jayne of Hobe Sound, Florida. "We were the dungaree Navy," he said. "I was seventeen years old, in charge of all foodstuffs. I served on LSTs for two and a half years as a gunner and storekeeper. We spent ten days at Iwo Jima." LSTs could carry up to 350 troops plus tracked landing vehicles, such as the amtracs, the Higgins boats, and the DUKWs (see page 255). They also carried pontoons for causeways, bulldozers, and Marston matting, a pierced steel planking that could be laid across the sand for traction.

With their relatively flat bottoms, they could pull right up to the beach, set a stern anchor, pump out the ballast, and open their bow doors so a vehicle theoretically could drive right out onto the sand. It should have been easy. With the steep, terrible sands and rugged surf on February 19, 1945, at Iwo, it wasn't that simple.

15

MACHINIST'S MATE THIRD CLASS
PERLE "DUSTY" WARD

133rd Seabee Battalion

Because I was born and raised on a farm and could run a tractor and drive horses, different things like that, they thought that I ought to be able to run a bulldozer.

Perle "Dusty" Ward, eighty-one, holds a statue of the flag raising while he stands next to the Joe Rosenthal photo at his home in El Cajon, California, in August 2007.
Photo by Carole Strasser

The young Seabee Seaman First Class Dusty Ward leans against a palm tree in Honolulu in 1944. He received an official commendation for helping evacuate casualties on D-day on Iwo Jima, working all night as a stretcher bearer to bring in wounded marines. "His activities contributed materially to the saving of many lives," the citation says.

I did not know, when I reached Dusty Ward by phone at his home near San Diego, that Mabel, his wife of fifty-four years, had died only days before, on April 7, 2007. "We just finished her memorial last Saturday at the Elks Lodge here in El Cajon," he said. "It turned out to be a beautiful one. I'm just sitting here looking at a bunch of flowers, and I started out this morning to write thank-you cards to all the people that sent flowers. I made up my mind I was going to get to it this morning and not stop till I'm done. She wasn't that old. She was only seventy-two. The poor gal had a lot of things went wrong with her."

"I came into Iwo Jima February 19, 1945, on an LST. Going into shore, I remember an LST coming in next to me, and as soon as they dropped the damn ramp, a mortar shell hit right on the ramp as guys were coming off. I don't know how many were killed, but it was right alongside me. So talk about being lucky, I feel that way. And that was the first day. No heavy machinery came in. They probably started moving it late in the second day. Our job was to help get other equipment inland.

"I got involved in a deal late in the afternoon of the first day where some officer from the Fourth Marine Division came and asked for volunteers to carry some wounded back. I was one of the four that volunteered. We carried them on litters, maybe as many as thirty guys, one after the other, after they had been treated by the corpsmen. Of course there were shells they were bombarding us with, but none came too close. The Japanese could shoot artillery or come out of their caves and rapidly fire off a couple mortars and duck back inside. They felt pretty safe. They had the range to hit any place on the island. Everything was bracketed.

"Well, this went on longer than we anticipated, way into the wee hours of the next morning, till two-thirty or three o'clock. We had left our outfit on the beach because we hadn't been landed too long, and when we came back, our outfit had moved. So there we were four of us, alone in enemy territory, and it was dark. We felt the enemy had a big advantage over us, knowing the terrain and one thing and another, so we were smart enough to dig a foxhole for the night. And that's where we stayed until the next morning.

"When daylight came, we went looking for our outfit, and after asking different people, we finally found them a few hundred yards up the beach, going away from Suribachi. When we got there, my CO [commanding officer] said one of us had to report. They designated me, and then he pointed up a hill and said, 'See those two officers standing up there? Report to them, and tell them briefly what happened last night and why you weren't with your outfit.'

"So I walked those fifty yards up the hill and talked to a Marine lieutenant colonel and a Marine major, probably from the Fourth Division. I briefly told them what had happened, how we came ashore and they asked for volunteers to carry wounded marines from inland to the beach to be sent out to the hospital ship. Turned out to be a longer job than we anticipated and we had to dig a foxhole and stay the night. When morning came, we started looking, and here we are, I said. One of them thanked me.

"This whole thing took probably a minute and a half. So I turned around and walked down the hill toward where my guys had already dug a foxhole for me near the beach. I got forty or fifty foot from them when a mortar landed just where the three of us had been standing. Of course it killed the major and the lieutenant colonel of Marines, and it blew me from that forty or fifty foot away clear on down, head first, into my foxhole. When I come up, I had a little blood on my left hand. Guys were kidding me about going down to the beach to the hospital tent and get it fixed. Anyway, I still can see a couple scars, so I don't know whether a piece of shrapnel hit me from that far away or whether the sand cut it when the concussion blew me into the foxhole. Turned out to be minor. But anyway, that was our first day and the first morning of our second day on Iwo. Why were they killed and me spared? The good Lord was looking out for me. It was also a good thing I didn't take too long to make my report.

"Seabees was kind of a moniker. It came from the NCB, which stood for Naval Construction Battalion. Our job was to unload ships and build or repair roads and airstrips. We were part of the Navy, but on Iwo Jima we were attached to the Fourth Marine Division. We wore Marine uniforms and were subject to Marine regulations.

"We also had the carryall, as we called it. Road graders they call them nowadays. I was born in 1926. I'm one of these dummies. I had some illnesses when I was young, and I quit school in eighth grade, when I was sixteen, and never got back to it. My dad had a sixty-acre farm, cows, horses, pigs, chickens, and a John Deere. Because I was born and raised on a farm and could run a tractor and drive horses, different things like that, they thought that I ought be able to run a bulldozer.

"I grew up near Armada in the Thumb district of Michigan. My given name was Perle, but somewhere along the line they took to calling me Dusty, because I used to get pretty dirty when I was a kid. I'm sure glad they didn't call me Dirty. But I lived with Dusty, and that's what most people know me as ever since."

Wouldn't Perle just confuse people anyway?

"Yeah. I was always mad at my grandmother on my father's side. That was her responsibility for giving me that name. I give my four kids all simple names like Pam, Deb, Bob, and Mike.

"Anyway, my older brother was in, and I knew it was just a matter of time before they'd draft me. It looked like the war was going to last for a while, so I just went down to the recruiting office in Detroit one day. I was going to join the Navy, but they talked about the Seabees and convinced me that was the way to go. I enlisted August 14 of 1943. I didn't know any better. I'd do it all over again, but I don't know if I'd have that much luck.

"We had basic training at Camp Perry in Virginia, and they give us the same training as they give the Marines. You had these drill instructors putting you through the ropes. Mainly it was just indoctrination, getting used to what the service was going be like, fundamentals. We didn't get into guns until we got to Camp Endicott at Providence, Rhode Island. We were there until the first part of 1944, and then we went to Biloxi, Mississippi, for more training, as I recall.

"We were trained with guns just like the Marines because we might get in a situation where we needed to defend ourselves, and then we were learning heavy equipment for road building and basic construction. The equipment was not armored. We crawled under live fire, through barricades, and learned how to knock down wire barriers. It was pretty advanced training as we moved along.

"We went from Biloxi to a camp in California between Oxnard and Ventura. We had bulldozers; we called them Cats for Caterpillar and road graders and road wheelers that tamped dirt on the airstrips. From there we went to Hickam Field in Hawaii. We were organized in platoons and companies. I was in the One Hundred Thirty-third Seabees, which turned out to have the most casualties, as I understand it, of any Seabee unit in history [reports vary, from 245 to 370, with at least 3 officers and 39 enlisted men killed].

"We had several more weeks' training at Hickam and then got on ships, headed out, and rendezvoused with the Fourth Marine Division, going to Iwo Jima. It was my first combat. I was just a wet-nosed kid, eighteen years old, a machinist's mate third class. The job was to defend yourself and build roads and airstrips. The equipment bogged down real fast in that coral ash when they tried to get it off the LSTs. We had these landing mats you put together to cross a bad area. They were folded and fit together by hooks. They were wide enough to drive over with jeeps or heavy equipment. We did the same thing on the airstrip, Motoyama No. 1, later on as temporary measure. We had the dozers or Cats; road graders and road tampers—heavy rollers—come in the belly of the LSTs later on.

"Before we could get our nose into things, you had to move the enemy out of there. We tried to stay alive and help organize things on the beach as we moved inland. Our job was to set up whatever they wanted, to assist the Fourth Marine Division, whatever their commanders wanted us to do, relayed to us through our officers."

According to a Seabee staff correspondent, Robert V. Evans, there were two battalions from the 41st Seabee Regiment at Iwo Jima, the 133rd, Dusty Ward's, attached to the Fourth Division, and the 31st Naval Construction Battalion, which was attached to the Fifth Marine Division. He reported that, following Seabee repairs, the southern airfield, Motoyama No. 1, was in use by February 26, a week after the invasion.

"We were there from February until the end of November. We stayed there long after the battle was over, built the airfields back up for B-29s to land, all that sort of stuff. We got shot at while driving the equipment, but that was about it. Those bulldozers were heavily made, so generally bullets would just glance off the blades and the metal parts. You were totally exposed, no armor other than the blade. Some guys got shot. Like I say, I was one of the lucky ones. We worked on Motoyama No.1 and No. 2, either rebuilding or refurbishing when there were bomb and shell craters, and then we maintained them as long as we were on the island. I saw *Dinah Might* land March 4, when it took out the telephone pole with one wing. I also saw B-29s come later with three motors gone, and I saw one hit the end of the runway where it dropped off onto a pretty steep bluff. It went right into the end of that thing and blew itself up.

"As far as what was on the island was concerned, there was no material value. Nobody would want that piece of land. But from the standpoint of strategic maneuvering, it was a good decision on America's part to take that island. They saved a lot of planes and a lot of lives coming back from bombing runs to Japan. They feel it saved something like twenty to twenty-five thousand lives, plus all those planes.

"When we left that November, we stopped by Guam on our way

back to the States. We were originally supposed to go to San Francisco, but for some reason, after we passed Hawaii, they decided to go to Seattle. We got there 19 December 1945. They gave us the choice to stay there and get discharged, which would delay our getting home for Christmas, or we could leave immediately, maybe make it home by Christmas, and get discharged later on. I chose to leave immediately. We took a train, and I'll always remember, after coming from the sunny South Pacific all that time, riding through these big snowbanks in Montana and places like that.

"Anyway, I walked into my family farmhouse at seven o'clock Christmas Eve 1945. My mom said I made quite a Christmas present. She was there and my father and younger brother would have been there. My older brother was Air Force, stationed in the Pacific. My discharge was delayed till the fourteenth of March 1946.

"I left Michigan before the winter of 1947 rolled around. I was spoiled by the Pacific, and I couldn't stand that cold weather anymore. My brother's got the farm, and he's got that same John Deere my dad owned. I ran it for a while after I got out of the service. It's still going strong. But then I went to California, and I've been here ever since."

Dusty fetched up in the San Fernando Valley and owned a gas station for a while, then went into real estate. He sold vacuum cleaners door-to-door, connected with Sears in the late forties and spent thirty-five years with the company, most of it in management, working all over California and Arizona. His last assignment took him to San Diego, and that was how he ended up in El Cajon, where he lives to this day.

He met Mabel in Riverside, California, during his first department manager job. He was told he was being promoted to a position in San Jose. Shortly after, he and Mabel were at dinner with one of her girlfriends one night.

"They knew I was going to San Jose, and I said something like, 'How are we going to work this?' And the girlfriend said, 'Well, why don't you guys up and go to Vegas and get married, and then you can go to San Jose together?'

"So that's what we did. It happened to be a Saturday night, and it happened to be my birthday, March 19, 1954. We went to Las Vegas and got married at the old Hitching Post, and that was it. We didn't think about it at the time, but had it worked out differently I wouldn't have wanted it on my birthday.

"I think the Seabees were a good outfit. Back on Iwo, we didn't have time to socialize much with other units. We stuck to our own area. It was pretty fast-paced, and they kept you pretty busy. I liked the bulldozer. All those years the Seabees never got credit for what they did. We should have received a Presidential Unit Citation, though. But I enjoyed my part in them. I'm glad it's behind me now; I feel lucky to be alive.

"My most vivid memory of Iwo was probably those six or seven seconds when I walked away from the major and the lieutenant colonel on the beach and how lucky I was. If I had been a long-winded guy and stood there another six seconds, I wouldn't be here today. I have probably lived that moment a thousand times since then and realize that no matter how good or bad in life you might be, luck has to play a very important part. The full realization of what happened to me that day has made me a better person, and I thank the good Lord for guiding me and putting me down the hill away from that artillery explosion. Of course the good part would be that I would have never known about it, because that Marine lieutenant colonel and major never knew what hit 'em. Their lives went out. There was no suffering there. There wouldn't have been with me either. I got to have a life instead."

16

PHARMACIST'S MATE THIRD CLASS
GEORGE WAHLEN

Navy Corpsman; Medal of Honor
Twenty-sixth Marines, Fifth Marine Division

[T]he last week aboard ship I think is the first time I ever prayed in my life. And in my prayer I always asked the Lord, I said, "If there's anything at all you can do, don't let me let one of my buddies down."

George Wahlen and Melba, his gracious and charming wife, in their Roy, Utah, home in May 2007. By the following August they had been married sixty-one years. A photo of George as a young corpsman hangs on the wall to his left.

Knees shaking, the last of fourteen men honored that afternoon, a petrified young pharmacist's mate, the first living corpsman to receive the Medal of Honor in World War II, is greeted by President Truman, who snatches his hand and says, "It's mighty good to see a pill pusher here in the middle of all these marines." Then he put the medal around George Wahlen's neck.

Two days before I was scheduled to fly to Roy, Utah, to visit George Wahlen in May 2007, he called to say he had just been hospitalized and maybe we should reschedule. When he found out my plane tickets were fixed, however, he offered to let me conduct the interview in his hospital room. Happily, he had been released by the time I got there, and I had a most enjoyable visit with him and his wife, Melba. Though George was not initially religious, he eventually joined the Church of Jesus Christ of the Latter-day Saints, and he and Melba went on to have five children, twenty-six grandchildren, and thirty-seven great grandchildren. I asked Melba how she handled all those birthdays. "It's simple," she said. "I just send each one a card and a two-dollar bill."

"I was born August 8, 1924. I was one of three boys. My father farmed, and later we moved into Ogden, Utah. My father had never been in the military, and he was kind of scared of what would happen to me if I went in, but he did let me quit school my senior year to take an aircraft engine mechanic's course at a college in Logan. Pearl Harbor was attacked the day after I enrolled. It was a six-month course, but I went for three and then had an opportunity to go to Hill Air Force Base near Ogden. I worked there several months. My dad still wouldn't let me join the service, but I went down and volunteered in June of 1943. I tried to join the Army Air Corps, but they said they were all filled up, so then I tried the Navy because I was told they had planes.

"I went by train to the Naval Training Center in San Diego for basic training June 18. I had a hard time learning to march. When I finished, they sent me to hospital corps school instead of aircraft mechanic's school. I tried to talk them out of it, but no one would listen. They told me if I did well, they might reconsider after I graduated, but that was baloney.

"I learned basic first aid; then they put me in a medical ward at the Naval Hospital in Balboa Park, San Diego, changing bedpans, cleaning floors, and being ordered around by female nurses. I was promoted to pharmacist's mate third class. I remember some nurse I didn't like got mad at me for not emptying some bedpans, and she said, 'If you don't shape up, I'm going to send you to the Marine Corps!'

"I thought about that and said to myself, 'I'm not going to be sent; I'll go volunteer.' I went and done it that day, and next morning I had my seabag all packed and went to the Marine Corps for seven weeks of further training. They sent me to Camp Elliott, gave me a Marine Corps uniform, and we had seven weeks of training, learning how to dress shrapnel wounds, splint bones, and treat an open belly wound. Instead of taking care of people in a ward and following a doctor or nurse's instruction, you had to learn how to treat wounds on the battlefield. Lots of times you get involved with sick ones too.

"I was in the Navy, but I was attached to the Marines and wore a Marine uniform. The Marine Corps medics were all Navy corpsmen. We had three months of training, including weapons. I trained with a carbine, the Browning automatic rifle, machine guns, hand grenades, forty-fives, everything. We got the same training as an infantryman. You were expected to know how to act in combat because you were in combat, same as the Marines. You were being shot at and exposed just the same as they was. You had no insignia showing you as a medic at all. You didn't want to; they claimed that was more dangerous. My pharmacist's rating translated me to a three-stripe sergeant. I was assigned to the Fifth Marine Division, which was activated January 1944. I was in Fox Company, Second Battalion, Twenty-sixth Marine Regiment.

"We sailed to Hawaii in late July 1944 and spent six months there at Camp Tarawa on the Big Island. We reached Saipan February 11, 1945, and left for Iwo on February 16.

"By now we knew where we were going. I remember the last

week aboard ship I think is the first time I ever prayed in my life. And in my prayer I always asked the Lord, I said, 'If there's anything at all you can do, don't let me let one of my buddies down.' For a nonreligious person, the comradeship you had with those marines was something that doesn't often happen in your lifetime. The thought of letting one of them down just really bothered me, and I think that's the feeling inside that I had. I would probably rather have been dead than let one of those guys down and know that I did. I worried about it before we went into combat.

"We went ashore late afternoon at Red Beach Two. There were bodies everywhere. We were in reserve, but we were also supposed to be protecting the left flank of the Twenty-seventh Marines. Three days went by without me having to treat a bad wound in my unit. The first one I treated, Lieutenant James Cassidy, died of a bullet wound near the heart.

"Then on D plus three, February 22, a shell blew the right leg off my platoon sergeant, Joe Malone. It also took the fingers of his right hand and the right side of his face. There was sand and thread from his dungarees in the stump of his leg, and I got a tourniquet on it and a battle dressing, wrapped his hand, and gave him a shot of morphine. Then I wrapped his face. The skin was peeled away, and his teeth, gums, and cheekbone were exposed. But he survived. A litter crew came and took him out of there.

"I was trying to catch up with my platoon after that, but then I heard another wounded marine moaning, and I crawled over to him. A machine gun had cut across his stomach, exposing his intestines. The important thing with this kind of wound is to keep it moist, so I soaked a battle dressing from my medical bag with canteen water and put that on and then gave him a shot. I went on from there and treated a man from my platoon. It went like that." [There were 120 killed from George's battalion that day alone.]

"I quit carrying my carbine, gave it away to a BAR man, because it just got in the way. About ten a.m. on the seventh day Fox Company was sent forward to relieve Easy Company. It started to rain. We'd move forward, but then the Japanese would follow in tunnels underneath and come out and attack us from the rear in areas we thought were secure.

"The Second Platoon was crossing a flat, open area about an acre in size when the Japanese waited for the right minute, then hit us with mortar and machine guns. I was trying to stay with my unit, but then I turned and saw about fifteen marines down, still under attack from mortars and artillery fire. My friend Eddie Monjaras was their corpsman, and I didn't see him out there.

"I crawled out and dragged a marine with a leg wound into a shell hole, wrapped him, then went out and crawled from man to man. I found Eddie, finally. He was hit in the chest and stomach. I treated him, but he died later. They tried to have two corpsmen assigned to a platoon, but they was lucky to have one, I think. Mortar kept falling, but I kept going until I got to them all, through about twenty minutes of it.

"I assessed the injuries, usually by the state of their clothes and by how much they were bleeding. As I remember, we did have scissors, but I don't remember using them. Under combat you'd do whatever you could to take care of the problem. Getting shot at and everything, you just didn't want to do any more than you had to to get the job done. Those I treated were all laying out there pretty much not moving, all exposed. I just crawled to each one of them, I think there were fourteen, and done that, took care of them. I remember I finally got back to my own team. I remember laying there thinking about what had happened. I was still there. I was amazed I survived. Not even scratched. How do you explain it? I've often wondered.

"I have no idea how or why I survived, without even a scratch. I crawled into a shell hole and got the shakes as I thought about it. I was worn out. But the platoon was moving again, so I followed. We were right near Hill 362A. Later that day a grenade went off as I was crawling, and several pieces of shrapnel cut my face. I couldn't see out of my right eye and I was bleeding, and I got a dressing out and wrapped the side of my face.

"I heard a call for a corpsman and I started crawling toward a wounded marine, but grenades kept landing near him. I finally saw a Japanese soldier come out of a cave on the hill and throw a fourth grenade. All I had was my forty-five, so I yelled down to some guys to throw me some grenades. They did so. Then I took some shrapnel in the rear and legs from another grenade as I crawled up toward the cave. I wanted to throw mine when he was coming out, but I couldn't pull the pin. The marine had bent it over, for safety. I straightened it with my Ka-Bar. I crawled up close enough, and after he threw out the next one, as I remember, I pulled it out and waited for a couple seconds before I threw it in, so it would go off right away. I knew those things could come back at you, and I didn't want to give him time to grab it and throw it.

"He jumped out, and my grenade got him. Then I went to treat the wounded marine, and I dragged him down the hill. His leg was torn up, the calf all exposed. Somebody came with a litter after a while, and we got him down and out. After that George Long, another corpsman, and I took care of several casualties. Then I went back for supplies because Long refused my order to go.

"My captain, Frank Caldwell, was at the command post, and he saw me all bloody with a bandage over my face and told me to go down to the aid station. But instead I just grabbed a bunch of bandages and battle dressings and things and headed back to my unit. He saw me two or three days later. I was still with my platoon, and he said, 'I thought I told you to go back.' I said, 'Sir, I was still needed.'

"I'll always remember one particular time when we had this marine brought back to me screaming and out of it. I was in a shell hole, and we held him down, and I gave him a shot of morphine. He got pretty quiet after laying there awhile; then I got involved taking care of more casualties up ahead. I finally come back to see if they got him evacuated, which I'd hoped to do. But he wasn't there, and I never seen him again until the reunions years later back here in the States. Our company commander asked everybody to speak a little bit, and so I did. A guy come up from the back of the group and started to cry. He said, 'Doc, you saved my life.' I didn't know who it was because he had a beard. I talked to him afterwards, and it turned out he was the guy who had cracked up. He says, 'If you hadn't of left me there, I would never have made it.' But he was one of the five out of two hundred fifty in my company that survived the whole thing."

By that night Wahlen had treated more than twenty of the forty-nine casualties suffered by Fox Company, according to his story, told in the book *The Quiet Hero*, by Gary Toyn. Eighteen were killed in action. The company was relieved the next day.

"We stayed in reserve until February 28, D plus nine, then it was back to 362A. We wound up alone on the front after the 327 pulled back, and Fox came under attack that night. Hill 362A was declared secure March 1. Fox Company had almost one hundred casualties with twenty-seven killed."

On D plus eleven Wahlen's company was in support of the 128 when several marines were shot and the corpsmen were busy. Near Hill 326B on Nishi Ridge, Wahlen crawled out to treat a marine whose legs were badly injured by a mortar shell. He was dragging the man to a safer spot when a shell went off behind and knocked George flying. When he came to, he could barely move, but he finally managed to crawl down the hill and into a shell hole, where he asked another marine to look at his back, which was badly gouged. He had the marine clean the wound and sprinkle sulfa powder on it, then wrap it with a battle dressing.

He continued to treat injured marines the next day as Fox Company was assigned to circle around Hill 362B as part of the assault. By noon it had gained three hundred yards, and by midafternoon it was moving up the hill. Then, around 4:00 p.m., Wahlen was rocked by a large artillery shell that landed on a number of marines in a shell hole.

"My strongest memory of Iwo was what turned out to be my last day in combat. As we were going up north, a group got hit with heavy fire, and as I was crawling up there, I got hit in the leg. There was casualties right in front of me, so I started to get up, but

I couldn't. I looked down at my foot, and part of my boot had been torn away, and my right leg was all bloody and broken just above the ankle. I pulled my boot off and put a battle dressing on it and give myself a shot of morphine. Then I crawled up to where the marines were. As I remember, there were about five of them, and they were all pretty well shot up. I think one guy lost a leg, and others were all beat up. I worked with them and bandaged them and give them morphine as long as I could. Finally they were evacuated. Then somebody out to our left flank got hit and started hollering for a corpsman, so I crawled out on hands and knees and took care of him too. He could have been forty or fifty yards out there, so I crawled out and bandaged him up, and we crawled to a shell hole. Finally we was both evacuated.

"The stretcher bearers came for us but then dropped me when rifle fire came. I got out my forty-five and started crawling toward the enemy. It was the morphine. They finally came and got me and took me to the aid station. Four of us went from there on a truck to the field hospital. My war was over. I think it was March 3. I was scared myself plenty of times. I always remember that feeling of being scared, but the thought of letting somebody down scared me even more." [Only 82 remained of the 250 in Fox Company that landed on D-day.]

"They finally got me on a ship next morning and took me to Guam. After several days there they flew me to Pearl Harbor. The leg was not healing well, and they sent me from there to a naval hospital in Oakland and then down to the U.S. Naval Hospital at Camp Pendleton. I had several surgeries because they couldn't get the blood to flow downward, and I was afraid I was going to lose my lower leg. It was months before I could walk on it.

"When I got home, I met my wife, and she was Mormon, so later on I joined the church. I had to give up smoking first, and that was a problem. I learned to smoke when I was with the Marines. I think when I got started, I was in the hospital there at Camp Pendleton. I remember spending all that time with those marines out on the porch, and they're all smoking. Every time you got up in the morning there'd be a pack of cigarettes on your bunk. I smoked whatever they gave me; I wasn't particular.

"I got the Navy Cross with a gold star [signifying two] when I was at Pendleton, and then in September they told me about the Medal of Honor. I flew to Washington, D.C., alone, and met my mother and father there and two aunts and uncles. There was fourteen Medals of Honor awarded that day, October 5, 1945, including Woody Williams [Chapter 5] and Franklin Sigler, who was in my company. Neither of us knew the other would be there. Here were all these generals and admirals and brass, and I was nervous. I believe I was the first living Navy corpsman in World War Two to get the Medal of Honor. I couldn't imagine something like that happening to me.

"As I remember, I was the last of the fourteen to receive my medal, and all that time here were all these high-ranking people sitting out there watching us. For a Navy corpsman to receive the Medal of Honor is almost unbelievable, so I was pretty nervous. Here's me, a lowly corpsman, shaking hands with the president. It was almost unimaginable. So when President Truman finally got to me, I started shaking. He saw it and grabbed my hand and said, 'It's mighty good to see a pill pusher here in the middle of all these marines.' Then he put the medal around my neck. I was not tall, five feet eight, and I weighed probably one hundred twenty."

Wahlen had violent nightmares for months after he came home. He went to junior college. Then an Army recruiter came after him, and once he was assured he could stay around as a recruiter himself, Wahlen went into the Army as a master sergeant.

"I kinda hesitated, thinking about going back to school. Then he promised me a tour on the recruiting side, and I wanted to get married, so I decided to go in. The medal was the reason they wanted me. Public speaking was a little tough on me, and I didn't like publicity, but I had to get over that."

He and Melba Holley married in August 1946, before he went back into the service. They had met on a blind date. Her father was opposed to the relationship at first because she was only seventeen, and George was a sailor, he took a drink now and then, and he smoked.

"I got sent to Japan from 1952 to '54,went to Korea in 1963, and I was in Vietnam during the Tet offensive in 1968. Somewhere along the line I ended up getting commissioned as a lieutenant. I retired in 1969, worked for the state, then spent ten years with the Veterans Administration in Salt Lake City."

Years went by before Melba even knew about George's Medal of Honor.

"She found out about it when we got our first invitation to go to a medal ceremony in the Rose Garden with President Kennedy. I didn't pass the word around."

Nobody ever asked him to return the Navy Cross and Gold Star, which were superseded by the Medal of Honor. And of course he holds two Purple Hearts.

George finally managed to quit smoking and became a full-fledged Mormon.

WAHLEN, GEORGE EDWARD

Rank and organization: *Pharmacist's Mate Second* [sic] *Class, U.S. Navy, serving with 2d Battalion, 26th Marines, 5th Marine Division.* **Place and date:** *Iwo Jima, Volcano Islands group, 3 March 1945.* **Entered service at:** *Utah.* **Born:** *8 August 1924, Ogden, Utah.*

Medal of Honor Citation:

For conspicuous gallantry and intrepidity at the risk of his life above and beyond the call of duty while serving with the 2d Battalion, 26th Marines, 5th Marine Division, during action against enemy Japanese forces on Iwo Jima in the Volcano group on 3 March 1945. Painfully wounded in the bitter action on 26 February, Wahlen remained on the battlefield, advancing well forward of the front-lines to aid a wounded marine and carrying him back to safety despite a terrific concentration of fire. Tireless in his ministrations, he consistently disregarded all danger to attend his fighting comrades as they fell under the devastating rain of shrapnel and bullets, and rendered prompt assistance to various elements of his combat group as required. When an adjacent platoon suffered heavy casualties, he defied the continuous pounding of heavy mortars and deadly fire of enemy rifles to care for the wounded, working rapidly in an area swept by constant fire and treating 14 casualties before returning to his own platoon. Wounded again on 2 March, he gallantly refused evacuation, moving out with his company the following day in a furious assault across 600 yards of open terrain and repeatedly rendering medical aid while exposed to the blasting fury of powerful Japanese guns. Stout-hearted and indomitable, he persevered in his determined efforts as his unit waged fierce battle and, unable to walk after sustaining a third agonizing wound, resolutely crawled 50 yards to administer first aid to still another fallen fighter. By his dauntless fortitude and valor, Wahlen served as a constant inspiration and contributed vitally to the high morale of his company during critical phases of this strategically important engagement. His heroic spirit of self-sacrifice in the face of overwhelming enemy fire upheld the highest traditions of the U.S. Naval Service.

17

SERGEANT CYRIL O'BRIEN

Combat Correspondent
Ninth Marines, Third Marine Division

Going ashore at Guam on D-day all I had was a forty-five-caliber pistol and a little Hermes; it was in my backpack. . . . Sheets of paper and everything. My whole office was in the backpack.

Cyril O'Brien at the Marine Corps Museum in Quantico in February 2007. He was eighty-seven at the time and writing regularly for such military magazines as *Leatherneck* and the *Marine Corps Gazette*.

Combat correspondent Cyril O'Brien interviews a marine holding a carbine "probably on our first day on Guam," O'Brien recalls, in June 1944. In O'Brien's left pocket is a hand grenade, still in its carton. "I guess I figured I could use it if I got in real trouble."

*Cy O'Brien, known to friends and acquaintances as Obie, is a
vigorous sprite of a man, not quite five feet five inches high,
energetic and vivacious at eighty-seven, still writing, still raising his voice. We met at the Iwo Jima Veterans Symposium in
Arlington, Virginia, in mid-February 2007, hit it off, and
started hanging out. He ended up telling me his story in my
hotel room. I offered him a scotch. He accepted. I joined him.
As our talk went on, we had a couple more, and then, as we
went down to dinner, I said something about martinis. "Martinis!" he exclaimed. "I just love martinis!" So we each had a
martini. Dinner followed, accompanied by wine. We both got
crocked.*

"My mother ran away from home in Newfoundland in the 1890s,
at the age of sixteen, and went to Camden, New Jersey, where she
worked as a chambermaid for several years. She said she saw the
great star Lillian Russell and her entourage sweep into some fancy
hotel in Atlantic City. Eventually she went back home and met
and married my father, who was a salty old son of a bitch. He was
a fisherman, and a good one. He had about a fourth-grade education, but intelligence and learning are not the same. He was very
intelligent. At the age of sixteen he went to sea, to Australia, all
over, and then came home to fish for cod. He was good at it. I was
born in Newfoundland in 1919, and we moved down to Massachusetts and then down to Camden, New Jersey, when I was nine.
I grew up in a blue collar part of town where nobody got any
higher education. My dad insisted I go to college. I don't think
there was anybody in four or five city blocks around me that went
to college.

"There was a Newfoundland guy in Camden who built docks.
Dad was used to the sea, and Dad was a carpenter, so it was easy
for him to get a job as a dock builder. I graduated from high

school in Camden 1938 and went to St. Joseph's, a Jesuit college in Philadelphia, across the Delaware River. I majored in English and philosophy. The Jesuits are big on philosophy. You had philosophy three days a week. You had Descartes! You had Spinoza! The Jesuits! Boy, they run you through it.

"At the same time I worked at the *Courier-Post* in Camden as a copyboy and then a reporter. I finished usually at one-thirty in the morning. I'd leave the college and go there at four in the afternoon. After they put the paper to bed, I studied there, or I went home and studied, or I didn't study at all. I made up for it on the weekends, cloistered myself, never went out, no fishing, no girls, no nothing. It was supreme discipline. You had to be motivated. But I knew it was the only way I could get through college. I think I made twenty-five dollars a week. My parents didn't have any money. I worked there the whole time I was in college. I did box while I was there. I always loved boxing. I took it for two years and never did learn to use the right hand.

"I managed to get hired because I always wanted to be a writer. Unlike other people who want to run things, I wanted to be a writer. At that time I wanted to do fiction, and right now I don't give a shit about fiction. I don't even read fiction. I thought I wanted fiction, but now I don't like it. I prefer reality. I was somewhere between quasi-reporter and copyboy. I took a course in typing in high school. I also learned shorthand. I wrote an article that appeared in *Family Circle* magazine; it was a handout in grocery stores.

"I wasn't heroic. I wasn't interested in the military. I didn't have a military mind. Had there been no war, I wouldn't have been a marine any more than I would have been a baker. But I knew I was going to be drafted. The only reason, really, why I went into the Marine Corps was . . . it's a shame sometimes how you do things just because you're challenged: The recruiters came out to the college seeking people for OCS, officer candidate school, and when they got to me, this recruiter said they wouldn't take me because I was too short, by less than half an inch! 'You're a half inch too short,' he told me. Those were his exact words. How chickenshit could you be? That was so chickenshit it was ridiculous! I mean that's childish, isn't it? Less than a half inch too short? That's crazy.

"So I got pissed off and I went down to the Marine Corps and complained. Rank didn't bother me. I didn't give a shit who they were. So I went into the colonel and shared my opinion with him, and he said, 'Well, if you're so interested in going into the Marine Corps, why don't you just enlist?' and I said, 'OK, I'll enlist.' So I went to Philadelphia, enlisted, had a month free, and I went in on July 21, 1942, and I landed on Guam July 21, in 1944, and I also got married on July 21—in 1950. Just coincidence.

"Parris Island was tough, it was challenging, but it was a wonderful experience. One night, in comes a runner: 'O'Brien!' He didn't say Mr. O'Brien. You weren't anything; you were a boot. He said, 'The record has it that you're a college graduate; why don't you go to officer candidates' school?' I was chagrined. I said, 'You turned me down!' He said, 'Well, look, you're in the Marine Corps now, so it doesn't make any difference. You wanna go to OCS?' I said sure, but I had a tendency to high blood pressure and I kept getting tested and everything got delayed, and I was training with the same guys, boondocking, and we completed boot camp in October.

"They had me doing sentry duty in Cape May, New Jersey, watching for subs, for a few months and then they sent us to New River and out to San Diego and Camp Pendleton, for more training, running up and down hills. Then we were all ready to go overseas. A day or two before we're going to leave, this guy comes into my tent and says, 'Obie, you're not going overseas. You're going back to OCS.' And I said, 'Horseshit! I'm going overseas!' Wouldn't you do the same thing? After all this training, I'm going for training again? Horseshit. So I went overseas. I don't know what kind of authority I had that way. I guess you can reject officers' school, can't you? Well, I did. I just rejected it.

"We arrived on Bougainville November 1943. It was fascinating going over the South Pacific, oh, my God! Why, I saw flying fish coming right up out of the water. I was a boot, and we came in as reserves, and they gave us all the lousy work. I was the number three mule in a mortar squad, humping ammo, out on patrol every day. You couldn't see, hear, or smell a man five feet away. It was the most dense jungle in the world. But I got off easy on two campaigns, Bougainville and Iwo Jima. But on Guam I made the assault, as a combat correspondent. I wanted to be a correspondent. It was in my mind, but I never knew where to go.

"Here's how that happened: After Bougainville we were sent to Guadalcanal for more training. Bill Burnette was a military correspondent, who had worked for the *Baltimore Sun.* He didn't know me at all, but I was walking by, and I saw he had a tent that said combat correspondent, and I went in and told him I was a newspaperman, and were there any chances, any opportunity for me? He says, 'You hit at just the right time. We're looking for a guy.' It was completely fortuitous, but that was how I became a combat writer. This was 1944. Pat Osheel was a newspaperman too, but he was a captain. He was the public relations director, and he took me on because I had been a reporter on the *Courier-Post* back in Camden. It was just completely fortunate that they needed somebody, a total accident. Correspondent! Just like that. The first job they gave me was a whole lot of medal citations. I had to find the guys who were being decorated and interview them and write them up and send them back to the hometown newspapers. It was doing rewrite in the city room. Most of them were for Bronze and Silver Stars. I'd write maybe five or six a day.

"I want to tell you what happened on Guam, but first I'll explain about Iwo Jima. I came in about March 12, after the second airfield was taken, and stayed about three weeks, writing up medal citations and going out with patrols. I had a forty-five caliber pistol and a little Hermes typewriter, and when I wanted to write something, I put it on my lap or on a box, anything I could find to hold it. They flew me in with a combat pack. We got fired on when I landed, and I had to get in under this jeep that was picking me up.

"Were they firing at me? I don't know, but whenever you hear firing, you get down. The fight was slowing down, but there were patrols that went out looking for Nips, and I went with them. This was mostly cleaning up, although there was some bitter fighting still to come. I used to love patrols. I went on patrols all the time. We never had night patrols. The reason I went on patrols is that you knew damn well something was going to happen, and the safest place you could be was behind a platoon of marines. I was behind the greatest bunch of marines in the world.

"And where was I going to use that forty-five? I did get into a fight. We were on a patrol, and all of a sudden I'll be damned the Japs started shooting at us from the bushes. The marines immediately put skirmishers out, and I had nothing but this goddamn forty-five. Soon they're heading toward the Japs. What the hell have I gotta move up for, with a forty-five? So I'm waitin' there, and all of a sudden, from behind this pile of logs, a Jap jumped up, and he's firing at me, and I said to myself, 'This son of a bitch, doesn't he know I'm a correspondent?'

"I know I was on Iwo March 26, the day the island was declared secured and those three hundred Japanese came down and killed all those pilots. I had been up around Kitano Point, but I went down the next day, when the bulldozers and three big Army trucks came loaded up with bodies. They buried them right down by Motoyama No. 1 airfield. They scooped out a big trench, laid them in neatly, then came along and dozed them over. The only reason I know I was there was because I saw them being buried.

"I had much more action at Bougainville, where I was infantry, and on Guam, July 21, 1944, by which time I had become a correspondent. I landed with the third assault wave on Guam. I wanted to cover the landing. I was thinking of the great epic of the war. But it was just a lot of fire, all confusion. I didn't know where to go or anything, so to play safe I jumped into a shell hole. All I had was a forty-five pistol and my Hermes; it was in my backpack. The top pack was my gear; the bottom pack was my Hermes. Sheets of paper and everything. My whole office was in the backpack.

"It was very hot, by which I mean artillery fire and mortars and machine guns were blazing from shore. The only thing is, it was unknowable. You landed, but you didn't know what was going on. You didn't know where to go. You only knew you had to get the hell off the beach because mortars are falling, and there's machine-gun fire all over hell, sparkling in the water. I therefore knew it was dangerous if I stood up, so I jumped into that shell hole. I stayed there awhile, and in true bravado I saw marines going by. Remember, I wasn't like them, I could go where I wanted to. But when I saw them going by, I said, 'Well, it must be safe,' so I got up and went with 'em.

"As I found my way around, a very interesting thing happened. Up on Chonito Ridge a marine says, 'Look over there, Obie.' And I saw a body tumbling down the ridge. He said, 'You know what, Obie? There's a Jap machine gun up there. A guy gets out there and shoots, and when he gets killed, they push him out and another guy takes over.' It was a kind of cliff face, and I just saw the body come tumbling down.

"I got ashore that first day with a guy who was the intelligence officer of the regiment, a very bright guy. I followed him. He says, 'Obie, we got a good spot.' He went up to the side of a cliff, side of a hill, and I dug the foxhole where the hill was going up. Well, he was so smart. You can't get hit by mortars there. You aren't getting attacked right there. It was like sleeping at home in bed. So all that night they battered the hell out of the beach, but they didn't bother me at all.

"I told you one time how, after you get used to danger, danger is danger? Later in that same day I remember a conversation. A marine was talking about Peoria, Illinois, and he says, 'Well, there's a church up there—' and all at once machine guns open up, and mortars are screaming in, and we all get down. Then it goes away, and he gets up and starts going on about Peoria again, calm as could be. What I mean to say is how even something as deadly as that can be kissed off. If that happened to you once, if you were a civilian, you'd remember it forever.

"The mentality amazes even me. Here I wanted to write this epic story of the landing, so I started to type, and I'll be damned, mortars started to fall in. And I said, 'Oh, shit!' I didn't say, 'Oh, shit,' because I was going to get killed. I said, 'Oh, shit,' because they were interrupting my writing. I hadn't even dug in: I was just typing. So when the mortars started falling, I jumped into a foxhole with a guy, and he said, 'Fine, Obie. It's fine.'

"It stops, and I go back to typing, and—God damn!—the mortars come again. So I jump in again. The third time he says, 'Obie, God damn, you got to dig your own foxhole!' The point I want to make is you got so interested in doing what you wanted to that you forgot about the danger. Isn't that something? They called me Obie, short for O'Brien. In the military all the emphasis is on the last name.

"I was wounded only once, on Guam during the landing. I felt wet and looked, and blood was running down my hand. I didn't know what had happened, never knew I was hit, never felt I got hit. All I did was see blood. As a correspondent you knew everybody, so I went up to the corpsman, and I didn't say 'wound,' I said, 'I got a cut here. Better put something on it.' I wouldn't have gone to a lot of trouble, but I was right with him, and he fixed it. Then he says, 'Obie, you're gonna get a Purple Heart.' I liked that, but then I looked around, and here was a guy with his leg split open, and there was a guy with his belly open. I says, 'Horseshit!' For a cut? I couldn't take it. He even wrote my name down, but I said no. Wouldn't you do the same thing? Had I been out on patrol and had been hit like that and nobody was around, I might have accepted it. But being right there with guys battered on the beach, I couldn't do it.

"I'll tell you when I felt bad. On Guam the biggest banzai charge that ever happened in the war was on July 26, 1944. I think they found three thousand bodies. It was like a flood. They came down at us, screaming and yelling. Somebody who wrote about it later said some of them knew they were going to die, so they tore up the pictures of their loved ones before they attacked. Maybe the banzai worked against the Chinese, but it would never work against serious marines. It was like shooting ducks in a barrel.

"You know I think the most wonderful, most highest journalistic praise I ever received, was on Guam. My company, Easy Company, Second Battalion, Third Marines, went up to outflank the Japanese who were holding the top of Chonito Ridge. Able Company had spent a day and a half in a frontal attack and couldn't do it. The Japs were so close, they couldn't throw grenades. They had to roll them down.

"My company went up the side. Three times our guys tried to assault that hill to get up there and was thrown back. Finally Easy Company flanked them, and we took the hill. I wrote about it, and it got published back in the States. It came back, and Captain Moore brought the company out, and with me standing there, the company commander had someone read the story out loud. Isn't that great? You couldn't get a better tribute than that.

"I went back to Guam from Iwo and stayed there till September of 1945. I got out in October of 1945. Back in the States, I returned to my old job at the *Courier-Post* in Camden. After a strike in 1947, I wound up at the *Long Island Press*, the most colorful newspaper I ever worked for. From there I went to the paper in Stroudsburg, Pennsylvania, where a combat correspondent name of Hamilton offered me a job covering the Capitol for the Irwin News Service.

"Journalism is fascinating, isn't it? I show up at the office, and he says, 'Obie, get up to the Capitol and to the Senate Cloakroom. Senator Taft's having a press conference on the price of natural gas at the wellhead.'

"What the hell did I know about natural gas at the wellhead? But as a reporter, when you're told to do a story, you do it, I don't care what it's about."

Cy O'Brien eventually moved on to do media work for the Applied Physics Lab at Johns Hopkins University in Baltimore. He and his wife adopted four children. She died in 1975. He never remarried. Obie retired from Johns Hopkins in 1985 but still maintained a weekly column for two newspapers and went on to write extensively for the *VFW Magazine*. He continues to write for such Marine Corps publications as *Leatherneck*. He is the author, among other things, of a definitive thirty-eight-page account of the battle of Guam for the World War II Commemorative Series entitled, *Liberation: Marines in the Recapture of Guam*.

Here is a sample of his reporting on Chonito Ridge, taken from a carbon copy he saved and donated to the Marine Corps. It is the piece Captain Moore had read out loud to the company:

Guam July 25 (Delayed) Nearly half my old company lies dead on the barren slopes of Chonito Cliff. Four times they tried to reach the top. Four times they were thrown back. They had to break out of a twenty yard beachhead to make way for later landing waves. They attacked up a 60-degree slope, protected only by sword grass, and were met by a storm of grenades and heavy rifle, machinegun and mortar fire.

The physical act of forward motion required the use of both hands. As a consequence they were unable to return the enemy fire effectively. Most of the casualties were at the bottom of the slope. They had been hit as they left cover.

There was Pappy, his name stenciled on his canteen cover. A bullet had ripped away the first "P" in his name.

My former assistant squad leader was beside him. He often had me on his working parties. I had seen those arms of his, which in death still clutched a splintered rifle, throw full ammunition cases about as if they were empty.

There was the first scout of my squad. We had shared the same tent for months. He was always promising himself "a white Christmas in forty-five." He was facing the sky, his hands at his sides. You'd think he was dreaming

Willie, who volunteered for mess duty so he "wouldn't have to stand inspections," was lying halfway up the slope. His feet were dug into the dirt. His arms were bent as if he were ready to charge again, but his Garand rifle was empty and thrown aside. The pistol in his hand was empty too. Perhaps he intended to club the enemy with the empty weapon.

The "Beast"—we called him that because he was so big—had charged his big frame to within five yards of an enemy machine gun nest. He caught a blast in the chest. The fancy lettering he always placed on the back of his dungaree blouse was torn by bullets.

There was Frankie, who had received a shiny, chrome-plated pistol from home. He had boasted he would get many Japs with it. Now the sun's rays from over the ridge glinted on the handle. The pistol was still in its holster.

Peter had a strong voice in camp. He had it in the face of death. He was halfway up the ridge, yelling something about the "bastards" on the top, when their fire cut him down.

The lieutenant we called "Chicken" because he seemed so young was the only one to reach the crest. A grenade smashed in the side of his head. Those skinny legs which had led me so often to exhaustion were white in the dried grass. Two Japs, five feet in front of him, had holes in their heads. An American grenade which the Chicken evidently had thrown was lying between the Japs. How often the lieutenant had drawled in his slow hesitant tone: "Now, a grenade—it explodes five seconds after you heave it." His hadn't.

Eddie was lying in a bed of mountain flowers. He was fond of flowers. He used to put them in his helmet for camouflage when others used grass. The hand that was not on a rifle was crushing a flower.

Behind the lieutenant, his face anxious as if awaiting an order, was Angelo. He loved to sing—but couldn't. He and I were penalized once for singing "Put on Your Old Gray Bonnet" after taps.

The company was still under fire when, on the ridge, I talked to the men who had made it. Private First Class Leon Slicner of Perth Amboy, New Jersey, tried to tell me how "Smokey" could have been saved had they been able to pull him out of the fire lane in time. His words came slow. Finally, he stopped in the middle of sentence, leaving the story in midair. He really didn't want to talk. Besides, he was pressing low into a foxhole, and he couldn't breathe well, for a machine gun was spitting fire over our heads.

Following are some samples of Sergeant O'Brien's combat correspondence on Iwo Jima, culled from carbon copies he had saved and donated to the Marine Corps:

Somewhere in the Marianas — How a Marine machine gun section repulsed a Jap night attack on Third Marine Division lines on Iwo Jima was told by Corporal Herbert J. Bovia, of New Orleans, La., the squad leader.

The 20-year-old Marine, who lives at 518 General Pershing Street, led a six man team which with two machine guns filled a gap between two platoon defenses. Due to the nature of the terrain, Corporal Bovia's unit dug in 20 yards beyond the rest of the front line.

Enemy small arms fire ceased at darkness, and, except for the pounding of artillery on the right flank, the front was quiet. It was nearly two in the morning when Bovia's gunner saw a figure crawling toward their position.

Bovia scanned the area to his front. Other figures hopped over a low ridge not twenty five yards from the muzzle of the corporal's machine gun. Crouching, the Japs moved toward the Marine lines. They did not see the machine guns that lay in their path until the raking fire cut into them. Three figures slumped dead on the volcanic rock.

Yelling and throwing grenades the others charged the exposed machine gun positions. Grenades exploded near Bovia's parapet and he was sprayed with dirt and stones. Two grenades exploded in the No. 2 gunpit, wounding the gunner and killing his two assistants.

The machine gun fire disorganized the night attackers, but they still rushed his position, and Bovia was in danger of being cut off from the rest of the Marine line.

"The Nips were trying to get behind us," Corporal Bovia said. "We killed three who almost made it. Our only choice was to get back to the lines, so I disabled the machine gun, and abandoned it. We dashed back to the company and the Nips were hot on our heels.

"From the lines we blasted the Nips again, but it was nearly fifteen minutes before the attack stopped."

When morning arrived fifteen Japs were found dead in front of the Marine guns. Blood trails on the jagged ledges showed that at least six Japs had staggered away seriously wounded.

Overseas for twenty-seven months, Bovia saw action on Bougainville and Guam. Before entering the Marine Corps in December 1941, the New Orleans marine was a doffer in a cotton mill near his home.

The next example describes an ambush:

Iwo Jima — We planned to trap the Japs tonight in a small ravine that sheltered several waterholes.

Under cover of dusk and the rising evening mists, we crept to our ambush position behind the boulders that ringed the waterholes, and waited.

Enemy stragglers, driven by thirst from their cave hideouts in the surrounding volcanic rock cliffs, ventured here nightly to drain the muddy puddles into their canteens. Their sandal tracks dotted the the moist sandy margins of the holes.

I hid with a 9th Marines machine gun squad, whose weapons pointed down a foot trail that led to the cliffs. The gunner, Private William E. Winkler, whispered a curse to the cold and pulled his blanket over his shoulders.

He had no time to enjoy the blanket's warmth, for he threw the cover off and stared behind him. Footsteps sounded to our rear. Japs were coming for water.

Privates Leo M. Chabod and Jack Woenne covered the rear approach from an adjacent foxhole.

Five figures, hugging the side of the trail, walked past the muzzles of the ambushers' rifles. The leader carried a mess tin, which tinkled on its handle as the Jap moved. Behind him the others carried canteens and bringing up the rear a stubby Jap, who continually glanced behind him, carried a water bucket.

Chabod let them enter the center of our ring. They cluttered around the waterhole and the leader was looking into it when Chabod's automatic rifle stuttered. The Jap carrying the bucket grabbed his back with both hands. The bucket rolled between his legs and the Jap pitched on his face. Another ran for the back trail but Woenne's fire followed him there, and he slumped in a heap on the trail's edge.

The Jap who carried the mess gear was already running down another trail, his mess gear clanging like a cheap bell. He swerved toward the cover of an overhanging ledge but was affronted by the foxhole of Pvts. Raymond Tenavitz and Thomas Cashin.

Cornered, the Jap pulled a grenade and was extracting the safety pin when Cashin's rifle fire sprung him into a somersault and the Jap rolled down an incline dead, the grenade still in his hand.

Two Japs still hid somewhere in the center of our ambush but Private Victor Schmidt soon routed them with a hand grenade.

The Japs leaped from the base of a dead tree. Resigned to sell their lives dearly, they rushed the foxhole occupied by Private First Class Robert Wolf and Private Fred Herrick Jr. The leader flung a grenade and was within ten yards of the foxhole with another in his left hand when Herrick's M-1 barked. The attacker spun and fell on his back. Herrick sprang from the hole and blasted the Jap again, to make sure.

Trapped and confused, the last Jap ran to the tree, changed his mind and charged back over the body of his dead companion and out of the ambush.

Silence fell again except for the occasional rasping scratch of a land crab or the moan of a tortured tree. An animal ran across the trail that was our fire lane, but that was all that came during my watch.

I had awakened Private Duane Wills to relieve me, when two carbine shots cracked in quick succession to our right. We turned in time to see Private First Class Dale Beckett dive into a rock pit as a hissing grenade passed over his head and exploded behind him.

In a draw below, a Jap slumped over an abandoned enemy satchel, two bullets through his neck. Another Jap hugged the shadowed sides of a draw from where he had thrown his grenade.

The Jap could not be seen in the shadows, but he made a frantic dash into the moonlight to escape from the draw. Two .30 caliber slugs passed through his head. Private First Class Harper R. Rudge guarded the ravine from the opposite wall. Rudge crawled to the edge of the draw, tossed a grenade, then disappeared behind the rock barricade.

Star shells were falling continually now over the beach area to our front, and in the distance a machine gun clattered.

"Doggies," [Army soldiers] Wells said. "The Nips are giving them trouble again." He stared back on the trail and hunched his body over the machine gun. I curled up at his feet in an attempt to sleep, but he soon tapped my helmet. Japs were again back on the trail.

Four walked boldly into our ring, gibbering among themselves. From behind a stone wall a burst of fire cut into the Japs. Two doubled over and fell. Private Patrick J. Cleary Jr. stood upright in his foxhole and cradled his Browning Automatic Rifle.

Shot through the legs, a Jap dragged his body with his elbows toward a grenade bag but before he had moved three feet another burst from Cleary's weapon caught him in the chest.

Another Jap, his right leg shattered, moved with surprising swiftness toward Chabod's position. The Marine dropped on the ground beside his companion as a grenade bounced off the parapet and exploded. The Jap was still rushing with a second grenade when a shot from Woenne's rifle caught him in the middle. He dropped in a sitting position, dead.

On the road, the first Jap caught in Cleary's surprise fire raised his body on his left arm. A grenade sputtered in his hand but this Jap was through fighting. He exploded the missile under his chest.

Dawn, and the ambushers stirred from cover in the crypts and behind the rocks. Through habit they still spoke in low tones.

Private First Class Ferdinand Leon found a bloody trail. Someone had dragged a wounded Jap away. He followed the trail for 20 yards but lost it on the jagged slope.

We filed back past the waterholes, and for the first time I looked in them. Eleven Japs had come carrying canteens, buckets and mess tins. Nine had died here.

There was not enough water in the well to fill a single canteen.— Sergeant C. O'Brien.

[In a note accompanying this story, O'Brien wrote that after the ambush in the dawn hours, "I went to the Japanese bodies and found one had been taken away. I found and followed the tracks of a dragged body up into a kind of field where I lost it. Whoever had rescued that body or person had come in under our guns to do it, and got away with it. There's heroism here. That was a waterhole and you know what water meant there and then."]

Finally, this one:

Somewhere in the Pacific — *A Memphis, Tenn., Marine, Corporal Kenneth R. Sigman, 22, is alive today because a Jap on Iwo Jima forgot to wear a helmet.*

The Jap was a member of a band of night attackers which crept from the well stocked caves in the north section of the island to harass Third Marine Division lines. All the Japs wore helmets except the soldier who attacked Sigman's position.

The Japs carried grenades, but before throwing them, they had to strike the missiles on their helmets to ignite the fuses. The bareheaded Jap hit the grenades on his bare head, then flung the explosives at Sigman.

But the Jap's head was not hard enough. The grenades landed harmlessly on the foxhole parapet, three feet from Sigman's head.

18

SERGEANT THOMAS HAYWOOD McPHATTER

Eighth Marine Ammo Company

Nobody in combat can live without food or ammunition.

"No cross, no crown," his mother used to say. Sitting in his San Diego home, a bust of the flag raising beside him, former Sergeant Thomas H. McPhatter, eighty-three, holds a copy of his self-published book *Caught in the Middle: A Dichotomy of an African-American Man (They Called Him Troublemaker)*. The back jacket says McPhatter "challenged injustice and racism wherever he encountered it, in the U.S. Marine Corps, the Navy, in civilian employment, in college and in the church." Photo by Carole Strasser

Commander Thomas H. McPhatter, fifty-three, of the Navy Chaplain Corps, photographed in San Diego in 1977. He retired as a captain in 1983.

I asked Thomas McPhatter over the phone at his home in San Diego if he had been a Montford Point Marine and whether he had known Hashmark Johnson and Edgar Huff. Yes, and yes, he replied. Montford Point was the segregated base where blacks were sent to be trained by the Marine Corps following the issuance of an order by President Franklin Roosevelt in June 1941 stipulating "full participation in the defense program by all persons regardless of color, race, creed or national origin." Johnson and Huff became well-known leaders at Montford Point. McPhatter and the roughly twenty thousand who trained there during the war were not considered suitable for combat, although they were trained to fire the rifle. Between fifteen hundred and two thousand blacks served on Iwo. Each Marine division had a regimental service battalion or field depot staffed by black marines, not to be confused with the Army DUKW drivers. There were stevedore units that were part of the shore party battalions. The depot companies' job was to move supplies from beachfront to supply dumps and from dumps to tractors and weasels (small tracked vehicles) and moved to the front by motor transport battalions. Blacks also worked in Graves Registration.

"I come from Lumberton, North Carolina, but I've called San Diego my home for over fifty years. We trained at Montford Point and practiced landings at New River. Second Lieutenant John D'Angelo had the first section of our platoon, and I was a sergeant and leader of the second section, First Platoon, Eighth Marine Ammo Company. We came ashore at Iwo Jima D plus one in an LST.

"I did not go up on the summit of Suribachi, but we were established at the foot of it. We had crawled from the LST up near

Suribachi to establish an ammo store to supply the Third, Fourth, and Fifth Divisions. They were running ammo on a conveyor out of the mouth of the LST onto the sand. My lieutenant, D'Angelo, and I crawled up there to find a secure place for the dump. We chose a spot, and he went back to get the rest of the troops.

"After growing up in Lumberton, I became a pretheological student at Johnson C. Smith University in Charlotte. I was the eleventh child in our family and the only male. My mother had ten girls. I didn't have to go into the military. I also worked during the summer for a dry dock company in a Newport News shipyard, so I had an exemption there too. But I was back on campus, and all my friends had got into the ERC, the Enlisted Reserve Corps, which was supposed to allow them to stay in college till they had finished their education and then go into the military. Well, the buses came up from Fort Jackson, South Carolina, one day and pulled them right out of class and took them away.

"This left me one of the very few males on campus, and I didn't feel right because I didn't know whether I was ministerial material. My mother wanted me to be a minister because she felt I was a godsend. My pastor wanted me to be a minister, but I didn't know if that was where I should be.

"I'm thinking: I don't want to be here because the war will be over and I'll be considered a draft dodger. I went to the Merchant Marines, but I was too young, I wasn't twenty-one. So then I went to the Marine Corps, and they said you have a 4D deferment. We can't take you unless you're reclassified to 1A. So I got myself reclassified and joined the Marines. So here I was on the train to New Bern with these black marines strutting through the train, walking on me like I was grit. At Jacksonville a big truck came, and the driver made me get in the back. It was cold, January of '43, and that was how I landed in Montford Point. They told me to say yes, sir, and no, sir, to every uniform and to salute them all.

"Hashmark Johnson and Edgar Huff were there. Hashmark was the top man, Huff was the battalion sergeant major. Boot camp lasted twelve weeks, and it was not difficult for me. I had just pledged a fraternity, and they did so much hazing on me that the way they treated me at Montford Point didn't bother me. I was used to it. I came out a PFC because I fired expert at the rifle range.

"I almost became a chaplain out of boot camp in March, and I was just getting snapped into the job when a man came in whose wife was about to have a baby, and he wanted the job. I said he could have my place. I said I'd rather be with the fellas I had come through boot camp with. So I gave that up to go with Eighth Ammo.

"We did part of our training at nearby New River, making landings and getting combat swimming instruction. They saw I had some college and they sent me to ammo tech school to learn about fusing rockets and mortars and propellants, how to store ammo, TNT, bangalore torpedoes, small arms, firing caps, that kind of stuff. We learned how to store ammo and how to move it. I had taught water safety back in Winston-Salem, so I volunteered and began teaching troops combat swimming, how to make life preservers out of mattress covers, pillowcases, or trousers. I was at Montford Point perhaps a total of six or seven months.

"We went to the West Coast late in 1943 and from there to Hawaii, at Camp Catlin, where we didn't feel we were being trained properly. The white boys were getting overnight liberty and weekends, and we had liberty for five, six, or seven hours. I wrote a letter to my mother and told her the very things I had got into the Marine Corps to get away from I'd run right into the middle of, which was racism. Well, all the letters were censored, and when they read that, they had me go see the captain and executive officer. The executive officer said, 'Did you write this, McPhatter?' 'Sir, yes, sir.' 'Why did you write it?' 'That's the way I felt, sir.'

"He said, 'Well, you're from Lumberton, and I'm from Asheville, and you've had more college than I.' I said, 'Sir, that's exactly what I'm talking about. You're the executive officer and a lieutenant, and I'm a sergeant.' He said, 'Well, the captain wants to see you.'

"The captain said, 'Did you write this letter?' 'Sir, yes, sir.' 'Well, what do you mean by you came into the corps and had more racism? Didn't you know this letter was going to be read? Why did you do that?' I said, 'It was the only way to let you know how I felt without being charged with insubordination.'

"I had more trouble when they wanted me and my men to move a big stack of corroded ammunition from an underground magazine, to be taken out to sea and dumped. I refused because it was too dangerous. Lieutenant D'Angelo stuck up for me, and that's what made me love the man. He was a man. He knew what I did was right, but he never said anything to me about it, just led us on a forced march to get us off the hook. My career was loaded with that.

"I was run up to the captain so many times, even on the ship to Iwo Jima. They had me up there, trying to get me busted. I had to do it. I had to insist on my rights.

"We landed on D plus one on Blue Beach right at the foot of Suribachi. We were standing by to go in the first day, but the Japanese just turned all hell loose after the first three waves came ashore. They came out of caves and holes, gun emplacements, everything else. You could hear men from ship to shore; you could see planes flying overhead trying to drop stuff and the big guns firing off the carriers. They killed a lot of our own men on that island.

"The beach was still very hot when we went in on the second day. Men were there dead and dying, still trying to get up off the beach, bodies bobbing in the surf. We worried about broaching and had to get pontoons off on the side so we could anchor the LST and get the tractors and trucks and guns out of the belly of the ship. They dropped some mats down as they landed. I had to go set up the ammo dump. You had to be very careful where you walked because of the mines.

"We were waiting for the DUKWs, big rubber-tired vehicles that could go through water, to move ammo up forward where we were putting it in store up by the first airfield. We had men who didn't want to go. They were afraid. They were saying, 'Shoot me,

I ain't going up there.' Lieutenant D'Angelo was my hero. He never asked me to do anything he wasn't willing to do first. So we went up there and got this dump and a perimeter set up. Nobody in combat can live without food or ammunition.

"We kept moving that ammo on up until one night here's a little gift, *pip pap pup*, mortar dropping into our ammo dump. Pretty soon a charge went off that shook the whole island. A captain came running up and told me to get a detail and go in there and put the fire out. I said, 'Sir, it is burning. I don't know how I can stop it. We need an armored bulldozer.' Lieutenant D'Angelo said, 'Let's go in,' so I started to run with him, but then that whole dump started going off, shells flying everywhere. A smoke shell fell near me and burned my face. We all started running for the beach, hollering the password for that night, which was American Trees. You didn't know who would shoot you. If you didn't give the password, they'd just blow you away.

"The next day the lieutenant told me to see how many men we had left, and I was going around to the ships in the harbor to see how many I could find. I told them we were going up to the dump to see what was left. Four or five of our men never got out of their holes. They were dead.

"Then a priority order came through for hand grenades, howitzer shells, and we didn't have any left. So they flew it in from Saipan, but the planes couldn't land, so they dropped it in parachutes. Lieutenant D'Angelo told me to get my sections up on the side of the airport and chase the parachutes. Now we're running after these parachutes of ammo scared to death. Then the Japanese spotted us and came in with a barrage of mortar fire, and now everybody's running for cover, and I jump into a bunker. A young white marine was there, holding on his chest pictures of his girlfriend, mother, and all. He had blood coming out of his mouth, his ears and his nose. He was dead. I had to try and scrape out a hole with my helmet out of that ash big enough to put my head in because that was the only thing I could protect.

"I lay there next to him and said the Lord's Prayer over and over, along with the Twenty-third Psalm, until the all clear was given. I made a promise to God if he let me live, I'd give my life to him in service. I never looked back. It may sound heroic, but it really wasn't. I wasn't in for the flash. I was a driver of men, and I knew if I got it, they would do the same thing."

After the war McPhatter went back to Johnson C. Smith University, became a pastor, and later entered the U.S. Navy Chaplain Corps and served in Vietnam as a captain. He retired from the military in 1983. He is a retired Presbyterian minister with a Doctor of Divinity from the Interfaith Theological Center in Atlanta.

Have things improved for blacks in the military since the days of Iwo Jima?

"They have improved, but you know I'm a marine and, if it's wrong, I think it ought to be right. There are no shades of right and wrong. Justice has no shades. Was it King who said justice prolonged [delayed] is justice denied? I'm eighty-three years old. If it's not here now, when am I going to see it? I just cannot be at ease with anybody being treated unjustly. I'm a champion of the underdog, right from the beginning of my life. I was known as a black Moses in the Chaplain Corps. They even kicked me out for a spell. I don't care what color they are. If it's unjust, let's make it just. My Lord says, 'Be in the world but not of the world.' I want the world to be different than it was before I came in here. I can't help myself."

The Army DUKW Drivers

Pat Mooney, who is associated with both Military Historical Tours and the Iwo Jima Veterans' Association, as well as the Marine Corps Museum in Quantico, has this to say about the Army's black soldiers, who were associated with the Marines on Iwo Jima:

"Each Marine division had an Army DUKW company assigned to it. These consisted of black enlisted personnel and black NCOs commanded by white officers. Sergeant Fred Gray was one of the unsung heroes of Iwo Jima. Fred was part of the 471st Amphibious, attached to the Fourth Marine Division.

"The contribution of these three Army amphibious companies really has gone unnoticed. They labored from D-day all the way through the battle with these vehicles, called DUKWs [pronounced *ducks*], which were absolutely phenomenal but very tippy. [The *D* meant it was designed in 1942, the *U* meant "utility," or also amphibious, and the *K* indicated four-wheel drive while the *W* meant there were two powered rear axles.] They were fifteen feet long, eight feet wide, usually mounted with a machine gun, and crewed by a driver and codriver.

"Their preliminary job was to bring guns in for the Marine artillery regiments, and they brought these ashore on D-day as well.

"They were plagued by the heavy plunging surf on the east beaches. The high freeboards were not meant for heavy surf, and the DUKWs themselves were not really meant for oceangoing traffic. Add to that the heavy loads of artillery and ammo and then float it ashore, bring it on land, and then unload a heavy one-oh-five-millimeter howitzer from the back of this DUKW via an A-frame that was either manhandled by a bulldozer or other vehicle to hoist this one-oh-five millimeter off the back. It was built on the chassis of the famous deuce and a half, the six-by truck, and classified as a two-and-a-half-ton truck. Propulsion through water was provided by an additional transmission with two screws, or propellers, in the back. Because of plunging surf and tidal conditions, the DUKWs had a tendency to broach to port. They would be pushed against the beach, and once a DUKW or any ship broached in that surf, it was only a matter of time before wave action would cause the vehicle to flip over.

"There were also many documented instances of these DUKWs coming heavily loaded off the bow of an LST and sinking. You had a combination of horror and excitement of coming off the bow of a ship in an amphibious vehicle where the vehicle actually submerges and you fervently pray it will rise back to the surface. Amtracs as well came off these ramps, and for whatever reason, the nose went under, and they plunged to the bottom of the ocean with their loads of equipment and any people who could not get out.

"This was about two miles offshore. I can only imagine the confusion. You watch the films and listen to the accounts and see these things plunge off the big boats and circle around and move in under fire. And they'd be stuck at sea, sometimes ramming into each other, missing the control boat, sailing around for hours in choppy water because crafts ahead had broached.

"Particular actions that strike me came after they had brought in supplies or artillery, and then their job was to reload under fire on that beach from some of the finest artillery ever massed in the Pacific. They had to load wounded on board and take them back to the ships, making that round-trip all day long. In one case, the stern anchor on this DUKW broke loose and the ship was broaching with wounded aboard, and the brave actions of the African American crew to go out and resecure anchors to bring that DUKW back from broaching saved the lives of every wounded marine and sailor aboard. Had they not done so, the DUKW surely would have been flipped in the surf and the men would have been crushed or drowned."

Bruce Jacobs of Alexandria, Virginia, was a combat historian from the Army's Central Pacific Command in Hawaii, assigned to record Army participation in the Iwo Jima campaign. But the only Army involvement initially consisted of the three DUKW companies. "They were the Four Hundred Fifty-second Amphibian Transportation Company and the Four Hundred Fifty-third and the Four Hundred Fifty-fourth. The Four Hundred Fifty-second, the one I was attached to, was with General Rockey's Fifth Marine Division. My recollection is that there were eighteen to twenty vehicles in each company, so sixty would have been involved altogether. I only remember hearing about two sinking on the way in from the ships, but I wasn't that peripatetic. I didn't get around that much.

"When you hit the beach, it was pretty much necessary to make sure the tires were deflated so you didn't skid on the sand, and then you have to know when to inflate them so you could keep moving. The requirement on D-day was to get some of General Rockey's seventy-five-millimeter-howitzers ashore. But when they got to our part of the beach, it wasn't soft and sandy, like the photos had led everybody to believe, it was an eighteen- to thirty-inch escarpment, and the tires couldn't make it up and over.

"Almost out of nowhere a Seabee in a little tractor of some kind came down the beach, and he was able to hook on to the DUKWs and get them up over the escarpment, where they could inflate their tires and take off. They worked with that Seabee all afternoon the first day until he got killed.

"The DUKW drivers were a terrific bunch of people. They had a lot to prove, and they knew it. A lot of the Army guys, between you and me, expected them to fail, and I think that when the word started to get back to our bosses in Hawaii as to how well they were doing, there was a considerable amount of surprise. You got to think a little bit about what the Army was like in those days. It was not necessarily the grandest moment in our national history.

"The Four Hundred Fifty-second got a Naval Unit Citation based on the recommendation of an amtrac battalion commander. The stories I heard about the other two companies indicated that they did just as well as the Four Hundred Fifty-second.

"The thing I have to say is that to me, Iwo Jima is the Marine Corps story, and I have always resisted anything that looked like the Army was trying to edge in. The Army contribution was tiny, and when you look at the casualties, it's just staggering when you consider the number of young marines who got killed up there. So I don't think the participation of the Army in the battle is worth more than a footnote to history, including the participation of the black DUKW drivers."

On March 4, 1945, *Dinah Might* becomes the first B-29 bomber to land on Iwo Jima
following the invasion. Hasty repairs were made in the thick of the battle, and she
took off half an hour later. No one was hurt, but the pilot and the entire crew
were killed when the plane was shot down over Kawasaki on April 14.

AP Wide World Photo, from the U.S. Marine Corps

PART SIX

The Planes That Came

The principal reason for invading Iwo Jima was to provide emergency landing strips, as Bob Merklein and Victor Chepeleff and Phil True point out, for the thousands of planes flying the three-thousand-mile round trip from Tinian and Saipan. Both True's and Chepeleff's B-29s stopped for repairs. Altogether 2,251 B-29s with 24,761 crew members landed on Iwo Jima. The first B-29, *Dinah Might*, landed on March 4, in the thick of the battle, made repairs, and got out of there. A number of other B-29s landed on Iwo before March 15. At one time there were as many as 300 B-29s on Iwo.

The *Midpacifican*, published in Honolulu during the war, ran an article on March 24, 1945, about a "blind" B-29 crash landing on Motoyama No. 1 on March 10. Its lead paragraph said: "Last night more than 200 Superforts raided Tokyo and today five of them landed on Iwo's recently won Airfield No. 1. One of them cracked up after an amazing seven-hour trip with only two engines run-

ning, no compass and no other navigational aids." It added that
clouds were so thick the plane was unable to fly above them to get
a fix from the stars and the pilot, Lieutenant G. S. Savage of
Collinsville, Illinois, "couldn't give enough praise" to its navigator,
Lieutenant. W. D. Born, "who just got us here somehow."

Departing from the Marianas at 2:00 a.m., the plane had
bombed Tokyo's "new business district" from a height of only
fifty-eight hundred feet, the article said. It was picked up by
searchlights from the ground, "and the Japs opened up with
everything they had. It looked like the Fourth of July and the end
of the world combined," Lieutenant Savage said.

"Sniping at the wounded giant," fighter planes pursued the
crippled B-29 as it headed back toward Iwo Jima. Somehow the
navigator got them there, and with the radio out, the pilot circled
Iwo Jima and, working only with hand signals from the ground,
saw to it that his plane "became the second Flying Fortress landing
on Motoyama No. 1."

Airfield No. 2 was extended for B-29s, veteran William Glaser
recalls, but it also housed P-51 fighters, as did Airfield No. 3.

The other reason for the invasion was to stop the radio trans-
missions warning Tokyo that the bombers were coming.

Was it justified? John Ripley points out that prior to the seizure
of Iwo, seventy-seven B-29 Superfortress were lost and that this
number dropped off drastically once Iwo Jima was captured.

19

LIEUTENANT ROBERT MERKLEIN

P-51 Pilot, Iwo Jima
46th Fighter Squadron, 21st Fighter Group,
7th Air Force

You hope you have the skill, that you can shoot straight and fly right and keep out of trouble, and that the bad one doesn't get you.

Bob and Laura, his wife of sixty-one years, in their new home in Sugar Land, Texas, late in 2006. He holds a photograph of himself standing beside a biplane trainer taken in the States before he was sent overseas.
Photo by Leba Shallenberger

Lieutenant Robert Merklein gets ready to take off in his P-51, *Available Jayne*, on the very first land-based fighter mission departing from Iwo Jima to attack mainland Japan on April 7, 1945.

I really wanted to find someone who had flown a plane at Iwo Jima during the war, and I first learned about Bob Merklein from his nephew, Jim Stanek, of Newport, Rhode Island. Merklein and I later spoke at length on the telephone in November 2006. He and his wife had recently moved from Houston to a retirement home in Sugar Land, Texas. In talking about his experiences during the war, he used the word luck *a lot, as it applied to his survival. But as his story indicates, it was clear that he had made a lot of his own luck. He was a handsome pilot, and he named his plane* Available Jayne. *This chapter tells why.*

"The battle started February 19, as everybody knows, and I arrived March 22, while it was still going on, four days before that last banzai attack, March 26. We'd been sitting down at Tinian, and that attack scared the hell out of us because we weren't prepared for it, you know, at five o'clock in the morning. The Japs would take over Motoyama No. 2 at night and the Americans had it during the daytime. There was a lot of fighting after they said the island was secure, before we even got there. From our tent area on up there was fighting on that north end, and then in the evening the marines would come right by our area with their dead and wounded. There was a bunch of 'em, I'll tell you. But it's war, you know. They still fought a hard battle for more than a month after I arrived.

"I was right in the middle of that banzai attack. For some reason or another when we landed there on the twenty-second, they had put up tents to the northwest. Why they put us up there, toward the area where the majority of fighting was still going on, I don't know. But anyway, on the twenty-sixth at five o'clock in the morning these three hundred Japs came out of the caves and hit our tent area."

While they were not supposed to take part in combat, black marines serving on Iwo played a significant part in defeating and killing the attackers. The Japanese, armed with automatic weapons, bayonets, swords, and hand grenades, had made their way underground from the northern end of the island to an assembly point just north of Motoyama No. 1, near the western beaches. Attacking in a gap between two garrisoned units preparing to debark the island, they struck the bivouac area, a tent city for the Seventh Fighter Command. Patrick Mooney, the historian and an expert on the battle, notes: "The Army Air Force units in the bivouac did not have observation or listening posts out. They were not prepared for combat. They were living aboveground, in tents. There were also Marine shore parties, supply troops, antiaircraft gunners, and Seabees. The Japanese came into that area and killed forty-four pilots in their sleep with swords and bayonets. Eighty-eight were wounded. The quick reaction of the Fifth Pioneer Battalion, a white unit, and the Eighth Ammo and Thirty-sixth Depot, both black, pinched off the Japanese and then swept through, methodically killing, wounding, or capturing the Japanese. They saved what could have been a real catastrophe for the troops in the area. Nine marines were killed, and thirty-one wounded. Eighteen Japanese were taken prisoner." Private James M. Whitlock and Private First Class James Davis of the Thirty-sixth Depot, both blacks, were awarded Bronze Stars. Private First Class Harold Smith was killed while several other black marines were wounded. First Lieutenant Harry L. Martin of Bucyrus, Ohio, led the fight against the infiltrators and was himself killed. The last marine to die in action on Iwo Jima, he posthumously received the twenty-sixth and last Medal of Honor awarded for the battle.

"It took the marines three hours to get us out of our tent because we had Japanese right outside in a shell hole," Merklein recalled. "We could hear them talking just like I'm talking to you. Of course bullets and shrapnel were flying around, and all we could do was hit the deck in our tent. Finally, when the sun came up, we heard a loudspeaker coming from the south, the direction our tent was facing, and they said, 'Anybody left in the pilots' area, yell out!'

"Well, the Japanese didn't know we were in the tent, and of course it was just a piece of canvas. They were so close, right on the other side of the canvas at the back wall of my tent. All they had to do was lift the tent and roll a hand grenade in there and we were done for. Later in that shell hole they found over twenty-five Japanese dead. Around our tent there were six more, just spread around, and everything from the ground up was just shrapnel holes and blood and guts on the tents and the ground pretty well blown apart. Most had already been wounded during the battle for Iwo because they came out of the caves. They had some American equipment on them. They came out of tunnels from the north.

"Anyway, finally, we saw some movement to the south, and we waved a towel or something, and they spotted us. They yelled over the speaker to get ready to get up and run. The order finally came about nine o'clock and we had one wounded guy in the tent. We drug him, and I remember diving into a garbage pit they had made. I landed on my flight surgeon, and he had a marine who was split wide open on his lap.

"A couple guys in my squadron actually did get to fire at the Japanese because they were on the farther side of the tent. My tent area got hit first, and that's why we were basically trapped there and couldn't do anything. We were lucky to get out. I was in the second row of tents. When we got there, I picked a tent out in the first row and then changed my mind and went back to the second row. Everybody in that first tent I picked out got killed. So you know you just luck out sometimes."

"I was born August 7, 1922, and graduated from high school in Madison, Wisconsin, in June of 1941. I wanted to join the service well before Pearl Harbor was attacked because my two brothers had already been in for a year. One was drafted, and the other belonged to the National Guard.

"The general sense was that we were going to be in the war; it was just a matter of time. Then, when the war broke out, I joined. At that particular time I was not interested in politics, so I wasn't paying much attention to the isolationist debate. I signed up with the Army Air Corps right after Pearl Harbor. They called me on January 20, 1942. I always wanted to fly, but I never expected it because I didn't have any college.

"After the preliminaries at Fort Sheridan, Illinois, we went down to Keesler Field in Biloxi, Mississippi, which they had just opened up. We took all kinds of exams to help decide what guys were going to be doing. It was decided that I would go to the Casey Jones School of Aeronautics in downtown Newark, New Jersey. It was a civilian school with a government contract. I was there about six months learning aircraft mechanics, and I enjoyed every minute of it. Then they sent me to Columbus, Mississippi, where I started working on advanced trainers, the AT-17 and AT-10. It was a flying school. The planes weren't armed.

"Things were building up fast in Army Air Corps. But I always had this thing about flying, and as far as I knew at that time you had to have the two years of college. I got my ratings pretty fast, and by the time I made buck sergeant I decided to sign up for gunnery school and at least be a crew member on a bomber, just a gunner or radio operator on a B-24 in combat, something like that. They had ten or eleven members in a crew, four officers and the rest enlisted. That's what I was going after. Turned out all you needed was a physical.

"Well, I got to know the girl at post headquarters, and I'd go over there every noon at lunchtime to check and see if they'd given me my orders, and she got to know me. I have no idea what her name was. This was November of 1942, and one day she said, 'Bob, why don't you try for aviation cadets?' And I said, 'I don't have the college.' She said, 'Well, they got this new program where you take eight hours of written exams, and if you pass, you can be a pilot. Why don't you do that?'

"I had just taken all this mechanical stuff, and I wasn't that long out of high school, so I was used to taking tests. Anyway, I passed and got accepted into the program, and January 1 of '43 I was at

Nashville, Tennessee, for a month. That was where they decided if you were going to be a pilot or a bombardier or whatever. Of course most of the guys wanted to be pilots. When it was time for the list to come out, we all ran to the bulletin board, and I was lucky enough to be chosen as a pilot. So nine months later, on October 1, 1943, I got my wings and became a second lieutenant.

"Of course it was one of the great experiences of my life, but the training was so intense and we'd all worked so hard as cadets we almost felt like we deserved the wings. But it was quite a thrill. Becoming a second lieutenant was fine, but the main thing was getting the silver wings. It was a dream come true because I had never thought it could happen.

"They sent us to Tallahassee [Florida], and from there they sent me to P-39 school, in Thomasville, Georgia. I had about ninety hours by the time we graduated in January. By the time I graduated I had the P-17 Stearman, an open-cockpit biplane, and the BT-13, the basic trainer, the AT-6, and ten hours of P-40 time. So I was on the road to fly anything. I hit it at just the right time. They moved you around, to Maxwell Field, to Douglas, Georgia, back to Alabama, then Marietta, Georgia, where I graduated from. The washout rate was 50 percent.

"It was up in Tallahassee where I met Sarah Jayne Pitts. Tallahassee was a pilot replacement pool, and they had the state teachers' college for women there, and all the guys would date the gals from the college. She said she was available for a date, so when I got to Iwo Jima, I decided to call my P-51 *Available Jayne*. That's the way she spelled her name. I dated her for several weeks.

"Then they shipped me to California to go overseas. We were there two or three weeks on Angel Island in San Francisco Bay, right next to Alcatraz. In fact, the ferry that took us out there stopped by Alcatraz to drop off prisoners.

"We got on a big Navy boat and thought we were going to combat. Everybody wanted to go to combat. I got off at the Hawaii Islands and said, 'Gee, I wouldn't mind spending a week or two here,' and by God I got stuck there for a whole year. I mean it was fun, but it wasn't combat. We went from P-39s to P-38s, and that's when we thought we were going to combat. Then, about November of '44, they said, no, you're going to get 51s. They put us aboard an aircraft carrier the first of February, I think. We went to Guam, where they off-loaded the 51s. We went up to Tinian, then to Saipan, and sat there waiting for number two airfield to open up on Iwo Jima.

"After the banzai attack, we lived in foxholes for three or four weeks. Hell, everybody was gun happy after dark, and everybody was shooting. So we dug down deep and lined the hole with sand-bags so our heads would still be below the surface when we'd lie on an army cot. We were living on C and K rations.

"I was in the Forty-sixth Fighter Squadron of the Twenty-first Fighter Group of the Seventh Air Force. There were three different squadrons to a group. There were about thirty in a squadron, so there were eighty to ninety planes in a group. They were all P-51s until the P-47s came along later.

"The P-51 was the most advanced fighter that I flew, and it was actually designed after the British got into the war with Germany. It carried six fifty-caliber guns, three on each wing. We had what we called practice missions to Chichi Jima and Haha Jima, one hundred to one hundred fifty miles away. We could take five hundred pounders with us and strafe because we didn't need drop tanks. But on the long missions we started off with heavy one-hundred-ten-gallon wing tanks, two of 'em. Then we graduated to two one-hundred-sixty-five-gallon tanks. We'd carry them as long as we could and then drop them before we went in to strafe.

"We had two airfields, all 51s, and the P-47s started coming in just about the time I left there. It was a big deal. You don't read about it, but we had a lot of planes there. Of course the Navy fighters were going in off aircraft carriers and strafing three or four weeks before we hit because they could get up pretty close.

"I was lucky enough to be on the very first land-based fighter mission to Japan. That was April 7, and we were one hundred fifty planes flying out of number two airfield on Iwo Jima, escorting B-

29s, which came from Guam and Tinian, over the target. It was seven hundred fifty miles to Japan from Iwo, fifteen hundred round trip. We were to rendezvous over Japan.

"They had a stripped-down B-29 we would meet over Iwo, and that plane would do the navigation for us on the way up. He'd get us up there, and we'd break off for our mission. We'd have a rendezvous point afterward, but a lot of times we never caught up to the B-29 on the way back. We also had what we called our Uncle Dog, a radio in the plane that we could home in on the B-29. All we had beyond that was a compass. It was all dead reckoning, and I was good at it.

"The missions, to different parts of Japan, lasted almost eight hours. Sometimes we escorted B-29s, sometimes we just strafed, depending on the mission. Then we had sea patrol off Iwo. Weather was our biggest problem. We always hit at least one front going up there or coming back. On June 5, 1945, we lost twenty-seven airplanes and twenty-five pilots just due to the weather. I happened not to be on that mission. There was always at least one weather front between Iwo and Japan, and we'd try to fly under it or we'd try to fly over it, and they just got discombooberated that day. The weather was so bad they shouldn't have even gone.

"But you do just luck out sometimes. My plane got hit three different times, but I didn't even know it till I got back. It was tracer fire from the ground: It was pretty; it had a curved arc coming up at you. I remember on one mission we strafed this airfield and pulled out over some water, and I happened to look down, and I said, 'My God, it looks like somebody's throwing gravel on the water,' and hell, those were shells hitting the water that they were firing at me.

"I finally did get to shoot down a plane. It was my last mission. It was on the east side of Tokyo Bay on May 29, 1945. I didn't know it was my last mission, but I was lucky enough to get one Japanese aircraft. It was a Tojo. I can't remember the number. We had a flight of four, and we had already escorted the B-29s, and we were heading for the rendezvous point where everybody shows up to fly back to Iwo, and as we were approaching the rendezvous point, we saw these two planes above us. We realized they were enemy planes, so we took off after them. Our flight leader took the one to the right, and I took the one to the left and just chased him down.

"He didn't fire back at me. He was trying to escape. He dove toward the ground, and I caught up with him and got him with the fifties. My wingman said he bailed out. We saw flames on the airplane where I hit him. I never did actually see him bailing out.

"The Tojo looked like a P-47, but it was one of the newer fighters. But by that time most of their pilots, the good ones, had been killed.

"For the return to Iwo, we didn't have cross runways. There was only one, and the fighters had to come in first because they had less gas than anybody: On that last mission all I had was five or ten gallons left when I landed after shooting down the Tojo. You had to be an optimist back then. You felt confident; you figured it was going to happen to somebody else, not yourself. That's why they wanted young guys, I guess.

"It was all very interesting. If we weren't on a mission and the B-29s were coming in low on fuel or damaged, we'd go up and watch them land with the engines shot up. We all gathered around for that. I don't know how many were saved, but it was a bunch. They were flying a lot of missions, and there were a lot of wrecked B-29s on Iwo Jima. They were just junked, too bad to try to fix up after they made their emergency landings."

While the seizure of Iwo Jima was intended largely to provide an emergency halfway stop for B-29s returning from attacks on Japan, space was extremely limited, and pilots were strongly encouraged to continue on to Saipan or Tinian if at all possible.

"They discouraged the B-29s from landing. They had a colonel in the tower, and if he thought they could make it back to Guam or Saipan, he wouldn't let them land. But I've seen B-29s bellying off the shore of Iwo. There were too many landings going on at one time, and they had to do something, so they ditched them. The

B-29 was a good airplane to ditch in shallow water. I saw one float for at least five days before it sank. The cabins were pressurized.

"When the war started, they used to give you a Distinguished Flying Cross for shooting down a plane. But then it got so common they'd give you the Air Medal instead. All I got was three Air Medals and some campaign ribbons, nothing real exciting. But anybody who's been in combat has been through that kind of crap. There's no hero stuff. I just lucked out. You hope you have the skill, that you can shoot straight and fly right and keep out of trouble, and that the bad one doesn't get you. I figured I at least paid for my cadet training because I shot one down. It was hard to find them. The higher ranks were always out in front. They were trying to get their glory, and you can't blame them.

"The reason that eighth trip was my last mission was we got back that night and the squadron commander came up to four of us who had been in the squadron over a year and he said, 'I've got to send somebody to Victoria, Texas, to learn about the K14 gunsight, a brand-new self-computing gunsight, and I need a volunteer to go learn it and then come back out here,' Well, the other guys were married, and I wasn't. He said 'I'll give you till tomorrow morning, and if nobody volunteers I'll have to choose somebody.' We'd all been out there at least eighteen months, and everybody was looking for a rotation back home. If you went to this gunnery school, you had to come back to Iwo. You had to learn this new gunsight and then come back, and that would extend your tour. So I talked it over with my buddy, and I said, 'Hell, I'll come back and probably get my captaincy.' I wanted to stay with the squadron.

"By golly, they sent me back and the war ended three days before school was out. I went to sign off the base to go back to Iwo, and I cleared the post, but the squadron commander wouldn't sign my papers. And all my records were on Iwo Jima. So I sat there and just junked airplanes up to Arkansas, stuff like that. I never got any of my stuff back.

"I had to wait from August 15 until November 29, and I finally got my records from Iwo, and by that time I was pretty well PO'ed from the delays and being pushed around, and then they closed the base. I couldn't even get my four hours of flying time in.

"I'd met my wife-to-be by then, so I said, 'Hell, I'll get out.' Which I did. We got married March 2, 1946, and then I joined the National Guard for about three and half years. That was the extent of my flying career."

It turned out his wife-to-be, Laura, had herself dated a pilot while she was a student at the University of Texas in Austin during the war. And just as Bob had christened his plane *Available Jayne*, that fellow Laura was dating had named his P-51 for her. There must have been a lot of that going around.

"I stayed in Texas. She was an only child, and I'd been out of snow country four years and just decided to stay down here in Houston. We raised our family here and made a living. I was in the lumber business about forty years. It was my father-in-law's. He didn't have any sons, and one day he called me up and said, 'Would you like to join me?' So my wife and I talked it over, and he was a man of his word and well liked in Houston. It just worked out."

Bob and Laura had a boy and two girls. By the winter of 2006 they had one grandchild, about the time they were downsizing into a retirement home.

"It's not home like we used to know, but it's working out. There's a bedroom and a study—nine hundred and twenty-five square feet. When you're downsizing from twenty-six hundred square feet and four bedrooms and a den, there's a lot to get rid of.

"I had wanted to rejoin my squadron because I figured they'd be going to Japan. I wanted to stay in the Air Corps. I loved flying, you know. But things just didn't work out, so the story's not too interesting."

20

STAFF SERGEANT VALENTINE CHEPELEFF

Radar Bombardier, B-29
40th Squadron, 6th Bomb Group

Had Iwo Jima not been there, we would either have had to ditch or bail out. We'd have never made it back to Tinian.

Valentine Chepeleff, eighty-five, in his Russian Orthodox priest's clothing in February 2007. Pinned to his jacket are his Distinguished Flying Cross and other medals relating to his service in the Pacific. "How did it feel, an individual bound for service in the church, to be dropping bombs on the Japanese people? I felt that since they had attacked us, we were defending ourselves. They were trying to take control of our country, which had not attacked them. What they were trying to do was get control of people. Germany was doing the same thing. Just like we saved all those lives that would have been lost invading Japan by dropping the atomic bomb."

I spoke with Valentine Chepeleff a couple of times on the phone and then visited him at his home in Wrentham, on the Massachusetts–Rhode Island border in February 2007, not long before he turned eighty-five. He walked with two canes, but he had dressed up in his black priest's clothes and had pinned smaller versions of five medals on his breast. One represented a two-time award of the Distinguished Flying Cross. He lived with his daughter Christine and her husband, Charlie, who made me a cup of tea. Christine brought a pizza home, and they shared it with me.

Valentine Chepeleff, who went on to a full career as a Russian Orthodox priest, was the radar bombardier on a B-29 that led dozens of bombers on thirty-five missions from Tinian to Japan between January and June of 1945. His plane was named *Earthquake McGoon*, after the Li'l Abner character. It made one stop at Iwo Jima.

"After several missions we had an emergency on the plane, and Iwo Jima is halfway between Tinian and Japan. We were coming back, and we had to land someplace. There was just water all over the place, and here they're fighting on Iwo Jima, but we called in and asked if they would have an airstrip maybe available.

"The answer was, 'Well, we got half an airstrip, but if you could wait a little bit, maybe we can get the rest of it.' We said, 'Thank you very much; we'll take the half.' And we landed the plane. We had a terrific crew. They repaired it, and we left right away. I don't remember what was wrong with the plane, but had Iwo not been there, we would either have had to ditch or bail out. We'd have never made it back to Tinian.

"My father and mother were Russian. I was born here, in Cohoes, New York, 1922, February 28. My father, Theodore, came over as a missionary priest in 1913, planning to stay for ten years, but then of course the Communists took over, so he never got back to Russia.

"When I was getting into the Army, I spoke Russian. I heard they were ferrying planes from Alaska to the Russians, and so I thought I might as well try that. As I was signing up for it, I talked to a Navy pilot, and he was trying to talk me into getting into the Navy program for pilots. And I said to myself: 'Let me think this over.' I had never thought of flying, but it sounded so interesting, flying a plane. But the thing that cautioned me was that if you're on a carrier and you go on a mission and you come back all battered and what if the ship is not there? Where do you land, in the water? So I thought: No, I'm going to go into the Army Air Force. You know, you're over land. [Laughs.] Well, there's a big surprise. I got into the Army program and got sent to the Pacific, where there was nothing but water.

"I signed up for a fifteen-week air cadet pilot training program September 8,1943, at Dickinson College near Hershey, Pennsylvania. But then they decided to take us out of there to learn radar bombing, this secret program for the B-29, which was brand-new at the time, and they needed a lot of things. You never saw a more dejected group of fellas. We were intent on flying and becoming pilots, and here we were being transferred to something else. We had to take special courses in radar, learning to apply it in combination with bombing. We were the first group when the whole thing started and we were supposed to get commissions, but they never came through. They sent us to Tyndall Field in Florida, May 8, 1944.

"In August they sent us to Lincoln, Nebraska, and from there we made trips to Puerto Rico to get the bugs out of the Superfortress and to get the crew accustomed to long-distance flights and to give the radar operator practice in navigating and bombing over land and water. We flew through some violent electrical storms, and it felt like the wings might be torn off. I was the only one armed to protect the equipment. If we had to land at some other airfield, I'd have to wait there till the MPs got there to protect the equipment because it was all so secret.

"I was in the middle of the plane in a little room with my radar equipment. In fact, they had a little control there where I could move the plane left or right after we were at altitude. I had the screens in front of me, and I had to make my calculations for altitude, airspeed, drift, from the IP [initial point] to the target; then you directed the plane either left or right. The bombardier was up front with his regular radar bombing equipment. I would just go along then, and if he could see something in a break in the clouds, he could make corrections.

"My job was to get to the target. I would get the target on my radar, zero in on it, make my calculations left or right, and release it. I don't know how it worked. As far as I know, I was releasing the bombs. I felt I was running the whole mission. [Actually, the radar operator or the navigator would provide the bombardier with the course to the IP. From there on, it was up to the bombardier to bring the plane the next fifteen or twenty miles to the target.]

"We went on to the West Coast in December and left for Hawaii January 17, arriving at Guam and then Tinian January 21. We were supposed to get commissions when we got through with this, but everything went so fast after we got out to the Pacific that they never came through. But after many missions, the replacements were coming in with commissions. I got to staff sergeant, but I should have been commissioned. At first we lived out of our helmets and canteens. Eventually we got water and power. We were stationed with the Twenty-first Bomber Command in the Marianas with the Three Hundred Thirteenth Bomb Wing. I don't remember when the raids started.

"There were eleven in the crew. The pilot, copilot, bombardier, navigator, flight engineer, and radar operator; the rest were gunners. When we first got there, we escorted some of the Marine fighter planes up to Iwo Jima so they could strafe it. So they must have had some navigational problems. We would bring them up, then hang out while they went in and did their job, strafing the targets. Then we would lead them home. Navigational problems were great for them. To navigate, you had to use your stars, your compass, anything you could pick up, any of the islands, because it was all water. It was not like in Europe, where you could find landmarks. In the Pacific you'd have to find an island or something. We had radar that would reach an island we could recognize fifty or one hundred miles out there so we knew where we were. I said that was a twist. In Europe the bombers were escorted and protected by fighter planes, and here we are escorting the fighter plane. We were just one plane; they didn't need any more than that to take them up there.

"We made thirty-five missions to Japan. Our first mission was a big operation, and I was deputy lead, meaning we were the second plane. But something happened to the lead plane on our bombing run, so we had to take over. The first plane is the one that picks out the target, and the rest drop their bombs when the first plane releases. Ours was the lead plane for the rest of my thirty-five missions. We were so good that after twenty-five missions we were supposed to get a rest leave in Australia, but instead they asked us to keep flying. We called our plane *Earthquake McGoon*."

"Originally we were going to fly at very high altitudes. The B-29 was built to fly at 33,000 feet where it would be out of reach of the ack-ack, the antiaircraft fire. But we found that the winds up there blew from one hundred fifty miles an hour so that, if you got a tailwind, you'd get over the target too fast, and if you got a headwind, you were practically standing still. So we started lowering, and we wound up flying much much lower.

"Our targets were mainly airfields, military installations, and industrial plants. You couldn't help but hit some civilian population in industrial areas, but they were not our target. We had strict instructions to avoid ancient temples or the palace in Tokyo."

In a raid on March 10, 1945, nearly 280 B-29s destroyed 267,171 buildings, one-fourth of urban Tokyo, killing 83,793 and wounding 40,918, exceeding the number of civilians killed in the firebombing of Dresden in Germany as well as those who died in the atom bomb explosion over Hiroshima. Fourteen planes were lost. All came from the 21st Bomber Command's 73rd, 313th, and

314th Bombardment Wings, based in Guam, Tinian, and Saipan. The planes flew at altitudes ranging from forty-nine hundred to ninety-two hundred feet.

"Whenever we went up to hit a target, I would take radar photos of that city so I could get more familiar with it in case we came back. I don't know what the other radar operators did, but whenever we left the target, I'd be scanning the area for any planes because we were all on our own to get back. We didn't go back in formation. We'd get together before the target, but we all flew back on our own.

"After I made my bombing run, I switched over to scanning the area three hundred sixty degrees. Many times I'd see a target [an enemy plane] coming in and we were on a collision course. I'd warn the crew and the pilot because they couldn't see through the cloud cover. Now I'm thinking: My God, I wonder how many planes we lost in collision with one another in a cloud cover? Later on we had Japanese suicide planes come after us, and I could pick them out as they were coming in. They would just try to crash into us. We used to laugh about it, say, 'Oh, they must have been pilots who washed out.'

"Many times, when we got back to base, the fellows would come to me and say, 'How are you?' I'd say, 'Why?' 'Well, we saw the flak burst right under your seat.' I said, 'I know. I felt the concussion.' We got a lot of flak, but it never penetrated. We took a look, but they were just scratches. None of it had penetrated. I said, 'Thank you, St. Nicholas.' My father had given me an icon of the saint, who is supposed to be the protector of seamen and maidens, and I had it with me on every mission. So many times the fellows came to ask and the plane was not damaged. The saint had to be out there praying for us. I had to miss one mission when my arm swelled up from an insect bite, and I thought: Oh, my God, the crew is going to think it is their time to go and I'm being saved by being left behind. So I took off my cross and gave it to my navigator. I said, 'You bring this back to me.' He did.

"So we never got our R and R in Australia, and on top of it all, after our thirty-five missions, I flew a War Weary back while the rest of the crew went by ship. A War Weary was a plane that needed repairs, had a lot of engine time, and was pulled out of combat to be sent back to the States. But when we were leaving Hawaii, this B-29 War Weary developed engine trouble. One engine was having trouble, and another engine was beginning to go, and I thought: Oh, my God, I got through thirty-five missions, and here I am on my way home, and we're going to have to ditch?

"On top of that we got news on the radio that the war had ended. So the war is over, and I'm in trouble on a B-29. Ha! They're celebrating in Hawaii, and I thought: Oh, my God . . . We made it eventually, but these little incidents kept your attention."

Back in the States, Valentine went to the seminary and became a priest and worked for years with his father, the Right Reverend Theodore Chepeleff, a mitered archpriest, in the Boston area. Valentine met and married Zinaida, or Zena, Martinoff, and they had five children. Zena died a few years ago.

"We were very active with the Roman Catholic Church. Father got to be well known among various denominations. He knew Cardinal Cushing. I knew Cardinal Cushing, Cardinal Law, and was close to a lot of the chaplains at the Veterans Administration. They know me and want me to speak here and there, but right now I got to get my medical health program set up. My mind is still active, but my body has slowed down quite a bit. I never officially retired. I'm the chaplain of the Disabled American Veterans here in Wrentham.

"When I got out of the service, I put it all behind me, never talked to anyone about what I did or anything for fifty years until I met Pete Santoro [Chapter 7] in a rehab pool and found out he had been at Iwo Jima. Then I started to think about it."

Earthquake McGoon's first citation for a Distinguished Flying Cross, dated June 1, 1945, cites her officers and one enlisted man, Valentine Chepeleff, "of the 40th Bombardment Squadron, 6th Bombardment Group" as "members of a lead crew bombing team which led three highly successful formation bombing missions against the Japanese Empire on the 17th and 22d of April and 10th of May 1945." It says they performed under rapidly changing and oftentimes adverse weather and under extremely difficult navigational problems over great expanses of ocean and unknown enemy territory. It also cites "varying degrees of enemy anti-aircraft fire and fighter opposition."

The second, this one an oak-leaf cluster awarded in lieu of the DFC, is dated August 2, 1945. It describes a daylight incendiary raid on June 5 against important industrial and shipping facilities in Kobe, Japan, in the course of a seven-hour flight. It says Valentine's plane was attacked "fourteen times by aggressive enemy fighters, and encountered heavy, intense and accurate anti-aircraft fire." It adds that this crew "led an exceptional formation, releasing their bombs over the briefed target with great accuracy" and says further that "over four square miles of the built-up portion of Kobe was destroyed." The captain, or airplane commander, is identified as Irvin M. Parsons. Lieutenant Hubert B. Connell was the navigator, and Lieutenant Carl J. Manone the bombardier. Also cited is Staff Sergeant Valentine Chepeleff of Brookline, Massachusetts.

21

LIEUTENANT PHIL TRUE

B-29 Navigator
99th Squadron, 9th Bomb Group

I gave a talk about the significance of Iwo for those of us in the Twentieth Air Force and the many lives saved, including mine, because of the Marines' heroism in taking that ugly piece of rock and sand. Yes, I did land there three times, and I am eternally grateful for the island and the Marines.

Phil True at eighty-one near his home in Fairfax, Virginia, in the fall of 2006

Second Lieutenant Phil True, nineteen, in a photo he says was probably taken at home in Jackson, Michigan, when he was given two weeks' leave after receiving his navigator wings, with a globe in the center, on December 15, 1944. On his lapel is the Army Air Forces insignia, a wing with a propeller through it.

I spoke with Phil True at length over the phone, and his feeling for the Marines was evident. In 1997, when he was talked into being chairman of a reunion for his 9th Bomb Group, he chose to honor the Marines for capturing Iwo Jima. "I organized a tribute featuring the Marine Drum and Bugle Corps," he told me, "and located members of the Third, Fourth, and Fifth Marine Divisions, who had invaded Iwo. They spoke, as did our commanding officer during the war and the colonel in charge of the Marine Barracks. We held it at the Marine Corps Memorial on August 28. We had close to three hundred people. Afterward I was asked to be an honorary Marine with Chapter Twenty-five of the Fourth Marine Division." He has continued his association with the Corps.

"I live in Fairfax, Virginia, now, but I grew up in southern Michigan, near Jackson. I was born April 14, 1925. I was the first person in my immediate family to graduate from high school. My father and mother, like most farmers, quit school in ninth or tenth grade. There was a junior college in town, and when I got out of high school, I decided to go there. When Pearl Harbor came, the draft age was twenty, and I really didn't think about going into the service. But then it was lowered in the fall of 1942, while I was in junior college, and I realized I'd be facing the draft the following spring, after I turned eighteen.

"Very few people went to college in those days, and the Navy and the Army assumed anybody in college was 'smart' and therefore officer training material. They had these specialized training programs, and I think in February of '43 the Army Air Forces, as it was called then, set up their aviation cadet program. Although almost every kid my age was interested in flying, for me it wasn't that I just *had* to fly. It wasn't that kind of thing. They had a little bonus. They said if you signed up, you could be called up some-

time after you were eighteen and there would be a five-month college program.

"I took the physical and a written test, and I was sworn into the
Army Air Forces three days before I turned eighteen. In fact, I was
the first seventeen-year-old to do that in Jackson. I was called up
August of 1943 and went through the entire training program.
The aviation program was roughly a year. You had to go through
basic, and then it depended on how you were classified: If you
were going to be a pilot, you went to primary training, then
advanced training. You'd be commissioned. Then, if you were
going to be a bomber pilot, you'd go through multiengine school.

"Of course taking it didn't mean you were in it. The washout
rates were maybe fifty percent. A lot of people didn't have the ability to do this.

"We did our basic training, from early September through early
November, in Miami Beach. The reason was that when the war
started, they simply did not have enough Army barracks built
throughout the country to house everybody. So they used the War
Powers Act to requisition hotels after the tourist season was over. I
think in April of 1942 about ninety percent of the hotels in Miami
Beach were being used. They had close to a hundred thousand
people undergoing basic training in South Florida.

"While I was down there, they decided to give us classification
tests, two days of written tests and what they called psychomotor
tests, devised to try to determine if you were best suited to be a
pilot, navigator, or a bombardier. Some people didn't qualify for
any, so they were sent to radio school or gunnery school.

"Anyhow, I qualified for all three, but my highest score was for
navigation. We had ten hours of dual flight instruction in little
two-seater Piper Cubs before we got sent up to Allegheny College
in Pennsylvania in mid-November of '43. I learned after the war
the college training program, the Army Air Forces cadet program,
was set up because the small liberal arts colleges had been drained
of students except for women. They sort of struck a deal that they
would put these training detachments in from the Air Forces, and

provide them with money. There were about four hundred of us and about a thousand coeds, so you could see the ratio was actually pretty good.

"As for the flying, I sort of enjoyed it, I guess, but I was rational enough to realize I wasn't a natural. I could put the plane in a stall and recover, but getting it to spin was not my forte. When I got down to preflight school in San Antonio in March of '44 I already knew my scores because when you were a student at Allegheny, you had to pull junior officer of the day, and so late at night, when no officers were around, you looked up your file. I discovered what my scores were and decided I would be a navigator.

"I went through preflight school, which ended in June of '44. Normally most people went on to gunnery school, but about four hundred of us in our class stayed on and went to the San Antonio Aviation Cadet Center, which is now Lackland Air Force Base. We waited around for shipping orders, and it got to be mid-August, and there was hardly anybody left when they received a direct call for people up at San Marcos near Austin. I was in this remaining group, so I went directly to navigation school instead of gunnery school. We were still not commissioned. We were essentially privates in the Army. There were fifty in my class, and I think thirty-one of us graduated. The attrition rate was high.

"We had actually four basic ways to navigate. One was through dead reckoning; that was simply through your instruments, using the compass and airspeed. You had to compute your drift, of course. You had to use maps, to figure out your declination in terms of your compass heading. We had a log, we called it a navigator's log. I had eight or ten columns of data that had to be entered in for any particular time to get your true airspeed. Then you got your ground position from that. Then you had radio, depending on where you were. Then you had celestial navigation, based on figuring your position from the stars. And finally you had what you called pilotage, which was just looking out the window. 'What do you see out there?' There were sectional air maps that provided good detail for what you were seeing on the ground.

"We actually had twenty practice missions. Each mission had three student navigators, and we'd have a three-legged triangular mission. One student would be lead navigator on each leg while the other two would follow what he was doing. The next student would plot the next leg and so on.

"We flew in a twin-engine Beechcraft, and it wasn't until the final mission or two that we were allowed to use all four navigational tools. If you had a zero zero mission, that meant you were perfect in figuring your ETA, your estimated time of arrival, and reaching your destination. You might be two minutes and five miles off, but that was considered reasonably good. It was a sixteen-week course. I graduated in December of 1944 and became a second lieutenant.

"We got some home leave, and I went back to San Marcos about New Year's. Somebody got sick, and an opening came up so I went to Lincoln, Nebraska, which was a classification center. They were making up crews to send to various bases for training. I didn't have any gunnery training, so they put me in a B-29 program because the navigator in a B-29 did not handle a gun. Our crew assembled about the first of February in Tucson, Arizona, and trained there until about the first of May.

"From there we went up to Wichita, Kansas, to pick up a B-29 to fly overseas. It took a couple of weeks to get it ready. We had to do a series of things, make sure the instruments were calibrated and so on. The citizens of Manhattan, Kansas, had had a bond drive to pay for a new B-29. It took about six hundred thousand bucks, if you can imagine that. They wanted to name the plane, and they had a contest and came up with *Nip Finale*, and that was painted on its nose. It's not politically correct now, of course, but that was our plane, and we enjoyed it.

"In late May we flew to California and took off from a field near Sacramento, then to Oahu, on to Johnson Island, and eventually we reached Kwajalein, which the Marines had taken I guess, in late 1944. It was just a flat atoll. The control tower there wasn't much. The airstrip was probably eight thousand feet long. I remember they had a sign up there in the operations office. It said: KWA-JALEIN ATOLL, ELEVATION EIGHT FEET, NO WHISKEY ATALL, NO WOMEN ATALL, NO NOTHING ATALL.

"Next day we flew out to Tinian, where the 313th Wing was located. We landed, and the pilot went to report, and one of the ground crew came up, dressed only in a pair of shorts, and he says, 'Where's the whiskey?' One of the guys, I guess the engineer, said, 'We didn't bring any whiskey.' What? No, we didn't bring anything. I heard the guy say, 'Didn't bring anything?' Whiskey was a great barter item. Actually one of our gunners had wanted to, but our pilot—he was a major—was very strict on rules and regulations.

"Anyway, we did not keep the plane. You make the mistake of thinking just because you fly a plane, it's yours. That plane was taken to one of the groups that needed it more than the 9th Bomb Group, where we were assigned. A number of years later, when I got reunited with my crew, I did some checking and discovered that *Nip Finale* had been taken over by the 504th Bomb Group, which was one of four in the 313th Wing. There was the 9th, the 504th, the 505th, and the 6th Bomb Group. Each group had about forty planes and crews. I learned the *Nip Finale* got in twenty missions. It was the third plane for that ground crew. Their previous two had been shot down."

Phil True was in the 99th Squadron of the 9th Bomb Group in the 313th Wing. Each bomb group consisted of three squadrons, each with fifteen planes. There were five bomb groups in the Pacific at the end of the war: the 73rd, in Saipan; the 313th, on Tinian; the 58th, on Tinian; the 314th Wing, on Guam; and the 315th, on Guam. Each wing had four bomb groups, for a total of twenty.

"We flew whatever plane was available. Crews didn't necessarily fly the same plane every time. Engines needed replacing frequently, and when your ship was in for repair, you flew whatever was available. Some crews flew as many as thirty-five missions, but they would fly maybe twenty-five or so on 'their' plane. So you never knew what plane you were going to fly. There would be an announcement that such and such crews would be briefing at eleven o'clock that night, twenty-three hundred, whatever; it was going to be a daylight mission. Then you would have a little breakfast, get in the truck, and go down the line. Then you'd find out which plane you were going to fly.

"We'd get down there, and one of the problems for the navigator was you had to take the astro compass and make sure everything was aligned correctly. You used the North Star normally to do that. On some planes the compass reading was maybe a couple of degrees off from what you were actually doing. You always had to make little corrections. Occasionally planes got caught in smoke thermals, and some of them got twisted two or three degrees, so you and the compass in the plane didn't quite agree.

"We flew some practice missions, bombing the airfield of an island called Pagan, in the Northern Marianas, about halfway between Iwo and Saipan and Tinian. I think there were a few Japanese left but no defenses. The B-29 could carry eight tons of bombs, but most missions you carried seven, depending on whether you had incendiaries. There were five hundred, thousand, and two thousand pounders.

"Our first mission over Japan was June 4 to 5. We took off on the fourth and bombed Kobe. We didn't fly in formation to Japan. That would have taken too much gasoline. We flew up separately, then used some sort of reference point; often it was just a compass point in the ocean. It was a very, very tricky job to get so many planes in formation once you got there. Each group had a slightly different certain altitude and a slightly different location. Then, at a certain time, they all had to fly to the IP, the initial point, from where you went on your bomb run. It was an intricate job.

"About four hundred fifty planes went over the target, in formation. There was a high overcast, so we flew a daylight mission at fourteen or fifteen thousand feet, which was very low. This put you in easy range of all the antiaircraft they had. The city was well defended, and the Japanese put up a couple of hundred fighter planes. About a dozen B-29s were shot down, and seventy-five were damaged.

"I went along as observer on that particular raid. I sat in a nose hatch right behind the pilot, copilot, and bombardier. Apparently what happened was the fighters came in after we dropped the bombs.

"They didn't attack during the bombing run, when they could get in the flak themselves. Normally the fighters would attack before you got in, or just after. Fighters came at us, usually in pairs. Mainly they'd fly head-on through the formations. The Japanese had three or four aces on B-29s. Some had shot down as many as fifteen planes.

"When the main force of Japanese fighters were coming from, say, twelve o'clock, straight overhead, there would be two or three of these aces, or better pilots, who would fly a couple thousand feet below a formation. They'd pick out a plane, and because the gunners were all looking ahead and because there was a slight dead spot on the B-29 right directly below, they would come right up under it to within a couple hundred feet and then fire their twenty-millimeter cannon shells into the wing tanks.

"That happened to our plane, although we didn't realize it at first. Then one of the gunners called in and said gasoline was coming out behind number three. Gasoline was from a wing tank, of course, and number three was the inboard engine on the right-hand side of plane. The pilot immediately shut down the engine and then feathered the propellers. Feathering meant you altered the pitch of the blades so they offered less air resistance. We feathered that engine, and then, ten or fifteen minutes later, the supply of gasoline to number four, which was the outboard engine on the right-hand side of the plane, ran out because the fuel tank had been hit. There was no way to transfer any additional fuel out there on this particular model B-29.

"So we feathered number four, and tried to restart number three, but I think the starter motor had burnt out. It may have been hit. Anyway, number three and number four engines were not working. By that time we were just leaving Japan, and a buddy ship flew with us for three or four hours. The pilot put the plane on what you'd call a climb setting, put the nose like he was going to climb, but because he didn't have enough power we just kind of mushed our way.

"We lost altitude till we got down around four or five thousand feet. Here the air was heavy enough so we could level off. But we still did not have much gasoline, and the pilot thought about having us bail out when we got to a picket ship, a Navy destroyer escort. But then he decided the water was too cold for him to jump. So he said we'd try to make Iwo.

"It was a stormy day. We got to Iwo, and the pilot was being very careful. He was too high, so the tower told him to do a go around, which was a little tricky. In fact, it was not recommended at all on a B-29. We had to go around the island with two dead engines. With that right-side wing down, it was very hard to control the plane.

"After the first go-round, we came in with flaps down, wheels down, and then, just a couple hundred feet above the runway, another B-29 cut right in front of us. In fact, I read a report many years later that said the air control was not good that day; pilots were not obeying the tower. Apparently this guy had wounded on board.

So we had to pull up. Any kind of little flicker on the remaining two engines would have been the end of us. The pilot said, 'If we can't get in this time, I'm going to dump you out over the ocean. I'll try to climb to fifteen hundred feet and let you out.' So we came around a third time, and this time, as we came in to land, visibility was essentially zero. But the tower had elementary radar, and they picked us up and guided us in. We screeched to a halt at the end of the fighter strip. We had maybe ten minutes of gas left. That was my first, and almost my last, mission. That's my story of getting saved on Iwo Jima.

"We landed twice again in June while on two other missions, but it was primarily because we were on the margins with our gas supply. If you were based on Tinian and you were returning with less than two thousand gallons, you were supposed to land on Iwo to take on more.

"Something wrong with the engines was discovered when we landed, and they said we had to hitchhike aboard another 29 that was going back to Tinian. And just as we took off, *boom*, one of its engines conked out. The pilot said, 'Hell, we can get back on three.' But then, an hour later, *ping*! another engine went out on the other side, and he said, 'Well, we gotta go back to Iwo now.' A friend of mine in college after the war had been in B-24s in Italy, and he was talking about planes. I said, 'Well you know, a B-29 can fly with two engines out on the same side,' and he said, 'You're nuts, you can't do that.' But I know, because we did.

"We flew twelve missions before our crew was selected in late July to come back and be trained as a lead crew to lead a group or squadron in bombing. There was so much bad weather over Japan you had to rely on radar bombing. About a dozen crews were being sent back each month. Then in August the war ended.

"Of course the first B-29 to land on Iwo was *Dinah Might*, on D plus thirteen, March 4. Lieutenant Raymond Malo, the pilot, was from my Ninth Bomb Group, Ninety-ninth Squadron. They had flown a mission over Tokyo, and their bomb bay doors had frozen open, and they had a fuel transfer problem. The Seabees said, 'You give us a couple hours, and we'll have another thousand feet of runway.' Malo said, 'No, thanks, I'm going to take off. I want to get out of here.' He didn't stay long.

"His plane was later shot down, on April 14, over Kawasaki. Malo and the entire crew were killed. Our group lost four planes that night. Another navigator took the cot of Malo's navigator in the Quonset hut where we were going to be living. Three or four days before we arrived in *Nip Finale*, the second navigator's plane was taking off on a night mining mission, and something happened on the runway: The plane skidded off, and the mines exploded. The tailgunner survived, but everybody else was killed. So when I got to this Quonset hut, I took this empty cot. After a few days the guy next to me told me the story. He said, 'You know, Malo's navigator had this cot, and then Caldwell's navigator had this cot, so welcome to the cot.'

"Do I think the seizure of Iwo Jima was worth the cost? Yes, I do, because around twenty-two hundred B-29s landed there after it was taken, although it's difficult to say how many crewmen would have been lost otherwise. Some planes were low on gas but would have got back anyway. And if you had to bail out, you had maybe a forty percent chance of survival. And the P-51 wing was located there as well.

"While we were sitting there at that reunion at the Marine Corps Memorial in 1997, two buses with Japanese calligraphy on the side came along, and out jumped a bunch of Japanese tourists. We had a dozen marines there, and one rushed over and told them to get back in the bus. I thought it was kind of ironic.

"I got discharged in mid-December 1945. I was only in for not quite two and a half years, but it seemed long enough to me. Besides, I was only eighteen when I started.

"I went back to Jackson, took a semester of junior college, then went to Western Michigan University in Kalamazoo. I graduated from there in 1948, ending up with a major in geography. I went on to the University of Chicago, where I got a master's in geography and taught for a year before a friend said they were hiring for the CIA, and I said, 'What's the CIA. Is that the CIO?' Anyhow, that's how I came to Washington.

"I worked forty-seven years in the CIA. I was on the analytic side, which meant I didn't go into phone booths and leave pencil marks. I worked primarily on China, and then I retired and worked on contract and then worked primarily in training and ran some courses. Most of the people I found at the CIA were very dedicated people. It's not a perfect organization, it's obvious. They certainly made a serious mistake in the 2002 October NIE [National Intelligence Estimate]. That's another story.

"I got married to Fern Brooks September 1949. I told this story at our fiftieth wedding anniversary: I was taking a speech class at the junior college in Jackson. It met early in the morning. It was wintertime; it was February 1946; it was cold. There were not many people in the class.

"I sat in the back row, and there was a young lady named Lenore Larsen. She was blond, pretty good-looking, liked to wear sweaters. She'd come in late most of the time, and she'd sit in the back of the room as well. She'd take off her coat, and then she'd stretch. So this friend, Warren Tisch, and I would kind of eyeball that. And after two or three weeks the professor said, 'Why don't we just move people around?' He said, 'Mr. True, there's an empty chair right up here.' And that's where my wife-to-be was sitting, though I didn't know her at that time. So it was proximity and Lenore Larsen that led me to my bride. She came from a farm family too. We had two boys and a girl.

"I was invited along with some other people four years ago when they opened up the Air and Space Museum out at Dulles. The *Enola Gay*, the B-29 that dropped the atom bomb on Hiroshima, was there. Eight or nine of us from the Ninth Bomb Group were going to get a picture taken next to the *Enola Gay*, and a Japanese TV crew came up and asked if they could interview me. I simply said, 'I think it [dropping the bomb] was cruel in many ways, but I think in the long run it saved more lives than were lost.' Despite the fact that their navy had been largely defeated, the Japanese were not in the mood to surrender.

"I was asked to say a few words at a memorial service on behalf of B-29s at a Fourth Marine Division reunion in Washington, D.C., in 2002. And at an Iwo symposium in 2005 I gave a talk about the significance of Iwo for those of us in the Twentieth Air Force and the many lives saved, including mine, because of the Marines' heroism in taking that ugly piece of rock and sand. Yes, I did land there three times, and I am eternally grateful for the island and the Marines."

The characters on this monument, erected on the summit of Mount Suribachi after Iwo Jima and the Ogasawara (Bonin) Islands were returned to Japan on June 26, 1968, say: "The Monument to Pay Tribute to the Soldiers Who Fought and Died on Iwo Jima." The map on the surface of the monument consists of stones from each pre- fecture of Japan, and an epitaph on an accompanying memorial reads:

A small force pitted against a mighty army
On a lonely island, where even the deities are in awe.
For thousands of years, love and hate disappear
And the fragrance of sincerity spreads over eternity.

(translated by Masahide Mizoguchi)

The small bottles and objects at the base of the
memorial represent offerings to the dead.

PART SEVEN

Aftermath

There was no glamour on Iwo. There were millions of flies. The bodies burned black. The smell was overpowering. The burials began as soon as possible. Two cemeteries were established for the thousands of marines slain. The Japanese dead lay where they fell or else were covered in anonymous graves plowed out by bulldozers. To this day thousands remain entombed in the caves and tunnels. All were memorably eulogized by Rabbi Roland B. Gitelsohn. The text of his remarkable speech is included in this part.

The Army took over as the Marines departed in March and April. There were up to thirty-five thousand Army and medical personnel stationed on Iwo until September, when the numbers began to decrease, according to William A. Glaser of New York City, who served as an emergency surgical nurse in an Army hospital and later as a clerk on Iwo from February 1945 to February 1946. Substantial numbers of Japanese soldiers remained in small groups in caves in the northeast. Many came out at night to steal food and clothing. Glaser tells of a group of soldiers coming out to surrender from behind a movie screen set up near Suribachi. He said they had been living in caves inside Suribachi for months. Many who surrendered were Korean slave laborers rather than uniformed soldiers. A huge hospital, the 232nd General Hospital, was planned to treat wounded expected from the invasion of Japan, scheduled for late 1945.

The island was returned to Japan by the United States in 1968. Various individuals from both nations, such as Tsunezo Wachi and John Ripley, acted to preserve the heritage of Iwo Jima, to venerate the dead and preserve the island as a shrine to the sacrifice of the fallen soldiers. Colonel Ripley was determined to find a way to sustain access to the island by Americans in general and the Marines in particular. Captain Wachi founded the Association of Iwo-Jima (Iwo-to Kyokai) and helped make possible the Reunions of Honor, which now occur annually on Iwo.

22

THE JAPANESE COMMANDERS—
Lieutenant General Tadamichi Kuribayashi
and Captain Tsunezo Wachi—
and the Years Afterward

My girl is waiting for me
And does not know
That my body will stay here
On the rocks of Mount Kamo.

—Hitomaro (From *100 Poems from the Japanese*,
translated by Kenneth Rexroth)

Captain Tsunezo Wachi, an Imperial
Navy commander, in March 1944
prior to his departure for Iwo Jima
as the garrison commander.
Photo supplied by his daughter, Rosa Ogawa

Lieutenant General Tadamichi
Kuribayashi, Imperial Japanese Army,
commanding general, 109th Division
and commander, Ogasawara Army
Group. He was fifty-three years old
at the time of the invasion. He fired
eighteen senior army officers, including his chief of staff, for opposing his
strategy for the defense of Iwo Jima.
He is believed to have died by ritual
suicide in his cave near Kitano Point
on March 23, 1945.

Iwo Jima today is a shrine, actually a vast graveyard where between 14,000 and 17,000 Japanese soldiers lay entombed in its honeycomb of caves and tunnels. Only the immediate family members of those soldiers are permitted to visit from Japan. There is no restriction on American visitors. Only about 20 of the original 1,023 Japanese survivors are alive today. Thousands of marine veterans of the campaign still live, but they are dying off as age overtakes them.

Key figures from the Japanese side of the story, alongside the more than twenty-one thousand soldiers who died there (some bodies have been recovered), are Lieutenant General Tadamichi Kuribayashi, their commander, and his predecessor, Captain Tsunezo Wachi, who became a Buddhist priest after the war and dedicated his life to the Japanese soldiers and sailors killed on Iwo Jima.

Kuribayashi, a brilliant strategist and an exemplary individual, earned the respect of his troops and very high regard of his enemy, even after his death in March 1945. Kuribayashi wrote a series of letters, forty-one in all, to his family during the nine months he was there. Much of his legacy is based on these letters, and they offer the best way to understand the Japanese commander. Clint Eastwood's second film about the battle, *Letters from Iwo Jima*, leans heavily on Kuribayashi's correspondence, as well as letters from the soldiers. For a man facing certain death, Kuribayashi's letters are a marvel of restraint amid expressions of concern for his wife and fatherly advice to the children. From the way they read, he might be returning home in a few days.

Kuribayshi actually took over from Captain Wachi, who commanded the naval garrison on Iwo during the early part of 1944 and left in October. Wachi left a lengthy memoir, which has been translated by his daughter, Rosa Ogawa. In May 2007, I wrote to Ms. Ogawa, who then sent me poems, photos, and other accounts of her father's life. He is also warmly remembered by American marines who worked with him to establish the

Reunion of Honor, now held once a year when American veterans come to visit.

Kuribayashi's story has been eloquently captured by Kumiko Kakehashi in *So Sad to Fall in Battle* (Presidio Press, 2007), based on his letters. She notes that as a captain in his late thirties Kuribayashi spent more than two years studying and traveling in the United States, from March 1928 to April 1930. He audited classes in English, American history, and current affairs at the University of Michigan and Harvard. He bought a Chevy and drove it from Kansas to Washington, D.C., where he met several American military men. Among his papers are forty-two letters, many illustrated by his drawings, that he wrote home to his family from the States.

Kuribayashi was samurai (a powerful military caste in feudal Japan), and some Japanese authorities resented his imperial connections. Kuribayashi bred greater animosity among his peers for his conviction that the United States was an unbeatable enemy and that Japan should steer clear of direct conflict with the Americans. It is thought that at least part of the reason he was sent to defend Iwo Jima was to get rid of him. This clearly was a fight that the Japanese were not going to win.

In 1944, as Guam and Saipan fell to the Americans, the Japanese knew very well that Iwo would be next. Its airfields, situated halfway between Saipan and Tokyo, would be crucial for the American bombing campaign. Wachi noted that many of the draftees on the island were civilians with no military training. He set about trying to remedy that before Kuribayashi even got there.

Kuribayashi arrived in June and began drastically reordering defensive priorities, assigning troops to help dig tunnels, a task that was purgatory itself since the troops had to endure sulfur gas and heat so intense they could work only in five- and ten-minute shifts. As he began to implement his defensive strategy, Kuribayashi established fields of fire that would blanket the invasion beaches.

Because the Americans had control of air and sea, he also

abandoned the standard tactic of heavily fortifying the water's edge because there was no way his men could sit there and fire at the incoming landing craft without being wiped out by planes and shelling. He also dismissed any notion of a banzai charge because it wasted too many men and had proved only marginally successful against American marines. Sensing the coming onslaught, Kuribayashi focused on his underground defensive positions, which could withstand bombing from planes and shelling from the ships. Indeed, the island was bombed for seventy-four straight days prior to the invasion. It caused a lot of headaches and obliterated every shred of greenery on the island but seems to have caused few, if any, casualties among Kuribayashi's men.

Kuribayashi also wrote and distributed six statements known as the "Courageous Battle Vows":

1. *We shall defend this place with all our strength to the end.*
2. *We shall fling ourselves against the enemy tanks, clutching explosives to destroy them.*
3. *We shall slaughter the enemy, dashing in among them to kill them.*
4. *Every one of our shots shall be on target and kill the enemy.*
5. *We shall not die until we have killed ten of the enemy.*
6. *We shall continue to harass the enemy with guerrilla tactics even if only one of us remains alive.*

On March 16, Kuribayashi sent a farewell telegram to the Imperial General Headquarters:

The battle is entering its final chapter. Since the enemy's landing, the gallant fighting of the men under my command has been such that even the gods would weep. In particular, I humbly rejoice in the fact that they have continued to fight bravely though utterly empty-handed and ill-equipped against a land, sea and air attack of material superiority such as surpasses the imagination.

One after another they are falling to the ceaseless and ferocious attacks of the enemy. For this reason the situation has arisen whereby I must disappoint your expectations and yield this important place to the hands of the enemy. With humility and sincerity, I offer my repeated apologies.

Our ammunition is gone and our water dried up. Now is the time for us all to make our final counterattack and fight gallantly, conscious of the emperor's favor, not begrudging our efforts though they turn our bones to powder and pulverize our bodies.

I believe that until this island is recaptured, the emperor's domain will be eternally insecure. I therefore swear that even when I have become a ghost, I shall look forward to turning the defeat of the Imperial Army into victory.

I stand now at the beginning of the end. At the same time as revealing my inmost feelings, I pray earnestly for the unfailing victory and the security of the Empire. Farewell for all eternity.

As regards Chichi Jima and Haha Jima, I am sure the men under my command there can completely crush any attack the enemy might make. I entrust that matter to you.

Finally, I append an inept work for your perusal below. Please forgive its clumsiness.

Kuribayashi's death poem follows:

> *Unable to complete this heavy task for our country*
> *Arrows and bullets all spent, so sad we fall.*
>
> *But unless I smite the enemy*
> *My body cannot rot in the field.*
> *Yea, I shall be born again seven times*
> *And grasp the sword in my hand.*
>
> *When ugly weeds cover this island,*
> *My only thought will be the Imperial Land.*

Kakehashi notes that the Imperial General Staff edited the telegram before releasing it to the newspapers, eliminating the phrase "utterly empty-handed and ill-equipped," and changing "so sad we fall" from his poem to "mortified, we fall." It's easy to see why. She goes on to suggest that Kuribayashi died leading the last charge, the attack on the pilots by Motoyama No. 1. This has been disputed, as Colonel John Ripley makes clear in Chapter 24 of this book.

Captain Wachi ended the war in southern Kyushu, in charge of a suicide torpedo boat training base, in which young volunteer trainees were to attack enemy vessels with only enough fuel for a one-way mission. In October, with demobilization under way, Wachi got off the home-bound train in Kyoto to visit a Buddhist monk. Wachi's daughter says that after he spoke of his determination to dedicate the rest of his life to mourn the war dead, including those lost on Iwo Jima, the monk ordained him on the spot. After a week's practice he became Jushoan Koami. He went on to write several poems under that name. During the occupation American troops imprisoned him for five months, presumably because of his wartime involvement.

As Jushoan Koami he founded and became president of the Association of Iwo-Jima and finally gained permission to return to Iwo to perform religious rituals. He wrote:

It was still under occupation when we first landed on Iwo Jima Feb. 1952 by L.S.T. While there I put up two Kannon (a popular Buddhist deity) statues at the north and south of the island for all the departed souls without distinction of nationality. My idea was to carry out religious services and pray and mourn for them as I had stated in my application based on Buddhism principle: to pray wholeheartedly for all the souls evenly for their eternal rest beyond human resentment.

In the meantime we went down into the raid-beaten and flame-thrower ruined caves to search and collect bodies and relics of the departed. We discovered to our sorrow that quite a number of skulls had been removed from the bodies. We immediately reported to the U.S. Marines there and asked them for measures to prevent further mishaps.

Later in December 1955 I was informed by a staff officer of the

U.S. Pacific Fleet Headquarters of the fact that the caves had been sealed with the bodies lying as they were. That might have helped prevent further removal of the skulls but it . . . made it almost impossible for us to collect other relics which had been sealed in with the bodies unless we used heavy machinery.

As the result of the defeat in the war which had never taken place in the long history of our nation, so-called "Democracy" came along. The idea had developed in the West but it was totally new to our nation. Many people took it as their golden rule to replace the august virtue of his imperial majesty which had always existed ever since the dawn of our national history.

His daughter adds that he offered prayers for the departed, crept into caves to pour water or sake, or smoked cigarettes as requested by the bereaved survivors aware of how the soldiers had died in "extreme shortage of their needs."

Ms. Ogawa notes that while the marines did not remove heads during or after the battle, soldiers recuperating on Iwo during the Korean conflict took skulls as souvenirs. Two American writers, Richard Newcomb, a wartime correspondent and author of six books, including *Iwo Jima*, and Bill Ross, who wrote *Iwo Jima: Legacy of Valor*, published with Wachi's address an appeal for the return of skulls and other relics, such as diaries, photos, and letters.

Wachi was instrumental in helping arrange the first Japanese-American memorial ceremony conducted on Iwo in February 1985, the fortieth anniversary of the invasion. The retired Marine general Jarvis Lynch was the liaison with Wachi for that event, and I heard him speak about Wachi at an Iwo Jima symposium in Arlington, Virginia, in February 2007. Lynch has also written about Wachi for *Naval History* magazine. He said it was doubtful that without Wachi's prestige in Japan, the memorial service or those that followed would have occurred. He also said that in the forty years before his death, Wachi had accounted for the remains of more than eight thousand Japanese soldiers and sailors.

Wachi died at the age of eighty-nine on February 2, 1990. Here is one of his poems, in both the original script and in translation, provided by Masahide Mizoguchi of the Bronx in September 2007, who says the poem was written in Kanji, one of the Japanese writing systems that use Chinese characters. According to Mizoguchi, this poetry format was very popular among the samurai class and, consequently, in the military before and during the war. The use of Kanji would enable one to convey deep meanings and nuances in a limited amount of space. Mizoguchi adds that notes written underneath the poem, part of a package sent to me by Wachi's daughter, indicate that Wachi wrote it while imprisoned by the Americans after the war. Wachi indicates in his notes that he wrote the poem after seeing a photo in the military newspaper *Stars and Stripes* showing the American flag flying from the summit of Suribachi. The Kanji script following the English version was reproduced by Mizoguchi on a computer.

To the Suribachi Monument

A new monument stands
At the top of the hill,
Where the Stars and Stripes still wave,
As it dominates the sea.

The foul smell of blood arises
From the stones it stained;
While mounds of bones
Cover the mountaintop.

The battle has been lost,
A year has now come around;
All ill will and vengeance
Have already ceased to exist.

'Tis hard to console the souls
Of the defeated,
While only the souls of the victor
Ascend to heaven.

題摺鉢山記念碑

丘上新碑影　星條圧海隅
血痕腥礫魂　累骨覆山顛
戰敗茲年有　怨讐既滅寫
我魂難供養　彼魂独昇天

A veteran Japanese journalist, Toshio Aritake, reports that it is not easy to get people to talk about the battle today. As a whole, they are concerned that if they speak out, they might end up bragging about their experiences or telling wrong or misleading stories. "History does not convey facts," says Kiyoshi Endo, eighty-four, a lieutenant of the Imperial Navy at the time of the battle and the chairman of the Association of Iwo-Jima.

A resident of Yokosuka, Endo expresses mixed emotions about the sudden resurgence of interest in Iwo Jima after Clint Eastwood's movie. Endo says the movie did help collect more information from Japan and the United States and contributed to the increasing return of belongings of the dead on the island. At the same time, he and the association began receiving commercially oriented inquiries. People suddenly wanted to travel to Iwo Jima. They wanted interviews for books and the chance to make films.

"I feel at a loss to see what happened in the island, what we did there, how we felt about our families and how our families and relatives felt about us during the battle are written and shown like ads. The battle had different meanings for everyone, and it is impossible to generalize those meanings and we should avoid such generalization," Endo says.

For young Japanese, the Hiroshima and Nagasaki atomic bomb attacks, which caused a huge number of casualties, are on the threshold of becoming ancient history. Likewise, for most Japanese, the Iwo Jima battle evokes blurred monotone images of soldiers from both countries sacrificing their lives for the causes of their respective countries.

For the Iwo Jima survivors, their families, and dependents, however, the battle is fresh and real, as the A-bombs are for those concerned, Endo says. "American troops were rescued [when they were injured], but for us, there was no rescue and we were just left to perish." He did not offer details but probably was referring to wounded Japanese soldiers who could not be treated or saved for the lack of medical supplies.

Endo feels awkward talking about his experiences of the battle because . . . "one person may say something while others may see it differently and say different things. Personal experiences cannot be accurately conveyed [in writing and images]. And when they speak, they may boast about their experiences, even though they did not do it." He says, "The only fact regarding that battle is that it was over and the war was over. Which side won mattered when it was being fought, but now, sixty-two years after the battle, won or lost—there is no such thing."

The journalist Aritake adds that like Endo, his late father, Asazo Aritake, who was assigned as a Navy Marine to Guadalcanal and other South Pacific islands "never talked about his experiences to us children. When he was running a sushi restaurant in downtown Tokyo, his wartime colleagues would come visit him begging him to tell war stories. He never reciprocated. He was among a very few who returned from there."

The bond between the veterans and other people concerned from both countries remains strong; they all actively participate in the annual memorial service held on the island. It is because "our mission is a common one—that is, to search and collect the belongings and jointly with the Japanese government, look for the remains of the dead," Endo says.

The Iwo Jima annual memorial is, as I understand it, the only ceremony for the war dead in the world that peoples of two former enemy countries hold. That in itself underscores how close the two countries are, says Yoshitaka Shindo, a member of the House of Representatives and a grandson of Lieutenant General Kuribayashi.

Veterans and others from the two countries hold an annual meeting at Yasukuni Shrine, the controversial Shinto pavilion where the war dead, including world war criminals, are buried. Endo visits the shrine every year to pay respects to the Iwo Jima battle dead buried in the shrine. "They dedicated their lives to the country."

Endo says there still are more than thirteen thousand remains uncollected, and the task is made difficult by the lack of regular air or sea travel. "I do not know how long it will take to collect all the remains, but we will continue. And if it is over, we want to collect the remains of Japanese soldiers and others who died in the South Pacific islands too."

Yasunori Nishi, eighty, is the son of the late Takeichi Baron Nishi, an Imperial Army officer and a 1932 Los Angeles Olympic equestrian athlete who died in the battle. He says the Iwo Jima Association, which at its peak had about five thousand members, has shrunk to about twelve hundred. But this does not mean the Japanese interest in the battle has waned. "It is going the opposite direction and becoming active again because of participation of grand-sons and granddaughters," he says. The survivors and their families are becoming fewer, but "there are grandsons and daughters asking to take them to the island to pay respects. Some of them, since they cannot go there for various restrictions, would go to Ogasawara [Bonin] Island, and there they would pray in the direction of Iwo, which is about two hundred fifty kilometers away."

Captain Wachi's daughter, Rosa, declares, "We appreciate that more people are developing an interest in Iwo Jima, but we do not want it to be used for business. . . . My father was sometimes bad-mouthed that he was collecting the remains of the Japanese sol-diers for money, but he just kept on doing it." She also questions the famous photo of the U.S. Marines' flag raising on the island, saying that it might be "a show probably asked by a photographer to model. . . . It is too good to be true!"

23

PATRICK MOONEY AND THE GRAVES

Deputy Director, Combat Veterans of Iwo Jima;
Director, National Museum of the Marine Corps,
Docent and Visitors' Services

*In the loading order for the LSTs, you see the list
for Graves Registration, you see the items that
were needed to process the dead. The crosses and
Stars of David were already manufactured and
stacked and brought in aboard the LSTs.*

The dedication ceremony for the Fifth Division cemetery comes to a close on March 21, 1945,
as taps is played and the flag is lowered to half-staff. Survivors of the campaign stand in the
distance at the southern end of the cemetery, where the remains of 2,280 marines, sailors, and
soldiers of the division and attached units are interred. It was during this ceremony that Lieutenant Roland Gittelsohn, USNR, a rabbi in the Fifth Marine Division, gave his memorable
eulogy. By the end of 1948, all the graves had been exhumed and the bodies sent home to local
cemeteries or interred in Hawaii by choice of their next of kin. USMC photograph

I grew acquainted with Patrick Mooney, himself a former marine, during my visit to Guam and Iwo Jima with Military Historical Tours in March of 2006, and spoke with him at length over the course of an Iwo Jima symposium in Alexandria, Virginia, in February 2007. He was invariably gracious and accommodating, and extremely knowledgeable in all aspects of the campaign.

"Every marine wore two dog tags. One was on the main cord, and the secondary tag was attached by a short suspension loop below the other dog tag, and that was the one that went on the cemetery cross.

"We [historians] count five thousand nine hundred thirty-one combat ground casualties on Iwo Jima, consisting of marines, Navy guys, and one coast guardsman. They all were buried on Iwo or lost on the island. The remains of one hundred seventeen are still missing, meaning they have been declared dead but their remains have not been recovered. A lot of them were lost in the sea when their boats were hit or shot as they tried to wade ashore. Others were incinerated by artillery explosions or blown to pieces. A few, like Bill Genaust and others, we know what happened to them, but we never recovered their remains. The actual number of graves in the two cemeteries came to forty-seven hundred.

"The burials began under fire. The battlefield was still proximate, and on Iwo Jima there was no rear area. The Third and Fourth Divisions adjoined each other in one large cemetery that was split in half. The Fifth Division cemetery was separate. The Third and Fourth Division cemetery was just off Blue Beach One and Two. The Fifth Division cemetery was on other side of the island south of Airfield No. 2, just north of Airfield No. 1.

"The first burials I recorded were dated about four days after the battle started. Until that point they were gathering the dead in the beachhead area. The bodies were sprayed with insecticide to keep the bugs off and the odor down, then wrapped in ponchos. There are photographs of them doing that. Then, about D plus three or four, they began to bury the first dead in temporary cemeteries around the regimental hospitals and divisional hospital sites. They established the sites of the permanent cemeteries even before the landing went in.

"In the operational orders, the sites of the hospitals and cemeteries were already established. In the loading order for the LSTs, you see the list for Graves Registration, you see the items that were needed to process the dead. The crosses and Stars of David were already manufactured and stacked and brought in aboard the LSTs.

"After about the fifth day they began to to inter the dead in the permanent cemeteries. The process was very well organized and regimented. You have to realize that by February of '45 we had been in ground combat for eighteen months and the Marine Corps had suffered sixty thousand killed and wounded. So they were well prepared by this point. About a quarter of that number would have been dead and buried in various places as they moved from island to island. And each island had its own cemetery or several cemeteries. The dead were always arranged by the unit, so you had the different divisional cemeteries, and within the cemeteries at each plot you can look at the burial dates *vice* the date of death. Date of death can vary by two weeks. There were cases of bodies not recovered for as long as two weeks before they were buried. That's how the plats go.

"The divisional battalions, mostly black units, would dig the trenches. They'd bring in bulldozers, D8 Caterpillar bulldozers, and dig long trenches. The width of the bulldozer blade was about eight feet. They dug from a sloping height down for a certain length, and then they would slope upward on the other end. The bottom height would be anywhere from four to six feet below surface, depending on the stability of the sand or earth they were on. They would dig down and scoop out that long section.

"The bodies would be arranged, again very regimented, even in death. The bodies were carried in ponchos or in mattress covers. There were no body bags; that was an invention for later wars. The bodies would be laid in these trenches with a uniform width between each body, I think it's twenty-four to twenty-eight inches depending on the different unit and how they buried. That also dictated later on when the graves were filled how the cemeteries were laid out and how the graves were marked and where the crosses went. Every marine had two dog tags, and a dog tag was left with the body and a dog tag was taken by the Graves Registration personnel. All personal effects on the body were gathered and put in a small green canvas bag with a white linen tag on the front. The white linen tag was filled out as completely as possible with the name, rank, serial number, date of death, any information that could be garnered from the body. All the personal effects on the body would be placed in this bag. All the combat equipment, helmet, weapons, web equipment would be placed in the salvage depots, where they were processed for destruction or reuse. Personal effects were sent home.

"The body was buried in whatever uniform it was in at the time so they would have their boondockers, leggings if they wore them, dungaree trousers, dungaree shirt, and then they were placed in the poncho or the mattress covers. They left the boondockers on. They did not remove footwear or any clothing items. Even if there was a field jacket on, they left that but took all the personal effects. The Marine Corps poncho was big enough to encircle the body. You can see in the photos that if the poncho was spread out from top to bottom, it would cover from head to toe everybody except the tallest individuals. Priority was always given to covering the head and the face, with the boondockers sticking out the other end.

"Depending on the layout of the different parts of the cemetery, the trenches could contain as many as forty or fifty bodies or as few as twenty bodies. Each segment would be dictated by the quality of the soil they were digging in. The top layers of sand, that volcanic pumice, is very loose, but as you dig down, it gets into sandstone; that was what gave the Japanese the ability to tunnel so extensively. The bulldozer dug right down into the sandstone and gouged it out. It would take numerous passes to get to the requisite depth.

"The Pioneer battalions were all white: the Fifth Pioneer Battalion for the Fifth Division, the Fourth Pioneers for the Fourth Division, and the Third Pioneers for Third. The Pioneer battalions did the road engineering, the building, the construction of what we would normally think of as an engineer unit. In the Marine Corps combat divisions in World War Two, combat engineers performed combat engineering tasks, which were road clearing and demolition of obstacles. On Iwo that would include the demolition of caves and also obstacle clearance like the anti-tank ditch at Hill 362 Able. That was done by the Fifth Combat Engineer Battalion, the one Al Abbatiello was in. Tom Cox; Colonel Charles Waterhouse, the famous Marine Corps artist: these guys were all Fifth Combat Engineers.

"The Fifth Pioneers were the same guys involved in that shoot-out the last day when the three hundred Japanese came down and killed all the pilots. One of their leaders, Lieutenant Harry Martin, received the last MOH on Iwo Jima. These guys are often mistaken for being black. In World War One, large Pioneer battalions, mainly black African American units, were used as road clearance. It's often assumed they operated the same way in the Marine Corps in World War Two. Gentlemen from the Fifth Pioneer Battalion will be quick to tell you it was an all-white outfit. African American units were very limited in the Marine Corps. It was still a very segregated service.

"Getting back to the graves. . . . As the bodies were brought in, they were carried down this long slope, not lowered, but carried in, and then the trench would be back-filled from one end to the other. From the photos and from what I've been able to uncover, after every other body was laid, the chaplain would be about two bodies behind the registrar, who was moving along as the bodies were laid to make sure they were put in the right order. So the men would call out, "Smith, John, Sergeant, two-one-four-six-nine-seven-two, and the registrar would make the note that he was in Plat one, Row one, Grave twenty-four.

"Two bodies behind, the chaplain would be giving the appropriate benediction for the Catholic, Protestant, or Jewish faith. So they would move along that line, and once the bodies were all laid in and the appropriate benedictions were made and services and honors rendered, the grave would be filled in from head or foot depending on where the dirt had been pushed and plowed out. That was done mostly by the bulldozers; it was a tremendous task to fill that. The crosses in the photos were placed at the head of the trench so they knew approximately where the body was laid. They knew when they put Private Jones in that his cross was laid here.

"After the trench was filled, they would raise the cross and sink it into the ground. It was wooden construction, a cross or a Star of David. The second dog tag for that individual was affixed to the cross. The first dog tag was on the body. A number was stenciled on the back of the cross. Sometimes you'll see the dog tag affixed to the front and sometimes to the back of the cross. The name of the individual was stenciled, his service, his service number, and the emblem appropriate to his branch: the eagle, globe, and anchor, a Navy shield, or the Coast Guard emblem.

"The notched dog tag was an Army invention, and the notion that it was designed to be placed in the teeth upon death and then kicked shut was a myth. The notch was meant to hold the tag steady in the machine when it was being made. Throughout World War Two, the Marine Corps by and large did not have the notched dog tags. They used solid aluminum ovals that would either be etched or stamped. By Iwo Jima they were stamped, a flat oval cylinder about the size of a silver dollar, with a single hole. They were affixed around the neck by a linen-coated wire which had a screw fixture. The Marine Corps did not come out with chains to hold the dog tags until very late.

"Starting in 1946, all the graves were exhumed and repatriated by the end of '47. There was a continuing effort in the latter half of the 1940s to go back and resolve as many missing in action cases, the unknowns, as possible, and a very elaborate process was followed. Burial mistakes were made under combat that might not have occurred in a calm peacetime situation."

According to Army Graves Registration, the coordinating entity for all services, what it dug up varied from mummified corpses to just bones and other human remains. This depended on the location of the grave, the cemetery, soil conditions. Because it was so dry and there was so much heat on Iwo, there was a wicking effect of moisture into that volcanic pumice that in effect pulled the fluids out and mummified the body.

"A number of graves were lost in the Fifth Marine Division cemetery because of the ground subsiding and collapsing in different areas because of the vast Japanese tunnel complex. Mortuary specialists and embalmers and forensic people from all the services were recovering bodies, and when they dug down the requisite depth to recover the bodies, they weren't there. They continued to dig, and they finally found that the tunnels below had collapsed in a particular section and a half dozen bodies had fallen four and half feet below the area where they were originally buried. They were recovered.

"In another case, they went to grave one and dug down where there was supposed to be Private Smith, but he wasn't there. Then they dug grave two, and there was Private Smith. So a row that was supposed to be fourteen individuals wide was actually thirteen wide, and all the bodies were off by one set. All were recovered. It was just that somehow, in the rush and mix of everything, they had shifted the bodies one down and incorrectly recorded the grave as being marked on another so that number two was actually number one. ID's were found on the bodies as they were exhumed, and forensic exams were done, compared with extensive personal data from the casualty reports, dental records, everything. They were very thorough.

"So we had fifty-nine hundred guys buried in two cemeteries in a five-week period. They stayed there until 1946, when the War Department began to repatriate the remains of battlefield casualties. At that point we had battlefield cemeteries all across the

Pacific. Every island battlefield and base area had a cemetery. So
New Caledonia had a cemetery. Ulithi. In New Zealand and Australia. Not only combat areas. An effort was begun to gather these
remains, come up with a consolidated cemetery plan, and to repatriate some remains whose survivors wished to have the bodies
brought back.

"Family members were given one chance: They could elect to
have the bodies brought back to their hometown cemetery or they
could have the bodies reinterred at a national cemetery. And the
two sites chosen in the Pacific were Honolulu and Manila. Or back
to their hometown. You had one chance to do it. It was decided
that the remains of those who fought in the central Pacific and
northern Pacific would be brought to Honolulu. Those who
served in the southwest Pacific or in the Philippines, to include
Peleliu, those remains would go to Manila. Those who died in,
around, and over Iwo Jima were brought back to Honolulu or
back to the States. The vast majority of the Iwo Jima casualties
were brought back to Honolulu, where they rest to this day.

"I have not found an instance in the record of a combat casualty who was brought back to Arlington. The family could choose
where they buried their marine, and if the family chose Arlington,
well, I would assume there are some. Never say never. The
Basilones and folks like that and of course one of the flag raisers,
Ira Hayes, are at Arlington. He died well after the war. A lot of
postwar guys ended up there. You had to be a combat vet. But
space is so limited now you have to have a medal of valor, such as
a Bronze Star, or a Purple Heart to qualify for interment now."

Ed White of New York City, a theater critic for the *Wall Street Journal* for many years, remembers this:

"A small group of us landed on Iwo two years to the day of the
first landing, February 19, 1947. I had gone into the Army on an
eighteen-month enlistment in the fall of '46. They kept putting
the draft on, then calling it off, and I wanted to get it over with.

"I was put to work in the port director's office, a Quonset hut,
overseeing things that were wrecked just offshore. The Japanese

were reclaiming vehicles and weaponry and taking them back to Japan for scrap metal, which was kind of ironic. There was very little to do. I taught myself to type on a manual typewriter there in the office.

"People had advised me get into Special Services, and there was a small radio station in two or three Quonset huts under the shadow of Suribachi. They had generators and played large platter-type records with fifteen minutes of shows that we were getting from the Armed Forces Radio Service, popular music, big bands like Tommy Dorsey's. It was strictly for entertainment. I volunteered and learned how to run the station. Then the man who had been running it was reassigned to the Philippines, and I was the only man on the island who knew how to run the place.

"It was while I was doing that that the gravedigging unit came in March or April of '47. They were an all-black unit, come to dig up the graves for movement back to the States or Hawaii. I vividly remember this graveyard of white crosses with a few Stars of David standing out against that black volcanic ash. It was quite an incredible sight, a field of crosses, very stark.

"One of the men in charge, a master sergeant or somebody, came to see me one day at the radio station and said, 'We got a chorus. We sing spirituals.' I said, 'That's terrific.' Because we had very few live shows on the station. So I put them on the air every Sunday afternoon. Eighteen or twenty of these guys would crowd into our little studio and do thirty minutes of spirituals and harmony, a cappella, of course. I don't think we even had a piano.

"They were still working on the graves when I left in July for Guam."

About fifteen hundred marines of Jewish faith took part in the battle of Iwo Jima. Rabbi Roland B. Gittelsohn, the first Jewish chaplain appointed by the Marine Corps, was assigned to the Fifth Marine Division, according to an article appearing November 6, 1998, in the newspaper *Forward*. He was asked by the division chaplain, Warren Cuthriell, a Protestant, to deliver the memorial sermon at a combined religious service dedicating the Fifth Division cemetery in March 1945. But, the article goes on, a majority of Christian chaplains did not want a rabbi preaching over predominantly Christian graves and blocked his participation. Ultimately three separate services took place. The rabbi delivered the eulogy he had written for the combined service. About seventy attended, including three Protestant chaplains incensed by the prejudice displayed by their colleagues.

As a consequence of their anger, copies of Gittelsohn's talk were widely circulated, including back in the States; it was read into the *Congressional Record*. The talk remains famous in Marine Corps circles and elsewhere to this day. Here is what the rabbi said:

> *This is perhaps the grimmest, and surely the holiest task we have faced since D-Day. Here before us lie the bodies of comrades and friends. Men who until yesterday or last week laughed with us, joked with us, trained with us. Men who were on the same ships with us, and went over the sides with us as we prepared to hit the beaches of this island. Men who fought with us and feared with us. Somewhere in this plot of ground there may lie the man who could have discovered the cure for cancer. Under one of these Christian crosses, or beneath a Jewish Star of David, there may now rest a man who was destined to be a great prophet—to find the way, perhaps, for all to live in plenty, with poverty and hardship for none. Now they lie here silently in this sacred soil, and we gather to consecrate this earth in their memory.*
>
> *It is not easy to do so. Some of us have buried our closest friends here. We saw these men killed before our very eyes. Any one of us might have died in their places. Indeed, some of us are alive and breathing at this very monent only because men who lie here beneath us had the courage and strength to give their lives for ours. To speak in memory of such men as these is not easy. Of them too can it be said with utter truth: "The world will little note, nor long remember what we say here. It can never forget what they did here." No, our poor power of speech can add nothing to what these men and the other dead of our Division who are not*

here have already done. All that we even hope to do is follow their example. To show the same selfless courage in peace that they did in war. To swear that by the grace of God and the stubborn strength and power of human will, their sons and ours shall never suffer these pains again. These men have done their jobs well. They have paid the ghastly price of freedom. If that freedom be once again lost, as it was after the last war, the unforgivable blame will be ours, not theirs. So it is we the living who are here to be dedicated and consecrated.

We dedicate ourselves, first, to live together in peace the way they fought and are buried in this war. Here lie men who loved America because their ancestors generations ago helped in her founding, and other men who loved her with equal passion because they themselves or their own fathers escaped from oppression to her blessed shores. Here lie officers and men, negroes and whites, rich men and poor—together. Here no man prefers another because of his faith or despises him because of his color. Here there are no quotas of how many from each group are admitted or allowed. Among these men there is no discrimination. No prejudices. No hatred. Theirs is the highest and purest democracy. Any man among us the living who fails to understand that will thereby betray those who lie here dead. Whoever of us lifts up his hand in hate against a brother, or thinks himself superior to those who happen to be in the minority, makes of this ceremony, and of the bloody sacrifice it commemorates, an empty, hollow mockery. To this, then, as our solemn, sacred duty, do we the living now dedicate ourselves: to the rights of Protestants, Catholics and Jews, of white men and negroes alike, to enjoy the democracy for which all of them here have paid the price.

To one thing more do we consecrate ourselves in memory of those who sleep beneath these crosses and stars. We shall not foolishly suppose, as did the last generation of America's fighting men, that victory on the battlefield will automatically guarantee the triumph of democracy at home. This war, with all its frightful heartache and suffering, is but the beginning of our generation's struggle for democracy. When the last battle has been won, there will be those at home, as there were the last time, who will want us to turn our backs in selfish isolation on the rest of organized humanity, and thus to sabotage the very peace for which we fight. We promise you who lie here: we will not do that! We will join hands with Britain, China, Russia in peace, even as we have in war, to build the kind of world for which you died.

When the last shot has been fired, there will still be those whose eyes are turned backward, not forward, who will be satisfied with those wide extremes of poverty and wealth in which the seeds of another war can breed. We promise you, our departed comrades: this too we will not permit. This war has been fought by the common man; its fruits of peace must be enjoyed by the common man! We promise, by all that is sacred and holy, that your sons, the sons of miners and millers, the sons of farmers and workers, the right to a living that is decent and secure.

When the final cross has been placed in the last cemetery, once again there will be those to whom profit is more important than peace, who will insist with the voice of sweet reasonableness and appeasement that it is better to trade with the enemies of mankind, than by crushing them, to lose their profit. To you who sleep here silently, we give our promise: we will not listen! We will not forget that some of you were burnt with oil that came from American wells, that many of you were killed with shells fashioned from American steel. We promise that when once again men profit at your expense, we shall remember how you looked when we placed you reverently, lovingly, in the ground.

Thus do we memorialize those who, having ceased living with us, now live within us. Thus do we consecrate ourselves the living to carry on the struggle they began. Too much blood has gone into this soil for us to let it lie barren. Too much pain and heartache have fertilized the earth on which we stand. We here solemnly swear: this shall not be in vain! Out of this, and from the suffering and sorrow of those who mourn this, will come—we promise—the birth of a new freedom for the sons of men everywhere. Amen.

24

COLONEL JOHN W. RIPLEY, USMC (RET.)

Former Director of History and Museums, Marine Corps
Iwo Jima, Then and Now

Our flag flies [over Iwo Jima] one day a year. The Marines bring it. We're not permitted to leave it there when we leave the mountain. We have to take it down.

Colonel John Ripley's most recent photo in uniform was taken around 1999, while he was president of Hargrove Military Academy. The large medals on the top row, from left to right, are the Navy Cross (blue with a white stripe), the Silver Star (red stripe), the Legion of Merit (two), the Bronze Star with Combat V (two), and the Purple Heart.

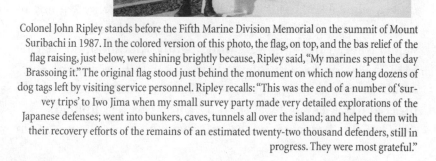

Colonel John Ripley stands before the Fifth Marine Division Memorial on the summit of Mount Suribachi in 1987. In the colored version of this photo, the flag, on top, and the bas relief of the flag raising, just below, were shining brightly because, Ripley said, "My marines spent the day Brassoing it." The original flag stood just behind the monument on which now hang dozens of dog tags left by visiting service personnel. Ripley recalls: "This was the end of a number of 'survey trips' to Iwo Jima when my small survey party made very detailed explorations of the Japanese defenses; went into bunkers, caves, tunnels all over the island; and helped them with their recovery efforts of the remains of an estimated twenty-two thousand defenders, still in progress. They were most grateful."

Colonel John Ripley, USMC (Ret.), was five years old when the Marines invaded Iwo Jima. After graduating from the Naval Academy in 1962, he served two years in Vietnam, participating in twenty-six major operations, and eventually was awarded the Navy Cross for almost single-handedly blowing up the bridge at Dong Ha during the 1972 North Vietnamese Easter invasion, a feat for which he should have received the Medal of Honor. He became involved with Iwo Jima as a colonel stationed in Japan and has visited the place more than fifteen times, always sleeping on the summit of Mount Suribachi. He later served as the director of history and museums for the Marine Corps. I was with him on March 5, 2006, as he knelt to pass a coin across the sawed-off circle at the base of the flagpole where the American flag first flew that morning of February 23, 1945. "To the Marines," he said, "this is Lourdes." Sacred ground.

"When we returned Iwo Jima to the Japanese in 1968, the Status of Forces Agreement and the treaty made it very clear that we, the Marine Corps, would always have the right to train there and we will always have the right to visit there.

"It all started during my watch, in the fall of 1987 in Okinawa, when I was a colonel, the G3 in charge of operations and planning for the Third Marine Amphibious Force. I said I wanted the Japanese to understand that although we hadn't been there in quite a while, I wanted them to understand that we were going to do this, establish more of a presence on the island. Prior to this, we would train in Iwo Jima very infrequently. An outbound Marine MEU [Marine Expeditionary Unit], a battalion aboard ship, would do a landing, wander around a bit, and then backload and proceed to Okinawa. It was training, but it was very limited.

"The G3 is the mover and shaker of everything that's happening in the force. So all the operations were set up and planned by my organization. I was responsible for everything the MEF [Marine Expeditionary Force] did. It was the Third MEF, which consists of all the elements—the division, the wing, all of the supply and ordnance. The purpose was to make sure the Japanese knew we were going to reassert our presence there. They were more than a little reluctant.

"The Navy wasn't all that keen to do it either, and finally the Marine Corps said, 'These are our MEUs, they need to have amphibious landings, to get as much training as they can, so we're going to schedule regular landings, training exercises, at Iwo, on the way out to Okinawa or on the way back.' This was 1987–88.

"So when I went back, the whole purpose of my going back was to walk around there, be seen, not be abrasive or offensive, but to let them know we were going to be around. We did send three Third Marine Division vehicles there. I've since made about a dozen trips to Iwo Jima, and I've stayed on the island for a couple weeks at a time.

"The Japanese used it for a similar purpose themselves, which is to say their war college and other units would come down and do battle studies at Iwo Jima. Every time I went over there I'd run into these guys. I was very cordial, very nice to them, never interfered with what they were doing. I would always take a party down there, say, three or four of our people, sometimes as many as ten, and we would do our own exploration.

"Soon the Japanese could see we were not a threat, and then two things happened that endeared us to them. One had to do with our using a wider area of the ocean there to practice Navy flights and simulated carrier landings, so we could keep away from Tokyo and Yokosuka. Our wing worked that out for them. The second thing was, their Home Office had just begun to disinter Japanese remains, all twenty-two thousand. That's a disputed figure, but I point out that at least a couple thousand were Korean laborers, and they're counted among the total losses on the Japanese side. In some cases they were killed, but mainly they were sealed off the same as the Japanese Army.

"My gang was going down into these caves in the fall of 1987 before the Japanese Home Office even got into it. We knew where they were, and we would go down there and find these incredible scenes. You would not believe the amount of equipment we found down in those caves.

"We found a hospital cave jammed with medical stuff, tons of medical supplies, cooking gear, rifles, Browning automatic rifles, a Lewis gun, records. We could only stay down there for twenty minutes. We had to rope up because it was so bloody hot you would collapse and couldn't get out of there. An artillery cave was packed with stuff, surveyors' kits, helmets.

"Then two things happened: We began to show these guys where this stuff was. They had nothing there but a backhoe or a couple diggers, and we never saw more than, say, two of these things with one or two other guys. I don't know what their progress was, but it was going to take forever to disinter them all. We'd go down there and find some remains, Japanese dead, and we'd go over and tell the guy, bring him over, and show him, and they appreciated that. And of course we were very solemn about it. We would uncover [remove hats] and render a salute, and I think that impressed them.

"The other thing was Hartzell. Staff Sergeant Hartzell was the one who found the body of what we called the chief of staff of General Kuribayashi. It was not so much the remains of the chief of staff, which actually had mummified, as something else he found.

"Everyone knew where Kuribayashi's cave was. It's still there, still marked. It was directly across the street from the Coast Guard station, and there was a beautiful mowed grass field right in front of the cave. It's all jungled up now, but then we stayed at the Coast Guard station. I kept all my vehicles there. Of course we all went over to the cave. Hartzell went in a couple times. He had done a considerable amount of exploring in Okinawa. He had an Okinawan wife; he could read and speak Japanese. He had a real sixth sense. This guy was quite a talent. When he got there, it was a treasure trove for him, and he walked into the cave. To enter, you had to lie on your back and turn around and come up over like a cornice into the main chamber of the cave.

"What wasn't seen initially was it had planking, kind of like duckboards, all covered with paper. Somebody had gone in there and trashed the hell out of it over the years, just souvenir hunting, I'm sure. Hartzell gets in there. It had a much higher ceiling than most of the caves we'd been in. You didn't have to stoop down. It was a command bunker. And almost as if he's getting some message, some divine message, Hartzell gets down and scoops all the paper away, and he's looking at the boards. Finally he gets all that out of the way, and there's the mummified remains of Kuribayashi's chief of staff.

"This was the man who had the honor of helping his chief with seppuku. Of course, knowing the importance of this, we back out. And Hartzell has found not Kuribayashi's diary but his combat journal, and that was a real treasure. We went right over to the airfield and told the air station commander of the maritime defense force there. He was a very nice fella. He couldn't speak English, but we showed him, opened it up, and he was dumbstruck.

"He called the Home Office, and they said they were going to send an aircraft down to pick it up and they wanted Hartzell to come with it. They wanted to honor Hartzell, which wasn't possible. I've seen him on a number of Iwo programs since he left the Marine Corps. I think he has some kind of official position in Okinawa at present.

"The last entry in the log was made the day Kuribayashi died. He had diagrams in there, exceedingly well done, with a fountain pen, for heaven's sake. The only thing we saw were diagrams of the defenses of Iwo Jima. It was in the possession of the chief of staff.

"How do we know the chief participated in seppuku? That brings up another very interesting question. They're now saying Kuribayashi died leading that last attack of the three hundred on the pilots, and I think all of this is a very obvious reconstruct or revisionist history. They want to somehow glorify Kuribayashi beyond the amazing man that he was. Yet virtually everything, sixty years of history, gives the account of him being killed by proper seppuku, and this chief of staff is mentioned in all this history, most of it Japanese.

"I have read in these various histories, which are translations, myself. I'm sure there's a degree of interpretation involved. I have never seen an actual Japanese document, and I'm not sure our Marine Corps archives would have it either. But over and over and over you see this account. The chief of staff killed himself. His body appeared to be undamaged, but there might have been a puncture somewhere.

"The thing which is the most irrefutable evidence of all is that Kuribayashi's body, which was a hot item, was never found. Every single body involved in that last attack was not necessarily identified, but they knew it wasn't Kuribayashi. Every single one. Because they were looking for him. And he wasn't there. Period. So that is the premier fact that refutes his involvement in that battle.

"We know the last attack originated in the naval forces area over by the Quarry. They came all the way down, heaven knows how, it had to be through tunnels. Because there was Hill 362 Charlie, Cushman's Pocket, the amphitheater, amazing fighting still going on over in those places. So how in the world did they manage to get past all these marines? The only way it can be understood is by tunnels. Because the actual fighting took place way over by the airfield on the other side of the island.

"Was Kuribayashi brilliant? No question. It's an overused term, but nevertheless it applies. He was a brilliant and a very determined strategist. He was chastised very heavily for his nondefense along the beach. This is all written in Japanese memoirs as well. His intent was to permit the landing force to get ashore, to let it get concentrated on the beach and then open up, which he did.

"Another point you never see written anywhere is this: If you stand at Suribachi to the south or at the Quarry to the north and look down that beach, you have linear plunging fire from any kind of weapon. He had both sides enfiladed from one end to the other, multiple lines of fire, and if he could hold that landing force right there, he could do a hell of a lot of damage, and he did.

"He got into a big brouhaha over that eight months before-hand. When he began to fortify the island we had not yet captured the Marianas. His superior was Lieutenant General Hideyoshi Obata, the Thirty-first Army commander, who was trying to get through the Marianas and back to Saipan in order to relieve Kuribayashi. Along comes the battle June the fifteenth, 1944, and he gets stuck in Guam. But his intent was to relieve Kuribayashi because he wasn't following bushido, the warrior's code. He refused to defend from the water's edge.

"That tells you Kuribayashi dug his heels in. He said, 'I know a hell of a lot about fighting and we damn sure ain't going to lose what paucity of people I have here by trying to defend at the water's edge, in open air.'

"Why weren't our Marine units annihilated on the beach? Several factors were involved. First of all the presumption of Kuribayashi and essentially the whole Japanese force was that we would, under fire, go to ground, dig in. Natural. That's what people do, go to ground. But that's not what we did. We kept moving. Our mentality at this point, from Guadalcanal all the way forward, was to get the hell off the beach.

"Well, this was one hell of a big wide beach. You couldn't get off just by running out of the boat, down the ramp and across the sand. It was too wide. He started that attack at ten-oh-three, fifty-nine minutes, one minute less than an hour after the landing force first came ashore.

"Another factor was we had almost two-thirds of the landing force ashore. That excludes Third Marine Division, which was still division reserve, but in that one hour's time we had gotten a hell of a lot of people on the beach. And Combat Team Twenty-eight, Fred Haynes's outfit, was assigned to get off Green Beach and cut the island. His battalion went straight across, in an hour and a half. They were by the airfield, not all the way across, but they were essentially unhampered by the bombardment.

"Those who had business to perform on the beach, beachmasters and mortarmen and artillerymen, were pretty much positioned, and their first reaction was to dig in. Unfortunately a number of them were lost because there was no way to dig in those damn terraces. They said that sand was like walking through wet coffee grounds.

"The Marine Corps never differentiated between the bombardment losses and the total losses, but I would say over half the losses were from the bombardment, anything twenty-five millimeter or greater. We could deal pretty much with infantry small arms, and we did. What Kuribayashi did was restrict the first hour to infantry small arms, and although we lost marines—no question about it—it was only when he started his bombardment an hour later that heavy casualties began to appear, and we're talking about not just dismounted infantry out of the boats, trying to get up the terraces. We're talking about the boats themselves; we're talking about ships, LSTs.

"He had hull-down tanks [buried up to the turret], we call them, which are not terribly effective. A tank weapon is designed for direct fire, so you can't really fire it like an artillery piece. It doesn't plunge. All of his eight-centimeter weapons, his big guns, he made the terrible mistake on D minus one of firing on the eight Navy gunboats, thinking that was the invasion. He fired on those gunboats, and we lost every single one, forty-three KIA, one hundred fifty-three WIA. Almost one hundred percent, all the gunboats were lost, and almost one hundred percent of the personnel were killed or wounded. These were wave guide boats, and they were the ones that accompanied the UDT, the underwater demolition teams, into the beach. They were spread all the way across the beach, two miles of beach, eight gunboats, and they accompanied the UDT in, and they were meant to protect.

"Kuribayashi thought this was the landing, so he unmasked his antiboat guns, and as a result, we knocked them out. The one we didn't knock out was one still standing at the bottom of Suribachi. I think he had eight or ten of those guns. The sacrifice of our boats saved a hell of a lot of lives. What if all those damn shore batteries had opened up on the landing force on D-day?

"But the biggest single reason our force was not annihilated goes to, we like to say, leadership, meaning gunnery sergeants: 'Get your ass off the beach! Get moving!' Small unit action at its finest. A very major factor. And if you bounce that off Normandy, they didn't. Those poor guys, especially the National Guard divisions, Twenty-ninth Division, they just went to ground, and they just got slaughtered because the enemy owned the heights. They just directed all their fire right smack down. These guys went to ground, and they were stuck. The only ones who had any degree of protection were the ones that had come far enough across the beach so they were masked from the cliff there.

"Another big irony was the sand, which intelligence had said would not pose a problem to men or machinery. It turned out to be a partial blessing in disguise because it absorbed shelling. You didn't get what we call point detonating rounds. That's a factor a lot of people don't understand. A point detonating round has all of its splash horizontal right when it hits. The round doesn't penetrate at all. The softer the soil, mud, or something like that, it's going to absorb part of that blast. These rounds, especially artillery rounds, even if they were point detonating rounds, still would have gone in deep enough so that almost the whole front end of the round would have been absorbed in that sand. That was a major factor.

"The biggest killer on the battlefield is the mortar. Not small arms. Overwhelmingly. Mortars got a bow end on 'em, and they don't penetrate. They generally hit pretty much vertically, and they stop right at the deck, and all that splash is horizontal. A sixty mortar's killing radius is fifteen meters, meaning anything within fifteen meters or forty-five feet is almost assuredly a casualty.

"Another thing to be aware of is this, and it's very important: There were no such things as snipers on Iwo, although you hear again and again that any man shot individually was hit by a sniper. A sniper is a trained marksman with a scope with a special weapon. Most of the so-called sniper losses on Iwo Jima were nothing more than a rifleman who happened to hit a guy. It's a good point because you hear it constantly, but these were nothing more than infantrymen doing exactly what they normally do, and they take out people.

"Kuribayashi opposed the attack on the United States. Another aspect of Kuribayashi that is not talked about and I'm not sure how it figures overall, but Kuribayashi was nobility. He was very highly regarded. He had access to the emperor, and that always causes problems with your superiors, and I daresay his were a bit jealous of him. He was sent to Manchuria. He spent most of the war in Manchuria. He was up there and went from there to China. The important thing about that is, these guys he brought to Iwo never had any really serious combat against marines in the Pacific. It was all against an inferior Chinese enemy.

"It [the slaughter in China] was one of the world's greatest atrocities when you stop to think about it, just the numbers alone and what they did to the Chinese. The Japanese forces up there were very arrogant, very self-assured, tremendously loyal to Kuribayashi. A bunch of them went to Iwo with him. The whole purpose of pointing this out is if you consider his presence in China in the light of the atrocities that took place there, which the Japanese have been very careful not to do, he would not be the hero that he is.

"They have managed to totally wipe over the fact that he was part of the Kwantum Army (Japanese armed forces in Manchuria), which participated in all that genocide. His reputation is almost exclusively Iwo Jima. If we were to make an effort to tie him to the Kwantum Army for the two or three years he was up there, he would probably have been hanged had he survived the war. That also has impact here. None of his troops had any experience in tough warfare such as the ones who had been in the Pacific from the very beginning. None of them. The Chinese were so poorly armed that it was murder. When they got to Iwo Jima, things were radically different.

"It was a great honor to be sent to Iwo Jima by the emperor, who personally wanted Kuribayashi to go there. That's when he wrote his letter to his wife and said, 'I shall not return. I know this is my last posting. Don't expect to see me anymore. Say hello to the kids.'

"Was it an honor to die? Sure. Still, having been washed in victory from all the time they were in China, it had to be a pretty stark change when they were sent to Iwo Jima knowing that this was the last stand. We do have some unit names and identification. They had the equivalent of eight infantry battalions, a tank regiment, two artillery and three heavy mortar battalions, naval infantry, a mixed brigade.

"Kuribayashi arrived at the East Boat Basin in June of 1944. They had been working on Iwo since 1938, fortifying it, building the airfields, getting it prepared. It was totally off-limits to anyone other than military. Kuribayashi got there, and he was unsatisfied with the defenses, and I think he was predominantly unsatisfied with surface defenses, how the artillery was unrevetted, weapons not dug in properly. So he declared Japanese soldiers had to do this in addition to what the Koreans were doing and had already done. He said everybody's got to work. He made a profound impact on the island's defenses.

"Rations up until the invasion were satisfactory, and that is a stretch, but it means everyone had a meal. Most of their supplies came down from Chichi Jima. They had an airfield there also. Of course everything was shut off once the battle started. Food was limited, and the soldiers received a half a cup of water per day. There's no natural water, but they had cisterns and runoff from rain, but even that was inadequate. It's amazing what you can survive on, and for the Japanese, it literally was survival. All or most of the reports you read about involving night attacks or night activity were Japanese going out trying to take water off American casualties. We put deep wells there when we left.

"Why is the battle significant? It is now considered the most important bloodletting of any battle of that size, of that scale, in the war. We consider seventy-five thousand marines in what was called the Fifth Amphibious Corps, consisting of three divisions, to be veterans of Iwo Jima. Of that number, twenty-five thousand became casualties, nearly seven thousand of whom were killed. Thirty-three percent of all the Marine Corps losses in World War Two took place at Iwo Jima.

"Of eighty-two Medals of Honor earned in World War Two, almost a third of them were earned on Iwo Jima. Of the total losses at Iwo Jima, eighty-two percent were solely marines. If you add the corpsmen and the doctors, we lost over three hundred corpsmen. We had fifteen doctors killed in action. These guys were brutally set upon the whole time they were ashore. There were three hundred sixty-five Seabees lost, and ships lost. The *Saratoga,* the *Bismarck Sea*, the *Lunga Point*, all these were attacked by Kamikazes on D plus one. We lost the *Bismarck Sea* damn near with all hands. Eight hundred went down. These are stunning figures when you stop to think about it.

"The writer James Bradley, whose father was one of the flag raisers, points out that by noon at Normandy, the day of the invasion, you could have had a picnic on Omaha Beach, whereas on Iwo Jima people were fighting and dying from the very beginning to the end, thirty-six days later. And an additional several thousand Japanese would be killed after we declared victory on the fifteenth of March, when they ran the colors up.

"That of course was subterfuge because Nimitz needed to get all that shipping back to put the force aboard to go invade Okinawa April 1. We'd lose another seven thousand people killed and wounded between there and the end of Iwo Jima, after Nimitz had determined the island was secure enough to pull the shipping out. It was a profound decision. Not only did he secure the shipping and take back . . . Well, the hospital ships left, a lot of the matériel that might have been used, might have been necessary, left.

"Of course we had the airfields in operation by then, and that was important because we could evacuate casualties by air and bring in critical material by air, but under no circumstances would that ever take place today, nor did it prior to Iwo Jima. You just would never do that. And with them went the Third Marines, the reserve. The Third Marines, that's probably the biggest remaining controversy. The Third Marine Regiment never went ashore. And they were asked for five times. Two division commanders and the force commander, General Schmidt, asked Holland Smith to please bring the Third Marines ashore.

"The kindest thing that has been said about that is Holland Smith expected we would be invading Japan and we needed to have some experienced troops to build a corps around. We had lost the equivalent of an entire Marine division in casualties. There were three divisions, but the Third Marine Division put only two regiments ashore, Ninth Marines and Twenty-first Marines. An entire regiment, the Third, was withheld.

"The biggest problem with that was the replacements. They went in there, honest to God, just like cannon fodder, because there were no real veterans there to show them how to do things. We lost replacements, I would say, on a scale of two to one compared to our veterans. Holland Smith's not permitting the force reserves, the Third Marines, to come ashore and enter the fight did several things: It relied too heavily on replacements who were untrained, grossly inexperienced, and not attached to the leadership. They had not bonded in their units the way they should have, and therefore their losses were horrendous. In addition, Smith's decision forced the units that stayed there to become even less combat-efficient, because they never got a break.

"If he had brought that additional regiment ashore, then we could have pulled units off the line and let them rotate and rest and get back in shape, move them in and out, which we always did in every other battle. That was simply not possible without a division reserve ashore.

"I view Iwo Jima as the signature battle in the history of the Marine Corps. There are several things that make Iwo Jima different. One, it was a tiny little three-by-five, eight-square mile island with two airfields on it, every inch of which had to be captured, every inch of which was contested. There was no such thing as Japanese falling back to another line, falling back and giving ground in order to stretch out the forces. There wasn't any consideration for surrender. They were a ferocious, violent, very, very formidable enemy that had one purpose: Kill Americans. There was no place to get out of their way to cover yourself from their fire. And they had an enormous amount of time to prepare the defenses for the island, which was not the case in several other battles we'd fought.

"Fighting and dying took place from D minus two (February 17) all the way through March and beyond. The last Japanese gave up in 1949.

"There were anywhere from eleven to seventeen miles of tunnels, also individual chambers, eight hundred of them, used as headquarters command positions, hospitals, barracks, living quarters, and so forth. In some of the tunnels we found mummified casualties lying on litters with intravenous drips still in their arms.

"The chambers were not interconnected. There would be a tunnel leading to this chamber, but it had a totally separate purpose. The tunnels were a combination of what we would call barracks or a position for troops to stay. The chambers, on the other hand, had a very separate purpose. When I went down in the artillery position on Nishi Ridge, the tunnel there was surrounded by maybe fifteen chambers, primarily for ammunition storage. Then there were spokes off that for the troops who supported that position.

"There were three levels of tunnels. I have a diagram of Hill 362 Able, and there are three separate levels thirty and forty feet down. Everyone asks about heat, and I did as well when I first went there. It is ferocious, worse than a damn sauna. I finally figured it out: They found a way to ventilate them, but that was closed off when we got there. We got the Japanese diggers to open one up, and all of a sudden we could feel this breeze coursing through. And that's the only way you could possibly survive in there.

"They used ladders to reach the different levels. There's a funny story about one of them. I was coming down a slope with no steps, just a carved slope. This was volcanic rock and sandstone, easy to shape or sculpt. This ramp went down, and at the bottom there was a vertical descent of maybe twenty feet, a big hole, and I could see the tunnel below. Their ladder was gone by this time, but I had us all roped up, and when we got to that point, I just did a seat rappel down to the tunnel.

"When I came back a month or so later, I had the commanding general with me, Lieutenant General Norm Smith. And he didn't want to rappel; he wanted to jump. I said, 'General, we don't know what's in these damn things. There's still ordnance in here.' Well, he still wanted to jump. The surface of the lower tunnel was sort of pebbled. I was down there and shined the light up so he could see when he jumped. He landed, and his foot, the arch of his foot, was right on a Japanese grenade. His boot was right on that damn grenade. And of course the fuse sticks out of the upper end, and it's a pressure detonator. They'd bang it against their helmet, and it would start the timing chain.

"And I said, 'Don't move.' I got the grenade out from under his foot. So the damn things were full of ordnance. Those caves actually went in one direction to a huge cliff face that looked over Hill 362 Able and Nishi Ridge itself. I have identified that as the location where most of Combat Team 2-28, all the heavy losses, all the flag raisers, were killed in that area."

I raised the question of atrocities committed by marines during the battle and told Colonel Ripley of one veteran who related to me how he had come home with a jarful of gold-studded teeth and dried ears he had cut off Japanese soldiers. He had said it was not uncommon for those back at Camp Lejeune to tell marines departing for the Pacific, "Bring us back some teeth and ears." Richard Nummer knew of a marine who collected teeth, and Sergeant McPhatter told of marines driving prisoners into the sea and shooting them.

"Ears didn't become popular until Vietnam, believe it or not, but teeth definitely. As for actual torture, I would say without question these things probably happened once or twice, but marines have a different focus. We're here to kill you and get on with the next guy and the next guy. We're not going to sit here and play cat and mouse with a casualty. It doesn't make any sense. I'm not saying it doesn't happen, but I am saying it is rare because there are too many other things we are dealing with. Now, at Iwo Jima, the Japanese atrocities that are probably more prominent to me involve James Bradley's example of his father's good friend Ignatz, Iggy, who was hideously tortured and mutilated, and then we think Bill Genaust was probably tortured. But he was shot. They saw him get shot. There wasn't any question that he was down. [See Norman Hatch, Chapter 13].

"I would say there are eighteen thousand soldiers still entombed on Iwo Jima, which the Japanese naturally consider a shrine. An easy way to determine for sure would be to find out how many they've shipped back, but I'd be surprised if they've even reached five thousand yet. [Some reports say eight thousand have been recovered.] There's the ossuary, where they store bones, on that little peak just over from 362 Charlie and right in front of Cushman's Pocket. Over the last five years they've built a massive memorial right next to the ossuary. The whole hill is now a very sacred spot. Even Japanese citizens are not permitted to go to the island unless they are the father, mother, or brother of someone who served. This is the Japanese definition of 'immediate family.'

"Of course Japanese are on the island full-time, probably not much more than two hundred. And American carrier pilots fly over from Japan and stay there while they practice touch-and-go's and maneuvers that wouldn't be possible over Japan because of airspace and noise restrictions. We have an American barracks there that will accommodate two hundred. That took place after I left, but I'm pretty proud of that because I'm sure all the work we did made it amenable to the Japanese.

"Our flag flies one day a year. The marines bring it. We are not permitted to leave it there when we leave the mountain. We have to take it down.

"The Japanese permit Military Historical Tours in Arlington, Virginia, to bring visitors one day a year, usually in March. A support element comes ashore with vehicles and tents and things solely to support this day, which is referred to as a Reunion of Honor. There was a lot of talk in the Marine Corps that after the sixtieth anniversary we'd have to stop doing that because our business now is war [in Iraq] and we can ill afford to be bringing that element over to Iwo Jima. The Navy complains about the shipping. 'We got a lot of things to do, and we don't want to have to bring all you guys to Iwo Jima.' Three ships generally. I would say there is constant complaining about it. One thing indisputable is the Japanese will not permit any other organization, so it's not as if they were beating out the competition.

"The reason we do it is everyone knows that Iwo Jima is *sanctum sanctorum* to the Marines, and the value that we get out of bringing those marines there, mainly from Okinawa, is so enormous that the commandant every single year says, 'Hey, we're going to continue this as long as we can.' For current and old marines. There's no frills associated with this, and it's the only way these veterans can get back to Iwo Jima. Even so, it would be hard to justify if we were just doing it for these old warriors. We love it, but it'd be damn hard to justify that kind of commitment by itself. But we can clearly justify it for the morale, the reenlistments, the tremendous lift these marines get by getting to go to Iwo Jima and support this reunion.

"Misconceptions? The main one, after you clear up the death of Kuribayashi, would be the battle for Suribachi. You constantly see references to the bloody battle for Suribachi, and it's always the flag raisers fighting their way up the mountain, fighting their way down, with terrible losses and so on. Well, the battle for Suribachi was at the bottom, and it was a hell of a fight: Nine hundred marines out of one regiment were lost in those first five days. In fact, the most decorated platoon in the Marine Corps was Third Platoon Easy 2-28 that took the colors up the mountain. A Medal of Honor and two Navy Crosses, just getting their way clear to get up the mountain. The greatest Marine of all, the only surviving flag raiser in 2007, was Chuck Lindberg, a flamethrower [Chapter 14]. He won a Silver Star that day.

"So although there was some action at the top of Suribachi, it was the three days prior to the actual patrol that went up on the fourth. The predominance of Suribachi's threat was really at its base. The USS *Pensacola* came in there and was whacked right smack in the bridge with an artillery shell fired from Suribachi, killing fifteen men, including the skipper, so Suribachi was lethal, a very tough nut. But it was not a tough trip when the very first patrol, Sergeant Watson's patrol, and Lieutenant Schrier's final flag raising patrol, which was a whole platoon, went up there. There are a billion myths and inaccuracies associated with the flag raising. Over a thousand people have laid claim to taking part in it.

"Talk to any veteran of Iwo Jima, and he's going tell you about his fight and the importance of his fight and the brutality and the difficulty, and, in other words, we had it far worse than anyone else. And you know what? Every single one of these guys is right. Their fight was tough. There wasn't any such thing as an easy run on Iwo Jima. The way that plays out now is the Fifth Division gets so much attention because of the flag raising, rightly or wrongly."

Latter-day revisionists have contended that the battle for Iwo Jima was wasteful and unnecessary and that only a small proportion of the 2,251 landings by B-29s afterward were for genuine emergencies.

"One of the things that such contentions overlook is that we lost seventy-seven Superforts before we even took Iwo, flying out of Tinian or Saipan straight to Tokyo and back. We never anticipated that kind of volume. Although American industry was magnificent in war production, they certainly couldn't sustain those kind of losses. Frankly the biggest issue with Iwo Jima was early warning, so Tokyo knew they were en route, and more important, there was the fighter cover, the CAP, the Combat Air Patrol, that they could put up from Japan to intercept the bombers. This originated when they saw them going over Iwo Jima.

"As to talk about how only a small portion of the two thousand two hundred fifty-one landings were genuine emergencies? Bull-crap! A landing for whatever reason is an emergency landing. Why the hell touch down on Iwo Jima unless you need to go to Iwo Jima? That wasn't their home base; they would have achieved nothing by being there. There was no room on the ramp for all these huge damn B-29s. They had to get back to the Marianas, had to get back to Tinian.

"So to hear some latter-day bobby-sox historian come along and say we didn't need Iwo Jima is just an ultimate insult. It makes no sense. I could go on and on with other examples, but the truth is this was nothing more than an academic exercise by some researcher poring over old unit archives and trying to make a case where none exists. Academics are the only ones that support this, meaning some professor says, 'Aha! This is recently revealed information.' They have no combat experience or understanding of our war aims, our strategy at the time. And then sixty years later they take the entire battle out of context and try to find fault with its underlying importance to victory, and even those who fought the battle! There's nothing new in here."

A question to Colonel Ripley on whether we were correct in returning the island to Japan led me to the following letter, which he wrote to a friend, Ross Mackenzie, on the night of November 17, 1987, from the summit of Suribachi.

Dear Ross:

From this most unlikely spot I am inspired to write you for reasons I can't fully explain. Certainly you have received no other letters from here I would wager, and you may find this interesting. It's the middle of the night—cold, windy, uncomfortable & profoundly moving. I'm looking down on a tiny island three miles wide and five miles long. Down there, and here where I'm writing by flashlight, over 7,000 Marines died. The mountain is Suribachi, the island, Iwo Jima. Of the hundreds of thousands of words written about this place, nothing close to describing its starkness, its inestimable cost and now, sadly, the poverty of its abandonment.

The entire island is a shrine, mostly Japanese, but a few

Americans—*only a few. Americans don't seem to care about such things when, as is the case here, it's inconvenient. And yet this island, its name and most especially this very spot where I sit— where the flag was raised—is immortalized in our national consciousness for as long as there is an America.*

The debris and detritus of war remain even after nearly 43 years. Rusty vehicle hulks, wrecked boats, sunken ships, canteens, mess kits, thousands of rounds of corroded ammunition, blockhouses, pillboxes, trenches, abandoned airfields, large naval shore guns, artillery, etc. And beneath my feet remains of 22,000 Japanese defenders, brave men who died at their posts; hated then, respected now.

Rupert Brooke said it perfectly: "Here in some small corner of forgotten field will be forever England."* And this brutally stinking sulfuric rock, depressing to see, demoralizing as it has lost its once vital importance and our nation's once great concern, will be forever America. It will be forever in the memory of those 75,000 Marines who fought here, the 25,000 who suffered wounds here and the 7,000 who gave their blood and lives to its black soil. Again Rupert Brooke. . . . "In that rich earth, a richer dust concealed." Their hopes, their happiness, their dreams ended here. And if we fail to honor them in our memory and our prayers, we should be damned to hell for such failure.

I brought a small team here to survey the island for future exercise use. The Japanese would prefer we did not exercise here, but that will be over my dead body. I find it hard to believe (and impossible to accept) that our government gave the island back to them. It's as if we gave them Gettysburg or Arlington National Cemetery. Americans died in such numbers here that in nine and a half months, had the battle lasted that long, it would have equalled our losses of 10 years in Vietnam.

---

*Brooke's original lines, from "The Soldier," read:

If I should die, think only this of me:
   That there's some corner of a foreign field
That is for ever England.

The Marine Corps must never lose its right to exercise here, and
I'm damned proud of having something to do with assuring that
will be so.
Yours aye,
John

In June 2007 Japan announced that it was going to restore to the island its original name, Iwo To, which means essentially the same thing as Iwo Jima, or Sulfur Island. I asked Colonel Ripley what he thought about that.

"My feeling is that the name change, perhaps important to the Japanese, is disingenuous and ultimately will make no difference. The Burma Road is still the Burma Road, and all of Napoleon's battle sites bear their original names despite the renaming of each locale. This is replicated worldwide.

"Many years ago the island center in Micronesia called the Gilberts decided to change the name of our famous Tarawa to Kiribati. Well, it has made no difference whatsoever as we, and everyone else, still call it Tarawa. By the same token, Iwo Jima is a hell of a lot more than just a Japanese piece of property. Changing the name sure as hell won't change the history—especially recent history—of the island. It will forever be Iwo Jima in the hearts of all marines and the American public as well, for all time."

[*Author's note*: John Ripley died of natural causes at his home in Annapolis, Maryland, October 28, 2008. He was sixty-nine.]

APPENDIX

Military Terminology

amtrac: Tracked amphibious vehicle used to transport the first waves of the invasion on Iwo Jima. Called an LVT for "landing vehicle, tracked," it was eight feet wide, nine feet tall, and twenty-seven feet long.

banzai: Usually suicidal infantry assault, which the commander of the Japanese forces refused to employ on Iwo Jima. Ironically, had Kuribayashi ordered a banzai attack on the first night of the invasion, it may very well have succeeded, because the landing forces were so disorganized.

BAR: Browning automatic rifle. This was the principal rapid-fire weapon for a regular infantry squad. It was a gas-operated .30-06 caliber and could be fired via tripod or standing up. Basically a "walking machine gun," its twenty-round magazine could be emptied in three seconds. Each BAR man had an assistant who carried ammunition for it. The .30-caliber round was interchangeable for the M1 rifle, the BAR, and the light and heavy machine guns, according to Mike Mervosh, who was on Iwo Jima for the entire campaign.

bazooka: Common name for the tubular 2.36 rocket launcher, fired over the shoulder, used against tanks or fortified positions. The 2.36 refers to the diameter of the shell. Each platoon had at least two. The assistant inserted the shell from the back, then tapped the gunner on the shoulder. Effective range was about one hundred meters.

Betty: Principal heavy bomber of the Japanese Navy, the G4M was referred to as the Betty by the Allies. It was remarkable for its long range, achieved by depriving it of armor and equipping it with huge fuel tanks in the wings. Because it tended to catch fire readily when hit, it acquired the nicknames One-Shot Lighter and the Flying Cigar.

boondockers: Marine field shoes, usually worn with canvas leggings.

boot: Marine recruit.

bulkhead: A wall.

C2: A puttylike plastic explosive that could be molded by hand; favored for use in satchel charges. A fuse set off a blasting cap that caused the C2 to explode.

cannon: A large, heavy piece of artillery of four basic calibers: the .57 millimeter, which could be dragged up to the line of combat by hand; the .75-millimeter pack howitzer, which could be broken down and carried by several marines; the 105; and the 155. The .57 millimeter could fire ten rounds a minute; it employed mostly canister, small bullets in one shell that spread out like shotgun pellets but with much more lethal effect.

carbine: This was a .30 caliber rifle with a fifteen-round clip. It lacked the stopping power of the M1.

Cincpac: The sort of acronym loved by the military, this one stood for Commander in Chief, Pacific Command.

Corsair: Single-engine Marine fighter plane.

D-day: Debarkation (invasion) day.

deck: The ground or the floor.

dog face or doggie: Soldier in the U.S. Army. Negative term used by marines to label Army counterparts.

DUKW: Manned by black soldiers and also white marines in separate DUKW companies—this amphibious vehicle, pronounced *duck*, was fifteen by eighteen feet, with four-wheel drive, rubber tires, and a propeller that drove it through the water. One company of Army DUKWs was assigned to each Marine division on Iwo.

ear-banger: Someone who seeks to curry favor with a superior.

flamethrower: A portable weapon carried by hand or fired from a (Zippo) tank, projecting an incendiary fuel such as jellied gasoline or a mixture of high-octane gas and diesel fuel. The hand-carried version weighed seventy-two pounds. It held five gallons of fuel, which burned up in about seven seconds.

gung ho: Based on a Chinese phrase that means "to work together," this phrase was adopted by the Marines to describe an overly zealous member of the Corps.

hand grenades: There were three types: fragmentation, incendiary, and smoke. After you pulled the pin—by hand and never with your teeth— and released the lever, you had three to five seconds prior to explosion. It was customary to let two seconds go by before throwing the device, so it could not be flung back by the enemy. Mike Mervosh said he threw more grenades than he fired bullets. The effective radius was about ten yards. The Japanese version was activated by rapping it on one's helmet or another hard object.

hatch: A doorway.

H hour: The hour at which an operation begins.

Higgins boat: The flat-bottomed landing craft devised by Andrew Higgins of New Orleans. Various types included the LCI (landing craft, infantry), LCT (landing craft, tank), the LCVP (landing craft, vehicles, personnel), and the LCM (landing craft, medium). The LVT was the amphibious tracked ship-to-shore vehicle known as the amtrac.

house apes: Children.

Ka-Bar: a solid, six-inch fixed blade knife carried by virtually every marine, primarily for combat but also useful for opening K rations.

KIA: Killed in action.

line of departure: A suitably marked offshore line intended to coordinate landing craft so they could land on designated beaches according to predetermined schedules.

LP: Listening post.

M1 Garand: The infantryman's favorite weapon, it was a gas-operated .30-06 caliber with an eight-shot clip. Called by General George Patton "the greatest battle implement ever devised," it could be fired repeatedly by just pulling the trigger. With its sixteen-inch bayonet attached, the rifle weighed almost ten pounds. "You snapped the bayonet on the end of the muzzle when you hit the beach, and you put it on when you were snooping around caves," Mike Mervosh said.

machine gun: There were two basic types: a .30 caliber, air-cooled version that could be fired standing up or on a ten-pound tripod (each gunner had an assistant to help carry the gun and the webbed canvas belt that held 250 rounds) and the .30 heavy version, which was water-cooled and rested on a fifty-one-pound tripod. It was brought up at night for perimeter defense. Each gun was manned by seven marines, including four ammo humpers. Two machine guns were assigned to each platoon. The water-cooled gun weighed ninety-one pounds.

Maggie's drawers: Red flag or disk raised at a firing range to indicate the shooter has completely missed the target. It was said to come from a 1940s song entitled "Those Old Red Flannel Drawers That Maggie Wore."

Marine units: A division included 20,000 men, consisting of four regiments, engineer, pioneer, tank, service, motor transport medical, amphibian tractor battalions, signal and laundry company, a war dog platoon, an observation squadron, and two replacement battalions. A regiment consisted of 3,300 men, broken into three battalions. A battalion numbered 1,100, consisting of three assault companies of about 250 each, plus a headquarters company and various support units. A rifle platoon held 45 men, 43 marines and 2 Navy corpsmen. Mortar platoons were smaller, 18 to 20, and machine-gun platoons held up to 56 men.

mortar: a short smooth-bore gun for firing shells at high angles. The sixty-millimeter mortar was manned by six: the gunner, his assistant, and four carriers. It was muzzle-loaded and could be elevated to forty-five degrees. It was very accurate from three hundred to seven hundred yards, and it would reach as far as eighteen hundred. There was also the eighty-one-millimeter mortar.

mustang: Enlisted man who leaves those ranks to become an officer.

Nambu: Japanese light machine gun.

noncom: Noncommissioned officers are the enlisted men, especially gunnery sergeants and the like, who really enable the Marine Corps to function.

Quonset hut: Building made of corrugated metal with semicircular cross section, first manufactured at Quonset Point, Rhode Island.

rifle grenade: An adapter on a rifle muzzle could launch this grenade up to

150 yards, whereas 30 yards was about maximum for one thrown by hand.

salt: A marine who has been in the Corps a long time; an old hand.

satchel charge: A hand-carried charge of dynamite or C2 or C4 plastic explosive that could be thrown once a flamethrower had been used to blast the occupants in a cave into retreat.

scuttlebutt: Drinking fountain gossip or rumor.

slop chute: Enlisted men's bar.

Springfield '03: The principal combat rifle used before the M1 Garand. It was a .30-caliber bolt action, which meant each shell had to be ejected manually. The M1 was semiautomatic, meaning it could be fired repeatedly by simply pulling the trigger. The Springfield held a five-round clip.

squadron: Consisted of two or more groupings of aircraft or divisions of ships.

swab jockey: Any sailor, also referred to as a swabby, squid, or anchor clanker. The term was not complimentary.

Thompson submachine gun: This was a hand-held .45-caliber submachine gun equipped with a stick magazine that held twenty rounds. It was useful in close combat at point-blank range; otherwise it was not much good. It was favored by tankers and artillery men.

Tojo: Single-seat, single engine aircraft used to intercept B-29 bombers. With its poor visibility on the ground, weak armament, and high landing speed, it was generally disliked by its pilots. This was the kind of plane shot down by Lieutenant Robert Merklein. Tojo was also the name of Japan's wartime prime minister.

tracer: Bullet with a phosphorous coating, designed to burn in flight to provide visual indication of trajectory.

weapons carrier: A one-ton vehicle, manufactured by Dodge, that looked like an oversized pickup truck. It was designed to carry its crew and mortars or machine guns.

Weasel: Small tracked vehicle used for towing .57-millimeter cannon and hauling supplies to advanced areas, among other things.

WIA: Wounded in action.

WW: Walking wounded.